Post-traumatic stress disorder

The management of PTSD
in adults and children
in primary and secondary care

National Clinical Practice Guideline Number 26

National Collaborating Centre for Mental Health

commissioned by the

National Institute for Clinical Excellence

published by

Gaskell and the British Psychological Society

Gaskell is an imprint of the Royal College of Psychiatrists. The views presented in this book do not necessarily reflect those of the Royal College of Psychiatrists, and the publishers are not responsible for any error of omission or fact. The Royal College of Psychiatrists is a registered charity (no. 228636).

British Library Cataloguing-in-Publication Data

A catalogue record for this book is available from the British Library.

ISBN 1-904671-25-X

Printed in Great Britain by Cromwell Press Limited, Trowbridge, Wiltshire.

Additional material: data CD–ROM created by Pixl8 (www.pixl8.co.uk).

developed by   National Collaborating Centre for Mental Health
Royal College of Psychiatrists' Research Unit
6th Floor
83 Victoria Street
London
SW1H 0HW

commissioned by   National Insitute for Clinical Excellence
MidCity Place
London
WC1V 6NA
www.nice.org.uk

published by   Royal College of Psychiatrists
17 Belgrave Square
London
SW1X 8PG
www.rcpsych.ac.uk

and

British Psychological Society
St Andrews House
48 Princess Road East
Leicester
LE1 7DR
www.bps.org.uk

The
British
Psychological
Society

Contents

Guideline Development Group membership

Dr Jonathan Bisson (Co-Chair)
Clinical Senior Lecturer in Psychiatry, Cardiff University

Mrs Pamela Dix
PTSD Sufferer Representative

Professor Anke Ehlers (Co-Chair)
Professor of Experimental Psychopathology, Institute of Psychiatry, King's College London

Mrs S. Janet Johnston, MBE
Clinical Director, Ashford Couselling Service
Retired senior social worker, Kent County Council
Founder, Dover Counselling Centre

Mr Christopher Jones
Health Economist, National Collaborating Centre for Mental Health

Ms Rebecca King
Project Manager, National Collaborating Centre for Mental Health

Ms Rosa Matthews
Systematic Reviewer, National Collaborating Centre for Mental Health

Mr Andrew Murphy
PTSD Sufferer Representative

Ms Peggy Nuttall
Research Assistant, National Collaborating Centre for Mental Health

Mr Cesar De Oliveira
Systematic Reviewer, National Collaborating Centre for Mental Health

Mr Stephen Pilling (Guideline Facilitator)
Co-Director, National Collaborating Centre for Mental Health
Director, Centre for Outcomes, Research and Effectiveness, University College London
Consultant Clinical Psychologist, Camden and Islington Mental Health and Social Care Trust

Professor David Richards
Professor of Mental Health, University of York

Dr Clare Taylor
Editor, National Collaborating Centre for Mental Health

Ms Lois Thomas
Research Assistant, National Collaborating Centre for Mental Health

Dr Stuart Turner
Consultant Psychiatrist, Capio Nightingale Hospital
Chair of Trustees, Refugee Therapy Centre
Honorary Senior Lecturer, University College London

Ms Heather Wilder
Information Scientist, National Collaborating Centre for Mental Health

Professor William Yule
Professor of Applied Child Psychology, Institute of Psychiatry, King's College London

Acknowledgements

The Post-Traumatic Stress Disorder Guideline Development Group and the National Collaborating Centre for Mental Health review team would like to thank the following people.

Those who wrote and submitted personal testimonies that have been included in chapter 3 of this guideline.

Those who acted as advisers on specialist topics:

Ms Cristel Amiss and Ms Fernande Sambura (Black Women's Rape Action Project)

Professor Chris Brewin (Professor of Clinical Psychology, University College London)

Dr Chris Freeman (Consultant Psychiatrist, Royal Edinburgh Hospital)

Ms Caroline Garland (Consultant Clinical Psychologist, Psychoanalyst, Tavistock and Portman NHS Trust, London)

Ms Ruth Hall and Ms Woini Samuel (Women Against Rape)

Dr John Spector (Consultant Clinical Psychologist, Watford General Hospital)

Dr Dave Tomson (General Practitioner and Consultant in Patient-Centred Primary Care, Collingwood Surgery, North Shields)

Dr Guinevere Tufnell (Consultant Child and Adolescent Psychiatrist, The Traumatic Stress Clinic, Great Ormond Street Hospital)

Dr Felicity de Zulueta (Consultant Psychiatrist, Psychotherapist, South London and Maudsley NHS Trust)

The healthcare professionals who participated in the primary care focus group:

Dr Dorothy Dunn (Psychologist in Primary Care)

Dr Lesley Duke (General Practitioner)

Dr Brian Fine (General Practitioner)

Dr Judy Leibowitz (Psychologist in Primary Care)

Dr Tim Owen (General Practitioner)

Dr Guy Pilkington (General Practitioner)

Mike Scanlon (Community Psychiatric Nurse and Primary Care Mental Health Worker)

Dr Dave Tomson (General Practitioner)

The authors of the following systematic reviews who allowed the NCCMH review team access to their data files:

Professor Chris Brewin (University College London)

Professor Emily Ozer (University of California)

Dr Paul Ramchandani (University of Oxford)

Dr Guinevere Tufnell (The Traumatic Stress Clinic, Great Ormond Street Hospital)

The following for granting permission to reproduce their material:

American Psychological Association

John Wiley & Sons Limited

Oxford University Press

World Health Organization

List of abbreviations

I, IIa, IIb, III, IV	levels of evidence forming the basis for an evidence statement (for full definitions, see Table 4.1, p. 47)
A, B, C, GPP	grades of evidence forming the basis for a guideline statement (for full definitions, see Table 4.1, p. 47)
A&E	accident and emergency
AGREE	appraisal of guidelines research and evaluation
CAMHS	child and adolescent mental health services
CAPS	Clinician-Administered PTSD Scale for DSM–IV
CBT	cognitive–behavioural therapy
CCTR	Cochrane Central Register of Controlled Trials
CDSR	Cochrane Database of Systematic Reviews
CI	confidence interval
CINAHL	Cumulative Index to Nursing and Allied Health Literature
CMHT	community mental health team
DARE	Database of Abstracts of Reviews of Effects
DTS	Davidson Trauma Scale
EMBASE	Exerpta Medica Database
EMDR	eye movement desensitisation and reprocessing
GP	general practitioner
GPP	good practice point
HTA	Health Technology Appraisal
ICD–10	International Classification of Diseases, 10th edn
IES (–R)	Impact of Event Scale (–Revised)
k	number of studies, the evidence from which has been used to compile an evidence statement
MAOI	monoamine oxidase inhibitor
n	number of participants
NCCMH	National Collaborating Centre for Mental Health
NHS	National Health Service
NICE	National Institute for Clinical Excellence
NSF	National Service Framework (for mental health)
PCL	PTSD Checklist
PDS	Post-traumatic Diagnostic Scale
PTSD	post-traumatic stress disorder
RCT	randomised controlled trial
RR	relative risk/risk ratio
SD	standard deviation
SMD	standard mean difference
SSRI	selective serotonin reuptake inhibitor
WHO	World Health Organization

1 Introduction

This guideline has been developed to advise on the treatment and management of post-traumatic stress disorder (PTSD). The guideline recommendations have been developed by a multidisciplinary team of healthcare professionals, PTSD sufferers and guideline methodologists after careful consideration of the best available evidence. (The term 'PTSD sufferer' was chosen for use in the guideline on the basis of a survey conducted by sufferer members of the Guideline Development Group. People with the disorder were presented with a range of options such as 'people with PTSD', 'patients with PTSD' and 'PTSD sufferer' and asked to indicate which term they preferred; 'PTSD sufferer' was the term favoured by the majority.) It is intended that the guideline will be useful to clinicians and service commissioners in providing and planning high-quality care for those with PTSD while also emphasising the importance of the experience of care for patients and their families.

1.1 National guidelines

1.1.1 What are clinical practice guidelines?

Clinical practice guidelines are 'systematically developed statements that assist clinicians and patients in making decisions about appropriate treatment for specific conditions' (Department of Health, 1996). They are derived from the best available research evidence, using predetermined and systematic methods to identify and evaluate all the evidence relating to the specific condition in question. Where evidence is lacking, the guidelines will incorporate statements and recommendations based upon the consensus statements developed by the guideline development group.

Clinical guidelines are intended to improve the process and outcomes of healthcare in a number of different ways. Clinical guidelines can:

- provide up-to-date evidence-based recommendations for the management of conditions and disorders by healthcare professionals
- be used as the basis to set standards to assess the practice of healthcare professionals
- form the basis for education and training of healthcare professionals
- assist patients and carers in making informed decisions about their treatment and care
- improve communication between healthcare professionals, patients and carers
- help identify priority areas for further research.

1.1.2 Uses and limitations of clinical guidelines

Guidelines are not a substitute for professional knowledge and clinical judgement. Guidelines can be limited in their usefulness and applicability by a number of different factors: the availability of high-quality research evidence, the quality of the methodology used in the development of the guideline, the generalisability of research findings and the uniqueness of individual patients.

Although the quality of research in PTSD is variable, the methodology used here reflects current international understanding on the appropriate practice for guideline development (AGREE Collaboration, 2001), ensuring the collection and selection of the best research evidence available and the systematic generation of treatment recommendations applicable to the majority of patients and situations. However, there will always be some patients for whom clinical guideline recommendations are not appropriate and situations in which the recommendations are not readily applicable. This guideline does not, therefore, override the individual responsibility of healthcare professionals to make appropriate decisions in the circumstances of the individual patient, in consultation with the patient and/or carer.

In addition to the clinical evidence, cost-effectiveness information, where available, is taken into account in the generation of statements and recommendations of the clinical guidelines.

Whereas national guidelines are concerned with clinical and cost-effectiveness, issues of affordability and implementation costs are to be determined by the National Health Service (NHS).

In using guidelines, it must be remembered that the absence of empirical evidence for the effectiveness of a particular intervention is not the same as evidence for ineffectiveness. In addition, and particularly relevant in mental health, evidence-based treatments are often delivered within the context of an overall treatment programme including a range of activities, the purpose of which may be to help engage the patient and provide an appropriate context for the delivery of specific interventions. It is important to maintain and enhance the service context in which these interventions are delivered, otherwise the specific benefits of effective interventions will be lost. Indeed, organising care so as to support and encourage a good therapeutic relationship is at times more important than the specific treatments offered.

1.1.3 Why develop national guidelines?

The National Institute for Clinical Excellence (NICE) was established as a Special Health Authority for England and Wales in 1999, with a remit to provide a single source of authoritative and reliable guidance for patients, professionals and the public. Its guidance aims to improve standards of care, to diminish unacceptable variations in the provision and quality of care across the NHS and to ensure that the health service is patient-centred. All guidance is developed in a transparent and collaborative manner using the best available evidence and involving all relevant stakeholders.

The National Institute for Clinical Excellence generates guidance in a number of different ways, two of which are relevant here. First, national guidance is produced by the Technology Appraisal Committee to give robust advice about a particular treatment, intervention, procedure or other health technology. Second, NICE commissions the production of national clinical practice guidelines, each focused upon the overall treatment and management of a specific condition. To enable this latter development, NICE established seven National Collaborating Centres in conjunction with a range of professional organisations involved in healthcare.

1.1.4 National Collaborating Centre for Mental Health

This guideline has been commissioned by NICE and developed within the National Collaborating Centre for Mental Health (NCCMH). This is a collaboration of the professional organisations involved in the field of mental health, national service-user and carer organisations, a number of academic institutions and NICE. The NCCMH is funded by NICE and led by a partnership between the Royal College of Psychiatrists' Research Unit and the British Psychological Society's equivalent unit, the Centre for Outcomes Research and Effectiveness. Members of the NCCMH reference group come from the following organisations:

- Royal College of Psychiatrists
- British Psychological Society
- Royal College of Nursing
- National Institute for Social Work
- College of Occupational Therapists, now replaced by the Clinical Effectiveness Forum for the Allied Health Professions
- Royal College of General Practitioners
- Royal Pharmaceutical Society
- Rethink Severe Mental Illness
- Manic Depression Fellowship
- Mind
- Centre for Evidence-based Mental Health
- Centre for Economics in Mental Health
- Institute of Psychiatry.

The NCCMH reference group provides advice on a full range of issues relating to the development of guidelines, including the membership of experts, professionals, patients and carers within guideline development groups.

1.1.5 From national guidelines to local protocols

Once a national guideline has been published and disseminated, local healthcare groups will be expected to produce a plan and identify resources for its implementation, along with appropriate timetables. Subsequently, a multidisciplinary group involving commissioners of healthcare, primary-care and specialist mental health professionals, patients and carers should undertake the translation of the implementation plan into local protocols. The nature and pace of the local plan will reflect local healthcare needs and the nature of existing services; full implementation may take a considerable time, especially where substantial training needs are identified.

1.1.6 Auditing the implementation of guidelines

This guideline identifies key areas of clinical practice and service delivery for local and national audit. Although the generation of audit standards is an important and necessary step in the implementation of this guidance, a more broadly based implementation strategy should be developed. Nevertheless, it should be noted that the Healthcare Commission will monitor the extent to which primary care trusts, trusts responsible for mental health and social care, and health authorities have implemented these guidelines.

1.2 The national PTSD guideline

1.2.1 Who has developed this guideline?

The Guideline Development Group was convened by the NCCMH and supported by funding from NICE. The Group consisted of PTSD sufferers and professionals from psychiatry, clinical psychology, nursing and social work services. Staff from the NCCMH provided leadership and support throughout the process of guideline development, undertaking systematic searches, information retrieval, appraisal and systematic review of the evidence. Members of the Group received training in the process of guideline development. The National Guidelines Support and Research Unit, also established by NICE, provided advice and assistance regarding aspects of the guideline development process.

All members of the Group made formal declarations of interest at the outset, updated at every meeting. The members met a total of 19 times throughout the process of guideline development. For ease of evidence identification and analysis, some members of the Group became topic leads, covering identifiable treatment approaches. The NCCMH technical team supported group members, with additional expert advice from special advisers where necessary. All statements and recommendations in this guideline have been generated and agreed by the whole Guideline Development Group.

1.2.2 For whom is this guideline intended?

This guideline will be of relevance to adults and children of all ages who suffer from PTSD.

The guideline covers the care provided by primary, secondary and other healthcare professionals who have direct contact with, and make decisions concerning the care of, PTSD sufferers. The guideline will also be relevant to the work (but will not cover the practice) of those in occupational health services, social services and the independent sector.

Traumatic experiences can affect the whole family and often the community. The guideline recognises the role of both family and community in the treatment and support of PTSD sufferers.

1.2.3 Specific aims of this guideline

The guideline makes recommendations and suggests good practice points for the treatment and management of PTSD. Specifically, it aims to:

- evaluate the role of specific psychological interventions in the treatment and management of PTSD

- evaluate the role of specific pharmacological interventions in the treatment and management of PTSD
- evaluate the role of early psychological and pharmacological interventions shortly after traumatic event
- address the issues of diagnosis, detection and the use of screening techniques in high-risk situations
- provide key review criteria for audit, which will enable objective measurements to be made of the extent and nature of local implementation of this guidance, particularly its impact upon practice and outcomes for people with PTSD.

The guideline does not cover treatments that are not normally available on the NHS.

2 Post-traumatic stress disorder

2.1 The disorder

This guideline is concerned with the diagnosis, early identification and treatment of post-traumatic stress disorder (PTSD) as defined in ICD–10 (World Health Organization, 1992), code number F43.1. This disorder is one that people may develop in response to one or more traumatic events such as deliberate acts of interpersonal violence, severe accidents, disasters or military action. The guideline is concerned with the care of people for whom PTSD is the *main* problem after experiencing a traumatic event. The disorder can occur at any age, including childhood.

The best-validated diagnostic instruments, and most randomised controlled treatment trials of PTSD, use the stricter diagnostic criteria for PTSD of DSM–IV (American Psychiatric Association, 1994). However, this does not limit the applicability of the results for the purposes of this guideline. The available evidence suggests that treatments that are effective for PTSD as defined in DSM–IV are also effective for PTSD as defined in ICD–10 (Blanchard *et al*, 2003*a*). In contrast to ICD–10, DSM–IV distinguishes between acute stress disorder (duration less than 1 month) and PTSD (symptom duration 1 month or longer). The literature on acute stress disorder was therefore included in the NICE review of the evidence, as it is relevant for early interventions in PTSD.

The guideline does not apply to people whose main problem is the ICD–10 diagnosis of 'Enduring personality changes after catastrophic experience' (F62.0), the concept corresponding to 'Disorders of extreme distress not otherwise specified/complex PTSD' (see definition 2.3.6.1), which may develop after extreme prolonged or repeated trauma, such as repeated childhood sexual abuse or prolonged captivity involving torture. The guideline does not address dissociative disorders, which may develop after traumatic events, or adjustment disorders (F43.2), which may develop after less severe stressors.

2.1.1 Traumatic stressors

The diagnosis of PTSD is restricted to people who have experienced exceptionally threatening and distressing events. The ICD–10 definition states that PTSD may develop after 'a stressful event or situation ... of an exceptionally threatening or catastrophic nature, which is likely to cause pervasive distress in almost anyone' (World Health Organization, 1992: p. 147). Thus, PTSD would not be diagnosed after other upsetting events that are described as 'traumatic' in everyday language, such as divorce, loss of a job or failing an examination. In these cases, a diagnosis of adjustment disorder may be considered.

The DSM–IV highlights that a traumatic stressor usually involves a perceived threat to life (either one's own life or that of another person) or physical integrity, and intense fear, helplessness or horror. Other emotional responses of trauma survivors with PTSD include guilt, shame, intense anger or emotional numbing.

Whether or not people develop PTSD depends on their subjective perception of the traumatic event as well as on the objective facts. For example, people who are threatened with a replica gun and believe that they are about to be shot, or people who only contract minor injuries during a road traffic accident but believe at the time that they are about to die, may develop PTSD. Furthermore, those at risk of PTSD include not only those who are directly affected by a horrific event, but also witnesses, perpetrators and those who help PTSD sufferers (vicarious traumatisation). People at risk of PTSD include:

- victims of violent crime (e.g. physical and sexual assaults, sexual abuse, bombings, riots)
- members of the armed forces, police, journalists and prison service, fire service, ambulance and emergency personnel, including those no longer in service
- victims of war, torture, state-sanctioned violence or terrorism, and refugees
- survivors of accidents and disasters
- women following traumatic childbirth, individuals diagnosed with a life-threatening illness.

2.1.2 Symptoms of PTSD

The most characteristic symptoms of PTSD are re-experiencing symptoms. Sufferers involuntarily re-experience aspects of the traumatic event in a vivid and distressing way. This includes flashbacks in which the person acts or feels as if the event is recurring; nightmares; and repetitive and distressing intrusive images or other sensory impressions from the event. Reminders of the traumatic event arouse intense distress and/or physiological reactions.

In children, re-experiencing symptoms may take the form of re-enacting the experience, repetitive play or frightening dreams without recognisable content. Chapter 9 addresses the recognition and treatment of PTSD in children and young people.

Avoidance of reminders of the trauma is another core symptom of PTSD. These reminders include people, situations or circumstances resembling or associated with the event. Sufferers from PTSD often try to push memories of the event out of their mind and avoid thinking or talking about it in detail, particularly about its worst moments. On the other hand, many ruminate excessively about questions that prevent them from coming to terms with the event, for example about why the event happened to them, about how it could have been prevented or about how they could take revenge.

Symptoms of hyperarousal include hypervigilance for threat, exaggerated startle responses, irritability, difficulty in concentrating and sleep problems.

However, PTSD sufferers also describe symptoms of emotional numbing. These include inability to have any feelings, feeling detached from other people, giving up previously significant activities and amnesia for significant parts of the event.

Many PTSD sufferers experience other associated symptoms, including depression, generalised anxiety, shame, guilt and reduced libido, which contribute to their distress and affect their functioning.

2.1.3 Course and prognosis

The onset of symptoms is usually in the first month after the traumatic event, but in a minority (less than 15%; McNally, 2003) there may be a delay of months or years before symptoms start to appear.

Post-traumatic stress disorder shows substantial natural recovery in the initial months and years after a traumatic event. Whereas a high proportion of trauma survivors will initially develop symptoms of PTSD, a substantial proportion of these individuals recover without treatment in the following years, with a steep decline in PTSD rates occurring in the first year (e.g. Breslau et al, 1991; Kessler et al, 1995). On the other hand, at least a third of the individuals who initially develop PTSD remain symptomatic for 3 years or longer, and are at risk of secondary problems such as substance misuse (e.g. Kessler et al, 1995). This raises the important questions of when treatment should be offered after a traumatic event and how people who are unlikely to recover on their own can be identified. These questions are addressed in the guideline sections on early intervention after trauma (Chapter 7) and screening for PTSD (Chapter 8). One important indicator of treatment need appears to be the severity of PTSD symptoms from around 2–4 weeks after the trauma onwards (e.g. Shalev et al, 1997; Harvey & Bryant, 1998). However, it is important to note that symptom severity in the initial days after trauma (up to about 1 week) is not a good predictor of persistent PTSD (Shalev, 1992; Murray et al, 2002). Importantly, evidence suggests that the chances that a PTSD sufferer will benefit from treatment do not decrease with time elapsed since the traumatic event (Gillespie et al, 2002; Resick et al, 2002).

2.1.4 Impairment, disability and secondary problems

Symptoms of PTSD cause considerable distress and can significantly interfere with social, educational and occupational functioning. It is not uncommon for PTSD sufferers to lose their jobs, either because re-experiencing symptoms, sleep and concentration problems make regular work difficult, or because they are unable to cope with reminders of the traumatic event they encounter at work. The resulting financial problems are a common source of additional stress, and may be a contributory factor leading to extreme hardship such as homelessness.

The disorder has adverse effects on the sufferer's social relationships, leading to social withdrawal. Problems in the family and break-up of significant relationships are not uncommon.

Sufferers may also develop further, secondary psychological disorders as complications of the PTSD. The most common complications are:

- substance use disorders: PTSD sufferers may use alcohol, drugs, caffeine or nicotine to cope with their symptoms, which may eventually lead to dependence
- depression, including the risk of suicide
- other anxiety disorders, such as panic disorder, which may lead to additional restrictions in the sufferer's life (for example, inability to use public transport).

Other possible complications of PTSD include somatisation, chronic pain and poor health (Schnurr & Green, 2003). Sufferers from PTSD are at greater risk of medical problems, including circulatory and musculoskeletal disorders, and have a greater number of medical conditions than people without PTSD (Ouimette *et al*, 2004).

2.2 Incidence and prevalence

The available estimates of PTSD prevalence and incidence so far stem mainly from large-scale epidemiological studies conducted in the USA and Australia, and are restricted to data on adults. It remains to be investigated whether these data apply to the UK, and to children (see Chapter 9). The main findings from the epidemiological research on PTSD are as follows:

- the majority of people will experience at least one traumatic event in their lifetime (Kessler *et al*, 1995)
- intentional acts of interpersonal violence, in particular sexual assault, and combat are more likely to lead to PTSD than accidents or disasters (Kessler *et al*, 1995; Stein *et al*, 1997; Creamer *et al*, 2001)
- men tend to experience more traumatic events than women, but women experience higher impact events (i.e. those that are more likely to lead to PTSD; Kessler *et al*, 1995; Stein *et al*, 1997)
- women are more likely to develop PTSD in response to a traumatic event than men; this enhanced risk is not explained by differences in the type of traumatic event (Kessler *et al*, 1995).

Examples of people at risk of PTSD in the UK include people who have been exposed to or have witnessed an extreme traumatic stressor, such as deliberate acts of violence, physical and sexual abuse, accidents, disaster or military action. This includes both direct personal experience of the trauma and the threat to physical integrity of the individual involved. People who have experienced threat to their own life or the life of others while in medical care, such as during anaesthesia, complications during childbirth or as a result of medical negligence, are also at risk.

Special populations such as people in military service, emergency workers and the police are likely to have an increased risk of exposure to trauma, and are thus at risk of PTSD. Many refugees have experienced a range of traumatic events and may therefore, among other problems, suffer from PTSD.

2.2.1 Prevalence

Post-traumatic stress disorder is common. In a large, representative sample in the USA, Kessler *et al* (1995) estimated a lifetime prevalence of PTSD of 7.8% (women 10.4%, men 5.0%), using DSM–III–R criteria. Estimates for 12-month prevalence range between 1.3% (Australia; Creamer *et al*, 2001) and 3.6% (USA; Narrow *et al*, 2002). Estimates for 1-month prevalence range between 1.5–1.8% using DSM–IV criteria (Stein *et al*, 1997; Andrews *et al*, 1999) and 3.4% using the less strict ICD–10 criteria (Andrews *et al*, 1999). The disorder remains common in later life, but with the suggestion of a greater proportion of sub-syndromal PTSD in the older age group (van Zelst *et al*, 2003).

2.2.2 Incidence

Kessler *et al* (1995) found that the risk of developing PTSD after a traumatic event is 8.1% for men and 20.4% for women. For young urban populations, higher risks have been reported:

Breslau and colleagues found an overall risk of 23.6% (Breslau *et al*, 1991) and a risk of 13% for men and 30.2% for women (Breslau *et al*, 1997).

2.2.3 Influence of type of traumatic event

Different types of traumatic events are associated with different PTSD rates. Rape was associated with the highest PTSD rates in several studies. For example, 65% of the men and 46% of the women who had been raped met PTSD criteria in the study by Kessler *et al* (1995). Other traumatic events associated with high PTSD rates included combat exposure, childhood neglect and physical abuse, sexual molestation and (for women only) physical attack and being threatened with a weapon, kidnapped or held hostage. Accidents, witnessing death or injury, and fire or natural disasters were associated with lower lifetime PTSD rates (Kessler *et al*, 1995). Other research has shown high PTSD rates for torture victims, survivors of the Holocaust and prisoners of war.

2.3 Diagnosis and differential diagnosis

2.3.1 Diagnostic criteria

The ICD–10 diagnosis of PTSD requires that the patient, first, has been exposed to a traumatic event, and second, suffers from distressing re-experiencing symptoms. Patients will usually also show avoidance of reminders of the event, and some symptoms of hyperarousal and/or emotional numbing. The ICD–10 research diagnostic criteria for PTSD are as follows (reproduced with permission from World Health Organization, 1993: pp. 99–100):

(A)   The patient must have been exposed to a stressful event or situation (either short or long-lasting) of exceptionally threatening or catastrophic nature, which would be likely to cause pervasive distress in almost anyone.

(B)   There must be persistent remembering or 'reliving' of the stressor in intrusive 'flashbacks', vivid memories, or recurring dreams, or in experiencing distress when exposed to circumstances resembling or associated with the stressor.

(C)   The patient must exhibit an actual or preferred avoidance of circumstances resembling or associated with the stressor, which was not present before exposure to the stressor.

(D)   Either of the following must be present:

    (1)   inability to recall, either partially or completely, some important aspects of the period of exposure to the stressor

    (2)   persistent symptoms of increased psychological sensitivity and arousal (not present before exposure to the stressor), shown by any two of the following:

        (a)   difficulty in falling or staying asleep

        (b)   irritability or outbursts of anger

        (c)   difficulty in concentrating

        (d)   hypervigilance

        (e)   exaggerated startle response.

(E)   Criteria B, C, and D must all be met within 6 months of the stressful event or the end of a period of stress. (For some purposes, onset delayed more than by 6 months may be included, but this should be clearly specified.)

The DSM–IV diagnosis of PTSD is stricter, in that it puts more emphasis on avoidance and emotional numbing symptoms. It requires a particular combination of symptoms (at least one re-experiencing symptom, three symptoms of avoidance and emotional numbing, and two hyperarousal symptoms). In addition, DSM–IV requires that the symptoms cause significant distress or interference with social or occupational functioning. Several studies have found that trauma survivors who experience most, but not all, DSM–IV symptoms of PTSD show significant distress and need treatment (e.g. Blanchard *et al*, 2003*b*).

In contrast to the ICD–10 definition, a DSM–IV diagnosis of PTSD further requires that the symptoms have persisted for at least 1 month. In the first month after trauma, trauma survivors may be diagnosed as having acute stress disorder according to DSM–IV, which is characterised by symptoms of PTSD and dissociative symptoms such as depersonalisation, derealisation and emotional numbing. The ICD–10 diagnosis does not require a minimum duration. For the purposes of this guideline, we include PTSD symptoms that occur in the first month after trauma. A special section on early intervention (Chapter 7) is dedicated to the management of these early PTSD reactions.

Appendix 13 (source: Ehlers, 2000) compares the diagnostic criteria for post-traumatic stress disorder in ICD–10 and DSM–IV.

2.3.2 Assessment instruments

Well-validated, structured clinical interviews that facilitate the diagnosis of PTSD include the Structured Clinical Interview for DSM–IV (SCID; First *et al*, 1995), the Clinician-Administered PTSD Scale (CAPS; Blake *et al*, 1995) and the PTSD Symptom Scale – Interview version (PSS–I; Foa *et al*, 1993). All these instruments are based on the DSM–IV definition of PTSD.

There is a range of useful self-report instruments of PTSD symptoms; these include:

- Impact of Event Scale (IES; Horowitz *et al*, 1979) and Impact of Event Scale – Revised (IES–R; Weiss & Marmar, 1997);
- Post-traumatic Diagnostic Scale (PDS; Foa *et al*, 1997)
- Davidson Trauma Scale (Davidson *et al*, 1997)
- PTSD Checklist (Weathers & Ford, 1996).

2.3.3 Clinical aspects of the diagnostic interview

When establishing the diagnosis of PTSD it is important to bear in mind that people with this disorder find talking about the traumatic experience very upsetting. They may find it hard to disclose the exact nature of the event and the associated re-experiencing symptoms and feelings, and may initially not be able to talk about the most distressing aspects of their experience. This may particularly be the case for people who experienced the trauma many years ago or have a delayed onset of their symptoms.

2.3.3.1   For PTSD sufferers presenting in primary care, GPs should take responsibility for the initial assessment and the initial coordination of care. This includes the determination of the need for emergency medical or psychiatric assessment. **C**

2.3.3.2   Assessment of PTSD sufferers should be conducted by competent individuals and be comprehensive, including physical, psychological and social needs and a risk assessment. **GPP**

2.3.3.3   When developing and agreeing a treatment plan with a PTSD sufferer, healthcare professionals should ensure that sufferers receive information about common reactions to traumatic events, including the symptoms of PTSD and its course and treatment. **GPP**

2.3.3.4   When seeking to identify PTSD, members of the primary care team should consider asking adults specific questions about re-experiencing (including flashbacks and nightmares) or hyperarousal (including an exaggerated startle response or sleep disturbance). For children, particularly younger children, consideration should be given to asking the child and/or the parents about sleep disturbance or significant changes in sleeping patterns. **C**

2.3.3.5   Healthcare professionals should be aware that many PTSD sufferers are anxious about and can avoid engaging in treatment. Healthcare professionals should also recognise the challenges that this presents and respond appropriately, for example by following up PTSD sufferers who miss scheduled appointments. **C**

2.3.3.6   Patient preference should be an important determinant of the choice among effective treatments. PTSD sufferers should be given sufficient information about the nature of these treatments to make an informed choice. **C**

2.3.3.7   Where management is shared between primary and secondary care, there should be clear agreement among individual healthcare professionals about the responsibility for monitoring patients with PTSD. This agreement should be in writing (where appropriate, using the Care Programme Approach) and should be shared with the patient and, where appropriate, their family and carers. **C**

2.3.4 Identification of PTSD in primary care

The main presenting complaint of sufferers does not necessarily include intrusive memories of the traumatic event. Patients may present with depression and general anxiety, fear of leaving their home, somatic complaints, irritability, inability to work or sleep problems. They may not relate their symptoms to the traumatic event, especially if significant time has elapsed since that event. Older adults report more frequently somatic and physical complaints (Gray & Acierno, 2002) and are often reluctant to report traumatic events or admit to emotional or psychological difficulties (Comijs *et al*, 1999). Practitioners may also need to distinguish PTSD from traumatic or complicated grief reactions that may develop a year or more following a bereavement, with symptoms including intense intrusive thoughts, pangs of severe emotion, distressing yearnings, feeling excessively alone and empty, excessively avoiding tasks reminiscent of the deceased, unusual sleep disturbances and maladaptive levels of loss of interest in personal activities (Horowitz *et al*, 1997).

Epidemiological research has shown that the diagnosis of PTSD is greatly underestimated if the interviewer does not directly ask about the occurrence of specific traumatic events (Solomon & Davidson, 1997).

2.3.4.1 For patients with unexplained physical symptoms who are repeated attendees to primary care, members of the primary care team should consider asking whether or not they have experienced a traumatic event, and provide specific examples of traumatic events (for example, assaults, rape, road traffic accidents, childhood sexual abuse and traumatic childbirth). **GPP**

Checklists of common traumatic experiences and symptoms may be helpful for some patients who find it hard to name them. Both the CAPS (Blake *et al*, 1995) and the PDS (Foa *et al*, 1997) include checklists.

2.3.5 Trauma and families

2.3.5.1 People who have lost a close friend or relative due to an unnatural or sudden death should be assessed for PTSD and traumatic grief. In most cases, healthcare professionals should treat the PTSD first without avoiding discussion of the grief. **C**

2.3.5.2 In all cases of PTSD, healthcare professionals should consider the impact of the traumatic event on all family members and, when appropriate, assess this impact and consider providing appropriate support. **GPP**

2.3.5.3 Healthcare professionals should ensure, where appropriate and with the consent of the PTSD sufferer where necessary, that the families of PTSD sufferers are fully informed about common reactions to traumatic events, including the symptoms of PTSD and its course and treatment. **GPP**

2.3.5.4 When a family is affected by a traumatic event, more than one family member may suffer from PTSD. If this is the case, healthcare professionals should ensure that the treatment of all family members is effectively coordinated. **GPP**

Please see also the special section on the assessment of children (Chapter 9).

2.3.6 Differential diagnoses

Post-traumatic stress disorder is not the only disorder that may be triggered by a traumatic event. Differential disorders (and indicators) to be considered are:
- depression (predominance of low mood, lack of energy, loss of interest, suicidal ideation)
- specific phobias (fear and avoidance restricted to certain situations)
- adjustment disorders (less severe stressor, different pattern of symptoms; see below)
- enduring personality changes after catastrophic experience (prolonged extreme stressor, different pattern of symptoms; see below)
- dissociative disorders

- neurological damage due to injuries sustained during the event
- psychosis (hallucinations, delusions).

Of course, PTSD may also exist comorbidly with many of the above disorders, in particular depression and anxiety disorders.

2.3.6.1 Enduring personality changes after catastrophic experience, DESNOS and 'complex' PTSD

Many trauma survivors have experienced a range of different traumatic experiences over their life span or have experienced prolonged traumas such as childhood sexual abuse or imprisonment with torture. Several authors have suggested that many of these people develop a range of other problems besides PTSD, for example depression, low self-esteem, self-destructive behaviours, poor impulse control, somatisation and chronic dissociation or depersonalisation. It has been controversial whether these reactions form a separate diagnostic category. Herman (1993) and others suggested a separate diagnosis of 'complex PTSD' or 'disorders of extreme distress not otherwise specified' (DESNOS) to describe a syndrome that is associated with repeated and prolonged trauma. Initial research has found some evidence for the validity of this concept (e.g. Pelcovitz *et al*, 1997). However, it was decided not to include DESNOS as a separate diagnostic category in DSM–IV: instead, the DESNOS criteria were included among the 'associated descriptive features' of PTSD. This reflects the view that these characteristics are not a unique feature of survivors of childhood sexual abuse or other prolonged trauma, but instead apply in varying degrees to most PTSD sufferers.

The ICD–10 distinguishes between PTSD and 'enduring personality changes after catastrophic experience' (F62.0). The latter diagnosis arose from clinical descriptions of concentration camp survivors and is characterised by a hostile or distrustful attitude towards the world, social withdrawal, feelings of emptiness or hopelessness, a chronic feeling of 'being on edge' as if constantly threatened, and estrangement. 'Enduring personality changes after catastrophic experience' can be an outcome of chronic PTSD, especially after experiences such as torture or being held for a long period as a hostage.

The ICD–10 research diagnostic criteria for 'enduring personality changes after catastrophic experience' require:

(A)   A definite and persistent change in the individual's pattern of perceiving, relating to and thinking about the environment and the self following exposure to extreme stress.

(B)   At least two of the following:

    (1)   a permanent hostile or distrustful attitude toward the world

    (2)   social withdrawal

    (3)   a constant feeling of emptiness or hopelessness

    (4)   an enduring feeling of being on edge or being threatened without external cause

    (5)   a permanent feeling of being changed or being different from others.

(C)   The personality change causes significant interference with personal or social functioning or significant distress.

(D)   The personality change developed after the catastrophic event, and the person did not have a personality disorder prior to the event that explains the current traits.

(E)   The personality change must have been present for at least 2 years, and is not related to episodes of any other mental disorder (other than PTSD) or brain damage or disease.

The NICE guideline focuses on the treatment of PTSD, as there is as yet little research on the treatment of 'enduring personality changes after catastrophic experience'. It is, however, recognised that many PTSD sufferers will have at least some of the features of this disorder or the corresponding concept of DESNOS (complex PTSD). The guideline therefore takes into account that these features need to be considered when treating PTSD sufferers. However, the guideline does not apply to individuals whose main problem is a diagnosis of 'enduring personality changes after catastrophic experience' rather than PTSD.

2.3.6.2 Dissociative disorders

Dissociative disorders are characterised by a partial or complete loss of the normal integration between memories of the past, awareness of identity and immediate sensations, and control of bodily movements. The ICD–10 dissociative (conversion) disorders include dissociative amnesia, dissociative fugue, dissociative disorders of movement and sensation, and other dissociative (conversion) disorders including multiple personality disorder. The disturbance may be sudden or gradual, transient or chronic. It is presumed that the ability to exercise a conscious and selective control is impaired in dissociative disorders, to a degree that can vary from day to day or even from hour to hour. However, it is usually difficult to assess the extent to which some of the loss of functions might be under voluntary control. Dissociative disorders are presumed to be psychogenic in origin, being associated closely in time with traumatic events, insoluble and intolerable problems, or disturbed relationships.

People with PTSD may experience a peri-traumatic dissociation (a dissociative reaction at the time of the trauma), which may subsequently be associated with the complaint of psychogenic amnesia for an aspect of the traumatic event. The disorder is also associated with an increased rate of other dissociative symptoms. Indeed, in the preparation for the publication of DSM–IV, there was discussion as to whether PTSD should be listed as a dissociative disorder rather than an anxiety disorder (see Brett, 1993).

2.3.6.3 Adjustment disorders

Adjustment disorders are states of subjective distress and emotional disturbance that arise in the period of adaptation to a significant life change or stressful life event. Stressors include those that affect the integrity of an individual's social network (e.g. bereavement, separation) or the wider system of social supports and values (e.g. migration, leaving the armed forces), or represent a major developmental transition or crisis (e.g. retirement). Manifestations vary and include depressed mood, anxiety or worry, a feeling of inability to cope, plan ahead or continue in the present situation, as well as some degree of disability in the performance of daily routine. Conduct problems may also occur.

2.3.7 Is PTSD the main problem?

This guideline applies to patients for whom PTSD is the main problem. Whether or not PTSD is the problem that should be the focus of treatment depends on the severity and urgency of other disorders and problems, such as social problems, health problems and safety issues. This may include practical problems such as safe housing, support in court cases, and a range of psychological symptoms. In order to establish whether or not PTSD is the main psychological problem, it is useful to ask trauma survivors:

- what symptoms or problems bother them the most
- whether they think that they would need help with their other symptoms or problems if the PTSD symptoms could be taken away
- whether or not the other problems were present before the traumatic event.

Individuals should be fully assessed before a management plan is devised. Other factors, for example suicide risk, may determine what the most important focus should be in the first instance. Simply because there is a trauma history, it should not be assumed that there is PTSD.

Epidemiological studies give further insight into common patterns of comorbidity.

Comorbid diagnoses

In two large epidemiological studies conducted in the USA and Australia, 85–88% of the men and 78–80% of the women with PTSD had comorbid psychiatric diagnoses (Kessler *et al*, 1995; Creamer *et al*, 2001). This raises the following clinically important questions:

- Is PTSD primary or secondary to comorbid disorders such as depression, substance misuse or anxiety disorders?
- Will the treatment of PTSD lead to improvement in the comorbid conditions?
- Which disorder should be treated first?

Whether or not the comorbid diagnoses are secondary to PTSD (i.e. are complications of the PTSD) can usually be determined by the time course of symptom onset and their functional relationship. Kessler *et al* (1995) showed that PTSD was primary to comorbid affective or substance use disorders in the majority of cases, and was primary to comorbid anxiety disorders in about half of the cases.

In many cases comorbid problems that are secondary to the PTSD, such as comorbid depression, general anxiety or alcohol or substance misuse, improve with trauma-focused psychological treatment. Treatment studies of PTSD show that with the successful treatment of PTSD, comorbid symptoms of depression and anxiety are also greatly reduced. For example, patients with comorbid secondary major depression no longer met diagnostic criteria for major depression after PTSD treatment (Blanchard *et al*, 2003*b*).

2.3.7.1   When a patient presents with PTSD and depression, healthcare professionals should consider treating the PTSD first, as the depression will often improve with successful treatment of the PTSD. C

However, in patients with a long history of PTSD or patients who have experienced multiple traumatic events and losses, the depression can become so severe that it needs immediate attention (i.e. it is a suicide risk), and dominates the clinical picture to the extent that it makes some forms of PTSD treatment impossible (for example, owing to extreme lack of energy, social withdrawal and inactivity). Psychological treatments for PTSD often involve discussing the traumatic events and their meanings in detail. Extremely severe depression would need to be treated before patients could benefit from such trauma-focused treatments. (We use the term 'trauma-focused' treatment for a range of psychological treatments of PTSD that help the patient come to terms with the traumatic event by working through the trauma memory and discussing the personal meanings of the traumatic event.)

2.3.7.2   For PTSD sufferers who are so severely depressed that this makes initial psychological treatment of PTSD very difficult (for example, as evidenced by extreme lack of energy and concentration, inactivity, or high suicide risk), healthcare professionals should treat the depression first. C

2.3.7.3   For PTSD sufferers whose assessment identifies a high risk of suicide or harm to others, healthcare professionals should first concentrate on management of this risk. C

Similarly, many patients with PTSD misuse both alcohol and a range of drugs in an attempt to cope with their symptoms, and treatment of their PTSD symptoms will help them with reducing their substance use. However, if substance dependence (i.e. withdrawal symptoms, tolerance) has developed, this will need to be treated before the patient can benefit from trauma-focused psychological treatments. In cases where the drug or alcohol dependence is severe, collaborative working with specialist substance misuse services may be required.

2.3.7.4   For PTSD sufferers with drug or alcohol dependence, or in whom alcohol or drug use may significantly interfere with effective treatment, healthcare professionals should treat the drug or alcohol problem first. C

Personality disorders

Patients with personality disorders may present two kinds of problems with regard to PTSD. First, as a result of their interpersonal difficulties they may at times find themselves in situations in which they are more likely to be harmed and suffer PTSD as a consequence of the harm suffered. Second, in some cases there is a history of abuse in childhood as a factor in the development of the personality disorder. This may also lead to adult PTSD, although the PTSD is unlikely to be the main focus of their presentation. It has been assumed by some therapists and researchers that personality disorder is a contraindication for many treatments. However, recent research suggests that individuals with personality disorder can benefit from structured psychological treatments for comorbid disorder such as anxiety and depression, although such treatments may not directly affect the problems associated with personality disorder (Dreessen & Arntz, 1998). Patients with personality disorder therefore could benefit from trauma-focused psychological interventions.

2.3.7.5   When offering trauma-focused psychological interventions to PTSD sufferers with comorbid personality disorder, healthcare professionals should consider extending the duration of treatment. C

Social and physical problems

People with PTSD often have difficult life circumstances. For example, they may have housing or serious financial problems, live under ongoing threat (e.g. still live with the perpetrator of violence) or experience continued trauma. Refugees face multiple problems of building up a new life and adjusting to a new culture and language. Chapter 10 addresses the special problems in the treatment of refugees.

These adverse life circumstances may be the PTSD sufferer's most pressing concern and, if so, will need to be addressed before treatment of the PTSD is indicated. Similarly, PTSD sufferers who were injured in the traumatic event might still be undergoing medical treatment, might be waiting for further surgery or might have to cope with permanent physical disability. These physical problems might be their most pressing concern at present and might also have an impact on treatment duration.

2.3.7.6   Healthcare professionals should consider offering help or advice to PTSD sufferers or relevant others on how continuing threats related to the traumatic event may be alleviated or removed. **GPP**

2.3.7.7   Healthcare professionals should normally only consider providing trauma-focused psychological treatment when the sufferer considers it safe to proceed. **GPP**

2.3.7.8   Healthcare professionals should identify the need for appropriate information about the range of emotional responses that may develop and provide practical advice on how to access appropriate services for these problems. They should also identify the need for social support and advocate for the meeting of this need. **GPP**

2.3.7.9   Where a PTSD sufferer has a different cultural or ethnic background from that of the healthcare professionals who are providing care, the healthcare professionals should familiarise themselves with the cultural background of the PTSD sufferer. **GPP**

2.3.7.10   Where differences of language or culture exist between healthcare professionals and PTSD sufferers, this should not be an obstacle to the provision of effective trauma-focused psychological interventions. **GPP**

2.3.7.11   Where language or culture differences present challenges to the use of trauma-focused psychological interventions in PTSD, healthcare professionals should consider the use of interpreters and bicultural therapists. **GPP**

2.3.7.12   Healthcare professionals should pay particular attention to the identification of individuals with PTSD where the culture of the working or living environment is resistant to recognition of the psychological consequences of trauma. **GPP**

2.4 Aetiology of PTSD

2.4.1 The traumatic event

It is now recognised that the traumatic event is a major cause of the symptoms of PTSD. Historically, this has been the subject of considerable debate. Charcot, Janet, Freud and Breuer suggested that hysterical symptoms were caused by psychological trauma, but their views were not widely accepted (see reviews by Gersons & Carlier, 1992; Kinzie & Goetz, 1996; van der Kolk *et al*, 1996). The dominant view was that a traumatic event in itself was not a sufficient cause of these symptoms, and experts searched for other explanations. Many suspected an organic cause. For example, damage to the spinal cord was suggested as the cause of the 'railway spine syndrome', micro-sections of exploded bombs entering the brain as the cause of 'shell shock' and starvation and brain damage as causes of the chronic psychological difficulties of concentration camp survivors. Others doubted the validity of the symptom reports and suggested that malingering and compensation-seeking ('compensation neurosis') were the major cause in most cases. Finally, the psychological symptoms were attributed to pre-existing psychological dysfunction. The predominant view was that reactions to traumatic events were transient, and that therefore only people with unstable personalities, pre-existing neurotic conflicts or mental illness would develop chronic symptoms (Gersons & Carlier, 1992; Kinzie & Goetz, 1996; van der Kolk *et al*, 1996).

It was the recognition of the long-standing psychological problems of many war veterans, especially Vietnam veterans, and of rape survivors that changed this view and convinced clinicians and researchers that even people with sound personalities could develop clinically significant psychological symptoms if they were exposed to horrific stressors. This prompted the introduction of post-traumatic stress disorder as a diagnostic category in DSM– III (American Psychiatric Association, 1980). It was thus recognised that traumatic events such as combat, rape and man-made or natural disasters give rise to a characteristic pattern of psychological symptoms. The ICD–10 classification emphasised the causal role of traumatic stressors in producing psychological dysfunction even more clearly, in that a specific group of disorders, 'reaction to severe stress, and adjustment disorders', was created. These disorders are 'thought to arise always as a direct consequence of the acute severe stress or continued trauma. The stressful event ... is the primary and overriding causal factor, and the disorder would not have occurred without its impact' (World Health Organization, 1992: p. 145).

The criteria of what constitutes a traumatic stressor have been modified since the diagnosis of PTSD was introduced. Initially PTSD was thought to occur only following an event 'outside the range of usual human experience'. However, epidemiological data showed that PTSD may develop in response to traumatic events such as road traffic accidents or assault, which are so widespread that they are not 'outside the range of usual human experience'. The criteria for what constitutes a traumatic stressor have therefore been modified over the years (reviewed by McNally *et al*, 2003). The DSM–IV now emphasises threat to physical integrity as a common element of trauma, and takes into account that the person's subjective response to the event is crucial in determining whether the event is experienced as traumatic, by specifying that the person must experience extreme fear, helplessness or horror during the event. The ICD–10 emphasises that the event must be of an 'exceptionally threatening or catastrophic nature'.

2.4.2 Trauma memories

The characteristic re-experiencing symptoms in PTSD appear to be the result of the way the traumatic event is laid down in memory. Trauma is overwhelming, and exceeds people's resources for information processing. The resulting memory for the event appears to be different from ordinary autobiographical memories. This has the effect that aspects of the memory can be easily triggered, and are re-experienced as if they were happening right now, rather than as memories of a past event. The exact mechanisms of the memory abnormalities are currently being investigated (Brewin *et al*, 1996; McNally, 2003; Brewin, 2005; Ehlers *et al*, 2004).

2.4.3 Fear conditioning

Classical conditioning theory suggests that stimuli experienced at the time of trauma become associated with fear. Consequently, stimuli resembling those present during the traumatic event trigger severe distress, and are avoided (see, for example, Keane *et al*, 1985).

2.4.4 Individual interpretations of the traumatic event and its consequences

The degree of threat that people perceive during a traumatic event depends on their interpretation of what is happening. For example, whether or not people perceive that their life is in danger during the traumatic event has a large impact on the likelihood of developing PTSD. Similarly, the conclusions they draw from the event are important factors in maintaining PTSD; for example, if PTSD sufferers feel guilty or ashamed about what happened, and blame themselves for things they think they are responsible for, they are unlikely to come to terms with the event and resume their former lives. If PTSD sufferers interpret the trauma as meaning that they are at great risk of further trauma, they continue to feel threatened in their everyday life. The interpretations characteristic of PTSD not only concern the traumatic event, but also its consequences, including responses of others in the aftermath of the event, initial PTSD symptoms and physical injuries (e.g. Foa *et al*, 1999; Ehlers & Clark, 2000).

2.4.5 Unhelpful coping strategies

Trauma memories are painful and PTSD symptoms are distressing. In their efforts to cope with the event and the symptoms they are experiencing, trauma survivors may resort to a range of coping strategies that appear to be helpful at the time, but prolong or exacerbate symptoms. These include effortful suppression of trauma memories and emotions, rumination about the event, dissociation, social withdrawal, avoidance and substance use (e.g. Ehlers & Clark, 2000).

2.4.6 Social support and relationships with significant others

Lack of social support in the aftermath of trauma is associated with greater risk of chronic PTSD (Brewin *et al*, 2000; Ozer *et al*, 2003). The experience of a traumatic event often has a negative impact on survivors' ability to trust other people and engage in close relationships, in particular if the event involved intentional harm by others. Sufferers may feel alienated from others and withdraw from previously significant relationships. This may contribute to the maintenance of the problem, and interfere with a trusting relationship with health professionals (e.g. Ehlers *et al*, 2000).

2.4.7 Litigation

The hypothesis that reports of PTSD symptoms are mainly due to malingering and compensation-seeking ('compensation neurosis') has not been supported by systematic research. On the other hand, protracted legal proceedings may exacerbate the distress of PTSD sufferers and make it difficult for them to put the event in the past (Blanchard *et al*, 1996; Ehlers *et al*, 1998). This may well explain much of the association between PTSD symptoms and litigation, but the relationship is a complex one and is more fully considered in Chapter 8.

2.4.8 Hypothalamic–pituitary–adrenal axis abnormalities

People with current PTSD may show abnormally low levels of cortisol compared with normal controls and with traumatised individuals without current PTSD (e.g. Yehuda *et al*, 1995). In addition, PTSD sufferers may also have an increased number of lymphocyte glucocorticoid receptors. When given a low dose of dexamethasone, PTSD sufferers exhibit hypersuppression of cortisol. Thus, PTSD sufferers tend to show a very different pattern of hypothalamic–pituitary–adrenal (HPA) axis response from patients with major depression. The pattern of findings suggests that the HPA axis in PTSD is characterised by enhanced negative feedback (Yehuda *et al*, 1995). There may also be a downregulation of corticotrophin-releasing factor receptors at the anterior pituitary due to chronic increases in corticotrophin-releasing factor (Bremner *et al*, 1997). Overall, the pattern of findings suggests that the HPA axis in PTSD is set to produce large responses to further stressors.

2.4.9 Neurochemical abnormalities

Several neurotransmitter systems may be dysregulated in PTSD. Research suggests a sensitisation of the noradrenergic system. Another subgroup of PTSD sufferers seems to be characterised by a sensitised serotonergic system. Endogenous opiates have been suspected to mediate the symptoms of emotional numbing and amnesia. The dopaminergic, gamma-aminobutyric acid (GABA) and *N*-methyl-D-aspartate systems have also been implicated in PTSD, but the evidence for these hypotheses is sparse at this stage (Charney *et al*, 1993).

2.4.10 Hippocampal size

People with long-standing PTSD may have a smaller hippocampus than controls. Latest findings suggest that small hippocampus size may be a vulnerability factor, rather than a consequence of trauma (Gilbertson *et al*, 2002; see McNally, 2003, for a review).

2.4.11 Vulnerability factors

A range of vulnerability factors for PTSD have been identified (Brewin *et al*, 2000; Ozer *et al*, 2003). These include a previous personal or family history of anxiety disorders or affective disorders, neuroticism, lower intelligence, female gender and a history of previous trauma. Genetic factors and the impact of early trauma on the neurobiological system may also have a role (Heim & Nemeroff, 2001). Overall, the amount of variance explained by these factors is small. Chapter 8 is dedicated to a systematic review of factors that may be useful in screening for people at risk for PTSD after traumatic events.

2.5 Treatment and management of PTSD in the NHS

Emotional reactions to traumatic events started to achieve a high priority in the UK after the disasters of the 1980s, including the Bradford football stadium fire, the sinking of the *Herald of Free Enterprise* ferry and the King's Cross fire. In the aftermath of each of these events, committed people established treatment services. Following research into the needs of UK citizens held in Kuwait and Iraq as the 'human shield' in the first Gulf War (Easton & Turner, 1991), the Department of Health established two national treatment facilities (on short-term contracts) to help promote the development of services in the UK. Since then, there has been an expansion of these specialist centres across the country and a model of cooperation has developed (e.g. through the UK Trauma Group; www.uktrauma.org.uk). Statutory services for certain specialist groups such as refugees and war veterans have lagged behind, and have often been supported primarily by the voluntary sector. Recently, statutory services have started to grow in these areas as well.

One of the challenges of recent years has been to help local services gain the skills to treat as many people with PTSD as possible. To an increasing degree this has been achieved, and now people with PTSD and related disorders are being treated in a range of National Health Service (NHS) and non-statutory settings, including primary care, general mental health services and specialist secondary care mental health services. However, the provision and uptake of such services still varies across England and Wales and reflects the demands of particular populations (for example, refugees or war veterans) and the presence or absence of specialist services. The decade prior to 2005 has seen a significant expansion of special services, but the provision is still subject to considerable local variation, and some PTSD sufferers may have to go through many steps before they can obtain referral to a treatment service, or they may face unreasonably long delays.

The challenge for the future will be to see services devolved into primary care settings, where this is feasible. There is a need to develop a pathway of care that offers prompt, evidence-based services in local communities, supported by specialist services for more refractory or complex problems. We hope that this guideline will be a stimulus to this process.

2.6 Primary care

2.6.1 First presentations

Many individuals will consult their general practitioner shortly after experiencing a traumatic event, but will not present a complaint or request for help specifically related to the psychological aspects of the trauma; for example, an individual who has been physically assaulted or involved in a road traffic accident or an accident at work might present requiring attention to the physical injuries sustained. This provides an opportunity for an assessment of the patient's psychological state. Similarly, individuals who have been involved in such events often present at local emergency departments, notification of which is sent to general practitioners. Others suffering from a potentially adverse psychological reaction to trauma include people who might have been traumatised as a result of domestic violence or childhood sexual abuse and might not necessarily have presented with complaints related to this previously. The key point here is that primary care staff should consider that PTSD can arise not simply from single events such as an assault or a road traffic accident but also from the repeated trauma associated with childhood sexual abuse, domestic violence or the repeated trauma associated with being a refugee.

A small proportion of PTSD cases have delayed onset (probably less than 15%; McNally, 2003). The assessment of such presentations is essentially the same as for non-delayed presentations. There is evidence to suggest that delayed presentations of PTSD, even those that occur some years after the traumatic event, are likely to respond to treatment (Foa *et al*, 1991; Gillespie *et al*, 2002; Resick *et al*, 2002). A long period between the trauma and the onset and presentation of symptoms should therefore not be a disincentive to the identification and referral for treatment.

2.6.1.1 PTSD may present with a range of symptoms (including re-experiencing, avoidance, hyperarousal, depression, emotional numbing, drug or alcohol misuse and anger) and therefore when assessing for PTSD, members of the primary care team should ask in a sensitive manner whether or not patients with such symptoms have suffered a traumatic experience (which might have occurred many months or years before), giving specific examples of traumatic events (for example, assaults, rape, road traffic accidents, childhood sexual abuse and traumatic childbirth). **GPP**

2.6.1.2 General practitioners and other members of the primary care team should be aware of traumas associated with the development of PTSD. These include single events such as assaults or road traffic accidents, and domestic violence or childhood sexual abuse. **GPP**

2.6.2 Repeated presentations

A number of people may previously have presented with PTSD and received treatment for it. Although the response to effective interventions for the treatment of PTSD is now generally good, a small but significant number do not respond to such treatment. It is important to reassess individuals who have not responded and to consider other diagnoses and comorbidity. There is some evidence to suggest that returning for a second period of treatment may be beneficial and it is important therefore not to assume that failure of a previous treatment means that a person will not respond well to treatment in the future. For example, the presence of a continuing threat might have impaired an individual's ability to benefit from previous treatment, the treatment provided might have been inadequate, or the patient might not have been able to tolerate the treatment offered at the time.

2.6.3 Comorbid presentations

Post-traumatic stress reactions are associated with significant comorbidities. Most prominent among these comorbidities is depression. Depression that does not respond to conventional treatments or that might have arisen following a traumatic event should alert the general practitioner or other primary care team member to the possibility of a post-traumatic stress reaction. The inappropriate use of prescribed drugs or the misuse of street drugs or alcohol, particularly if associated with avoidance of certain situations, to facilitate sleep or to avoid other psychological difficulties, should also alert the practitioner to the possibility of PTSD.

As detailed in the section on screening and assessment (2.3.2 and 2.3.3), a few simple questions may be required to identify patients who require further and more detailed assessment.

2.6.4 Watchful waiting

A significant number of people presenting with acute reactions or established PTSD can be expected to recover within a relatively short space of time (Rothbaum et al, 1992; Bryant, 2003). The rate of remission is higher for those with milder symptoms. For such people some element of brief education, support and advice in the context of their presentation followed by watchful waiting may be most appropriate, with the individual either encouraged to return for further assessment or offered a specific appointment time if there is sufficient concern on the part of the general practitioner or the primary care team member.

2.6.4.1 Where symptoms are mild and have been present for less than 4 weeks after the trauma, watchful waiting, as a way of managing the difficulties presented by individual sufferers, should be considered by healthcare professionals. A follow-up contact should be arranged within 1 month. **C**

2.6.5 Immediate management of PTSD

The immediate management of PTSD in part depends upon the nature of the trauma and the circumstances in which it arose. In the rare event that it arose as part of a major disaster, man-made or natural, specific resources to support individuals involved in this may be available and it will be for the general practitioner and other members of the primary care mental health team to facilitate the individual's access to such services as may be available. More usually, however, the trauma will arise as a result of a smaller-scale incident. In the latter circumstances a number of treatment options are available. For some people relatively low-key brief interventions provided in primary care can offer the appropriate level of intervention. For others, more complex and long-standing interventions are required; inevitably some of these people will be required to wait for treatment, and this will leave the general practitioner and other members of the primary care mental health team with a potentially significant management problem. This might relate to specific PTSD symptoms, for example intrusive recollections or nightmares concerning the event, specific sleep disturbance, social withdrawal, irritability or more generalised distress. In such circumstances strategies such as advice on sleep hygiene, advice to rely on the natural support from their families and others available (including, where appropriate, support groups) and where possible pharmacological interventions (see Chapter 6) should be considered. Depending on the waiting time for appropriate psychological or other specialist interventions, the general practitioner may also consider regular reviewing of individual patients.

2.6.6 Persisting PTSD and chronic disease management

Regardless of offers of treatment or actual courses of treatment, a number of individuals with PTSD will achieve negligible or only partial recovery and will continue to suffer from PTSD symptoms for a considerable period. The degree of disability that people with chronic PTSD suffer can be significant and can considerably impair functioning in an individual's personal, social and occupational life. This may be associated with problems such as chronic sleep disturbance and occasionally with alcohol or drug misuse. More often it is characterised by significant social avoidance. In these circumstances the focus of management in primary care may be on the disabling symptoms rather than the underlying PTSD. Advice on sleep hygiene and (where appropriate) pharmacological interventions may have some benefit in dealing with sleep-related problems. An encouragement to engage in structured and supported activities with some facilitation from primary or secondary care mental health staff may also be of value to people with the chronic social avoidance associated with PTSD, as may contact with other individuals who have undergone a similar experience. In some areas support groups exist and individuals should be made aware of these and of national organisations.

Chronic disease management models, where the practice identifies and helps individuals develop appropriate coping strategies to cope with their chronic problems, should be considered. Models such as those that have been developed for the treatment of depression (Katon et al, 2001), drawing on previous work for the treatment of chronic physical conditions such as diabetes or arthritis, offer some promise. Regular routine contact, often through members of the primary care staff other than the general practitioner, and regular if not frequent reviews with the general practitioner, offer a real opportunity.

2.6.6.1   Chronic disease management models should be considered for the management of people with chronic PTSD who have not benefited from a number of courses of evidence-based treatment. C

2.7 Economic burden of PTSD

Methods of economic evaluation command a fairly high level of consensus and are reported by Drummond et al (1997). However, costing data for PTSD treatments and their consequent outcomes are scarce to non-existent. In the absence of known quantity-of-life or quality-of-life data, the preferred approach is to conduct a cost-effectiveness analysis to examine alternative interventions. In this form of economic evaluation, alternatives are assessed by both their impact on costs and meaningful health-related gains. This approach delivers the incremental cost per unit of benefit achieved.

In the case of PTSD, as with other disorders for which multiple treatments are practised, it is useful to examine the additional costs that one intervention or programme imposes over the other, compared with the additional effects or benefits each delivers (Drummond et al, 1997). Since there may be a significant difference in cost between patients at first presentation and patients continuing a treatment programme, there is a pressing need to compare incremental costs with incremental outcomes, and future studies should present these in a cost-effectiveness analysis with allowance for uncertainty of costs and consequences. Unfortunately, despite efforts to prevent and treat the condition, the majority of economic evaluations of PTSD fail to meet rigorous criteria for health economic appraisal.

'Neurotic disorders' have been estimated to cost the NHS up to £5600 million per year (Holmes, 1994). In addition, the Department of Health (1995) estimated that 91 million working days each year in the UK are lost through stress-related illness, at a cost to industry of £3700 million. In 2003–4, social and welfare costs of claims for incapacitation and severe disablement from severe stress and PTSD amounted to £103 million, which is £55 million more than was claimed 5 years previously (Hansard, 2004). Therefore, PTSD presents an enormous economic burden on families, the national health services and society as a whole.

To remedy this situation, there is a need for robust efficacy data and reliable cost estimates for alternative treatments. Prospective studies should report direct costs alongside indirect costs, which can be significant. For example, a patient who prior to leaving work garnered the average national earnings of £25170 per year (Incomes Data Services, 2003) would lose £483.04 for every week of absence, as well as opportunities for career advancement. At an estimated, approximate cost to the NHS of £825 for ten treatment sessions (1–1½ h in duration), every month of work absence would equate to an amount that could pay for more than 25 sessions of therapy.

Post-traumatic stress disorder presents an excessive health and economic burden on patients, families, healthcare workers, hospitals and society as a whole. Its effects extend far beyond the healthcare sector, and affect the quality of life as well as the ability to function socially and occupationally. The economic and social impact of PTSD is felt not only by those who experience the disorder, but also by families, co-workers, employers and the wider society (McCrone et al, 2003).

As was done in the case of bipolar disorder (Birnbaum et al, 2003), the totality of direct and indirect costs surrounding PTSD should be analysed and compared with other mental health disorders. Considerations of whether patients have equal access to treatment must be included alongside rigorous cost-effectiveness analyses of alternative programmes for distinct types of trauma and socio-demographic factors. Indirect costs to other sectors also must be measured, including those borne by schools, social care agencies, employers and the welfare system, to name but the major ones (Knapp, 2003).

The problem is identifying which patients are likely to benefit from certain treatments, and traumatic events present different patterns of onset and remission. Depending on a number of factors, including individual susceptibilities to a given trauma, the normal range of those exposed to traumatic events who will develop PTSD is 15–71% (Kessler et al, 1995; Breslau et al, 1998; L. G. Ost, personal communication, 2004).

Other traumatic events imbue different patterns of PTSD. For instance, it has been reported that the lifetime prevalence of PTSD following the murder of a family member is 71%, assault of a family member 63%, experiencing physical life threat or being seriously injured 63%, physical assault 58%, rape 57%, rape of a family member 50% and sexual molestation 17% (as reported by Ost and colleagues; L. G. Ost, personal communication, 2004). Thus, the type of trauma appears to influence significantly one's likelihood of experiencing PTSD as well as its pattern of remission and responsiveness to treatment (Breslau et al, 1998).

Therefore, treating populations of individuals who are most likely to need treatment is expected to be more cost-effective than treating the chronic condition at a later stage. As can be seen from the above, chronic PTSD limits years and quality of life as well as functional independence. Efficient service utilisation based upon additional rigorous health economic evaluations would reduce this social and economic burden of PTSD, to ensure the optimal care is delivered within the constraints of the national budget.

3 Experiences of PTSD sufferers and carers

This chapter describes the experiences of a number of PTSD sufferers and also those involved as family members or carers of PTSD sufferers. The testimonies set out below, which present both positive and negative experiences of services and treatment, were chosen because they illustrate a range of experience of sufferers and carers, and because they encompass both the initial trauma and the subsequent impact it had on people's lives. Sufferers' (and carers') struggles to obtain appropriate treatment and the benefit derived from such treatments are also described.

These testimonies and the subsequent commentaries are a central element of this guideline, as they provide an important context in which the effective treatment and management of PTSD can be understood. Many of the recommendations in Chapter 2 and in other parts of the guideline were developed in response to or shaped by the concerns and experiences of the sufferers represented here.

3.1 Personal testimonies from PTSD sufferers

3.1.1 Testimony one

I am a survivor of an industrial disaster that took place over 30 years ago, in which 144 people died, most of them children. I was 8 years old at the time. The disaster happened on the last day of school before the half-term holiday. During the first lesson of the morning there was a rumbling sound, which got progressively louder. The teacher assured us that there was nothing to worry about – it was only thunder. The next thing I remember was waking up covered in material. I could see a small aperture of light above me and I could hear screams for help, but could not move. Those screams got less and less as time went on. I was pinned down with my desk against my stomach. My right leg was caught in the radiator and hot water was coming out of it. On my left shoulder was a fellow pupil's head – she was dead and as time went on her eyes became more sunken into her head and her face became puffy.

The rescuers saw me through the aperture above me. As the firemen pulled me out I was passed in a human chain out into the schoolyard, where I was seen by medics before being sent to hospital. The rescue operation itself was somewhat of a chaotic affair, with miners from the local colliery, emergency services and voluntary bodies all coming to help. Debris was moved from one part to another with no indication as to whether anyone was under it. I was the last to come out of the school alive. Only four out of the 34 pupils in the class survived.

I had to grow up very quickly – one minute I was a young boy with no cares in the world. The next minute I had death on my shoulder; I couldn't play because the majority of my friends were gone, and I had recurrent nightmares. I sustained physical injuries to my head and stomach but these would heal with time – it was the psychological injuries that would go on for much longer and still have an impact over 30 years later.

At first, I could not go to school, as I feared that the disaster would happen again. In addition, my ability to concentrate was extremely poor. It was not until my O levels some 6 years later that I really settled down into education, eventually getting my degree. The attitude of the education authority at the time was not to push individuals back into education but to let them find their way back into the system.

After the disaster, psychological and psychiatric services – in their infancy at that time – were offered to the survivors. I always remember visiting a child psychologist and being told by her that whenever I had bad thoughts I should think of nice things like birthday parties and balloons. As an 8-year-old at the time, I wondered who needed the help. In fact much of the burden for the aftermath of the disaster fell on the local general practitioners and they really had to pick up the pieces and are to be praised for the role they played in the community.

I had nightmares for many years, flashbacks of what happened on that day (the girl's face on my shoulder), a fear of noise (particularly thunder), a fear of crowds, and a sense of guilt as to why I survived and others had died. The absolute torment of these issues engulfed my whole person, sending me into the depths of despair and depression.

Events (such as the earthquakes in Turkey) can trigger off flashbacks and deep depression. The depression totally immobilises me. I can't even pick up a razor to shave, unable to look in the mirror; I question my existence. It becomes so intense that I have to go to bed for a couple of days and wait for it to pass.

How have I overcome or come to terms with these issues? The answer is that I haven't – I have learnt to live with them. The effect of the disaster will be with me until I die. Some survivors have been able to manage it and come to terms with it better than others. I have found that over the years I have been able to talk about it more easily without getting upset. Indeed, talking about it has helped me to come to terms with it and it's surprising how often new facts come out, having been released from my subconscious. My advice to any one involved in a traumatic event is to speak about it and to release the anger and frustration that inevitably builds up within you.

3.1.2 Testimony two

After my final tour of duty in the military, I came home in 1993 feeling like my whole life had changed and that my attitude to my friends and life in general had changed. I had flashbacks, problems sleeping, was absolutely terrified of bangs and fireworks, and felt guilty and ashamed that I was the only one who seemed to be affected. My self-confidence had gone, I struggled with mood swings and had difficulty socialising.

I had my first breakdown in 1995, which resulted in my GP [general practitioner] prescribing Seroxat [paroxetine] that made me act in a frenzied and uncontrollable way when I had either forgotten to take it or tried to come off it. I was not offered any counselling or a referral to a psychiatrist and no investigations were conducted to find the cause of my problems.

I had a second major breakdown in 1999. I could no longer cope with my job because I couldn't deal with any confrontational issues, and was desperate to commit suicide. My life consisted of these spiralling periods of self-doubt, self-hate and worthlessness. I had no idea what was wrong, only that I felt I was going mad. I had many other problems, including anxiety, hyperventilating, sweating and social phobia, to name just a few. There were no clinics I could go to and no support groups. All I wanted to do was talk to someone and tell them how I felt and what I was going through, and how I could not cope. I went to my GP after I admitted to my wife that I wanted to kill myself.

In the end I saw a critical incident debriefer for 10 sessions (funded by my employer on the recommendation of SSAFA [Soldiers, Sailors, Airmen and Families Association] Forces Help) who eventually diagnosed PTSD in 1999. I cried for hours because for the first time in 6 years someone had told me I was ill. When PTSD was explained to me, I fitted every criterion. I knew then that I was not going mad, that I was not the only one who felt this way, and that my problems were normal responses to abnormal occurrences. I was prescribed more drugs (dothiepin [dosulepin]) that were steadily increased until I reached the maximum limit, but they turned me into a zombie. Again no psychological intervention was offered.

When I was first referred to a CMHT [community mental health team] in 1999, the CPN [community psychiatric nurse] would stare at the ceiling and fidget while I tried to explain to him what happened and how I felt. I didn't feel that I could build up any trust with him and he admitted that he did not have the skills or understanding to help me. On one occasion I explained that I had had a problem with Seroxat and as a result was scared to go back to the GP who had prescribed it. It seemed that the CPN did not at first believe me when I said that I found Seroxat to be addictive because he had to ask his colleague to confirm what I had told him. Imagine how I felt when he said this, implying that he did not believe a thing I said? I refused to go back after that and was sent a letter saying that because I had not attended my last appointment they considered me fully recovered and were not going to send me any more appointments. Maybe a questionnaire or a visit to ascertain why I had stopped going might have been better?

It was about a year before I saw anyone again, but I never once got to see a consultant psychiatrist, only the junior doctors who rotated every 6 months. Every time they changed, the new one never read my notes; it was always, 'OK, let's start by you telling me about yourself'. I could never build up any relationship of mutual trust and understanding. Once my wife came with me to see a junior psychiatrist because she was very concerned about my high dose of medication (250 mg of dothiepin [dosulepin]), which made me sleep extremely heavily and for long periods. The psychiatrist agreed to reduce my medication to 225 mg, but I was dumbfounded when on my next visit she asked me if our sex life was now better as she felt that my wife's concerns were due to her being sexually frustrated.

By now I had been to Combat Stress (a charity that helps ex-service personnel who are suffering from mental health problems) for a 1-week residential stay. This helped but initially was only a week at a time with a 6-month gap of nothing. I needed more help.

One psychiatrist had written to my GP and told him that they could no longer provide help for me because they had done everything they could and did not have the skills or resources in this area to help me further and recommended that I visit Combat Stress again, as they were the specialists who could really help me. My GP unfortunately did not agree and as a result I was denied my right to treatment. My GP also denied that he had even received letters from the CMHT when I questioned his decisions. After making a complaint to the senior partner I changed my doctor because I could no longer trust him.

When I needed help the most, I was let down. I was taken off the psychiatrist's books but was not told that I was no longer going to be getting any appointments. When I phoned 4 weeks later needing to see a psychiatrist I was told that I had to be re-referred via my GP. I went to him and was re-referred only to a CPN, not to a psychiatrist, who had clearly not read my notes. I refused to go over what I had been through again and told the CPN to read my notes because it was all in there. I was then informed that this was an initial appointment and that because his books were full they could not see me for another 2 to 3 months. I never did get an appointment from him. This was when I lost all hope in the NHS.

After this I reduced my own medication and using some of my war pension I set up a website about PTSD which explained about the different ways people can help themselves with techniques I had been taught and learnt myself. I wrote everything in a language that anybody could understand and included links to other groups around the world that could help PTSD sufferers wherever they came from. It revived very painful and upsetting memories but my whole motive was to provide information and support to fellow PTSD sufferers so that they did not have to go through the hell that I had to endure. I thought that if I could save just one life, prevent one person from committing suicide, then it was all worth while. My website is now the number one PTSD self-help/information (non-medical) website in the world and I have had many hundreds of thousands of visits to its pages and hundreds of messages of thanks and support.

After another year of being unemployable, I slowly managed to begin a new, 'drug free', life, and with the support of my family I started a new job. Now I have been taken on full-time at work and although I still have to deal with the anxiety, stress, shakings, avoidance and sweating on a daily basis, I am slowly rebuilding a life that just 3 years ago I thought was impossible.

There is hope for people who suffer from PTSD: you can rebuild a life again with the support of your family and friends. I have proven this, but it is not easy and there will be many times when you want to give in. Just accept that you will never be the person who you were before your problems started and accept the new you, warts and all (that's hard, I know, but it is possible).

I feel that healthcare professionals need training and education to understand PTSD (that it can arise as a result of military action) and that it can and should be treated. It is their responsibility to provide treatment in a sensitive, caring and understanding way and not to put PTSD sufferers on medication without adequate review or to reject us as the Ministry of Defence and our communities have done.

3.1.3 Testimony three

The death of my brother in a mass disaster catapulted me out of normality into another world for which I was totally unprepared. Visiting the scene a few days later was one surreal experience of many. Seeing the debris, being at what was basically an enormous gravesite, was something I needed to do. But it had an effect on me that even now, so many years later, remains almost impossible to put into words. What I needed was information, as well as practical help and support to get me through the hideous first days. What I mostly got instead, sometimes from well-intentioned people, ranged from insensitivity to overprotection. They seemed to have expectations of the 'right' way for people in my position to behave – and I didn't fulfil those expectations.

I first went to see my GP several weeks later. I used the excuse of not feeling well to see her and during the appointment I told her what had happened. She said that anger was an inappropriate emotion – she wasn't uncaring, but she seemed to have no understanding of what I might need. I didn't even know this myself, but I left the surgery feeling even angrier than when I had gone to see her – she was the professional and I expected that she would have some clue about what to suggest to make me feel better.

I tried to get on with my life while becoming very involved in trying to find out why the disaster had happened. I got to know other people whose relatives were killed in the disaster and we formed a support group of our own. We once invited a therapist from a trauma clinic to come and talk to us about post-traumatic stress disorder. While she was describing how we might be feeling I felt I couldn't stand it and left the room. Others did the same or put their heads down on the table and cried. Some of it was relief at the recognition that maybe someone understood and was acknowledging what we felt. Some of it was dread – how could we survive feeling this way?

At social events with friends and people from work, I couldn't relate to the ordinary things that were supposed to be amusing and meaningful any more. My experience put me in another category – I felt like I was never going to be the same again.

The next crunch time came for me when I was sitting on the tube [the London Underground] 8 months after the disaster. I was reading a newspaper article that was describing what might have happened to the bodies of those who had been killed – what they could have felt, how they would have been conscious before they died. As I looked around at the other people on the train I felt desperately trapped and wanted to scream at them.

I went to see a therapist at the trauma clinic I had found out about at the support group. I had to fill in a lengthy questionnaire about how I was feeling, without any explanation as to why I was doing it. I felt like screaming all over again – couldn't someone just help me? In the session with the therapist I didn't feel capable of saying what I wanted because I had no rapport with him. The gap between my experience and him seemed to me unbridgeable. I felt as if I was of more use to him than he was to me and so I didn't go back.

I felt more and more incapable of relating to people who didn't share my experience. The constant effort of behaving 'normally' put a huge strain on my life – I was always on edge, bad-tempered and intolerant, highly apprehensive about something happening to my children or my husband. Getting a decent night's sleep seemed impossible. Words beginning with 'd' always became 'death' and 'destruction'. The rest of the world seemed to want me to 'put it behind me', to 'get over it'. I veered between avoiding things that reminded me of what had happened and thinking obsessively about it.

The fifth anniversary brought another crisis. How could I carry on a normal life feeling as I did? I decided to seek help again – six sessions with a local counsellor who listened to what I had to say and tried to help me find ways of calming down. I saw this as a good way to spend the waiting time while I got an appointment at the trauma clinic to see another therapist. The sessions I had with him were definitely of benefit and much more productive than my first attempt. We had a rapport and he was completely non-judgemental of me in a way that I found really helpful.

I can see now that it was terribly frustrating not to have it sufficiently acknowledged by the first doctors and therapists I saw that there was something badly wrong. It seemed to be a real struggle – I felt like I had to jump through a number of hoops to 'prove' that something was wrong with me. At the same time, I resented the idea that the rest of the world was somehow 'normal' and I was not! How much did my brother's death contribute to how I felt? How much was it to do with the fact that so many others had been killed at the same time? How much was it to do with the way people had responded to me afterwards? I still can't be sure, but I do know that most of what happened in the aftermath made it worse. Those to whom I will always be grateful, however, are the people who offered not sympathy but practical help. What would also have been of benefit to me was straightforward, objective, non-judgemental medical information and advice.

Sixteen years on, life remains stressful but mostly manageable. I have joy in my family and find the work that I do to help others in similar circumstances very rewarding. I was right in thinking that I would never be the same again. I still have extremely strong feelings about what happened and sometimes wonder if I should – with the information I have now about trauma and PTSD – try some form of therapy again. I am sure it is never too late to try.

3.1.4 Testimony four

Other than two paramedics I was the first medic (I am a nurse) on the scene of a mass disaster. I had good reason to believe that members of my immediate family were involved. I was involved in resuscitation, had a person die in my arms and witnessed trauma and death, while looking for my loved ones among the carnage. I prepared equipment, stretchered casualties, and moved and helped to identify dead bodies. I later found out that my loved ones were not directly involved.

My feelings about what I had witnessed and experienced changed over time – through disbelief, numbness and a sinking feeling, reactions common after something so traumatic. The impact increased as time moved on – the reality, enormity and the closeness of losing loved ones are almost indescribable. I have gone through many phases of this condition and my PTSD has been determined by psychiatrists as being moderate to severe, and chronic (it is 8 years since it happened). PTSD has affected every aspect of my life and my family.

In the immediate aftermath of the disaster I could not find any help. There were no counsellors at the scene or available afterwards, and my local health centre kept usual hours. I went there the next day at 6.30 a.m. in a drunken state to seek assistance, but there was no one to talk to. I later returned to the health centre, demanding to see a doctor. A young locum advised me to 'see it through' and did not offer help, counselling or sedation.

The next day a local GP came to see me, but she spent more time telling me about her own experiences of the disaster. This was frustrating because I desperately wanted to let off steam. In the end I spoke to the police on the third day to 'let it out'. I also rang my employers, who at first were empathetic; they suggested occupational health, but I didn't see the point, as all they would do would be to refer me to a psychiatrist, nurse or a therapist. When they rang back the next day I was told that two professionals were vying for my case, although I had to wait to see them.

The next day I rang and said that if I didn't get help I was either going to go ballistic or knock someone's door down. The following day I met a therapist who was nice, empathetic, but ineffectual. She told me that she had not dealt with PTSD before but would like to try desensitising treatment that she had 'read about'. Her attempts to try and get me to relive the event while waving hands and lights in my face caused nothing but anguish.

I saw this therapist for months, but after making no progress I saw the other therapist who had previously been interested. When her interventions also failed, she wrote in my notes 'Mr — is not responding, or is unwilling to respond to treatment'! I also felt that the GPs were also clearly out of their depth. They were not willing in many cases to refer on to others as they believed that no treatment should be offered for PTSD for at least 3 months as most people would get better with no intervention. However, I felt that I desperately needed help in the days following the disaster.

I feel I irritated all the professionals that I contacted because I openly admitted the problem, cried for help, admitted that I was sleepless and drinking too much. But I had no help of any kind from them. Months later I saw a psychiatrist, who told me that he had read things on the internet! The only useful thing he did was to prescribe Prozac [fluoxetine] (although I found this hard to understand as I was suffering from PTSD not depression). The dose was ineffectual at first but he doubled the dose, which flattened my emotions and helped me to sleep. At the time that was useful, although perhaps inappropriate. Nothing else happened with this man.

At first my employers pledged their support, but were soon eager to have me back at work. Fourteen months after the event I was sacked on the grounds of ill health (I had hardly attended work during this time). Years later I sought another referral – I had to wait 10 months to be seen. Again this person was nice, but repeated visits proved fruitless. This therapist referred me to another psychiatrist. This man was the most sensible of all; he said 'given [my] history of unsuccessful interventions, there was little else that could be done, save chemical intervention'.

Now, this wasn't good news, but he was realistic, with no rubbish, so I appreciated this. I was prescribed Cipramil [citalopram] in varying doses, until I settled on 20 mg twice daily. The troublesome side-effects are lowering of libido and increasingly vivid nightmares, but on balance my quality of life is at its best since the event. I feel this is down to the medication, the passage of time and being able to work again part time.

I also meet with a few other people who were closely involved in the disaster. This 'self-help' group is perhaps the best 'intervention' I have had because it is with people who have had the same experience, really understand and do not patronise me.

3.1.5 Testimony five

In 2000 I was arrested for being part of a group fighting for democracy in my home country. I was held in prison for 2 months, during which time the police raped me. They beat me around the head so badly that my eardrum was perforated. I was released, but later they arrested my husband and took him away in the middle of the night. I don't know if he is alive or not. Officials kept coming to my house to interrogate me. They threatened to imprison me again, so in 2002 I fled the country, leaving my daughter with my mother.

On arrival in the UK I was interviewed by immigration officials. My English is not good, so an interpreter, who was a man from my community, was present. But I couldn't tell them what had happened because we can't talk about rape in my community – it is so shameful. I couldn't even tell my solicitor what had happened – he was also a man and I felt uncomfortable speaking to him. I was refused asylum.

I couldn't understand why I was being treated so badly and found that I was always crying. At my appeal hearing I still couldn't speak about the rape, but I told them I had been in prison and tortured. They didn't ask me any questions about where I had come from or what I had been through. I was really upset during the hearing and I cried. My appeal was refused some months later. My solicitor didn't do anything more to help me.

I had a friend who came with me to the appeal hearing. She saw that I was crying all the time and suggested I should go to Women Against Rape (WAR) and tell them what happened. So I did and it was the first time I had been able to talk about it and it helped me a lot. The Home Office wanted to send me out of London but I was referred to the Medical Foundation who took me on for counselling, so I was allowed to stay in London. And WAR found me a new solicitor who made a fresh appeal on my behalf. But after about 6 months the Home Office closed my file, and I had to leave the flat where I was living and lost my money.

My solicitor arranged some emergency accommodation through social services, but I was only allowed to stay for 2 weeks. I had a specialist report about my ear and a psychological report, which diagnosed that I was suffering from post-traumatic stress disorder. But although some people in social services wanted to house me, others decided my medical evidence was not enough. After the two weeks, I was homeless again. It was awful – it was just before Christmas and the weather was freezing.

When I was homeless I had many problems. I was sleeping in a park and my bag was stolen by two boys. I went to the police for help, but they arrested me! I went to many charities that are meant to help asylum seekers but no one would help me. The Refugee Arrivals Project let me stay a few nights but then told me to leave, saying I could sleep at the airport. When I asked the Medical Foundation for help they said I was not an emergency. What is the point of trying to make someone feel better with counselling if you know they have nowhere to sleep that night? I slept at the airport, on the street, in a church corridor. I just wanted to die. Fortunately after a while some nuns took me in to their hostel.

Because of the torture I suffered I have physical and mental health problems.

I suffer from repeated ear infections and terrible headaches. When my ear is infected it is so painful I can't see (I am awaiting a third operation). I am also nervous, angry and want to be alone. I can't watch TV or speak to anyone. I tried to get help from a GP because I was crying all the time and I couldn't sleep. I keep seeing what happened back home, reliving the rape over and over. I have bad memories and I can't get these things from my mind. And I really miss my husband and my daughter. But the GP was not good or sympathetic. I told him that I am upset, and that I have other problems like constipation. He just told me that I have depression, and gave me sleeping pills and told me to eat vegetables. I then saw another GP, who was more understanding. He changed my pills. He recognised that I have flashbacks and that I need help. I still see a psychologist every 2 weeks and she makes practical suggestions about my health. She told me to come off the tablets gradually.

WAR contacted my MP and then eventually I won the right to stay in the UK. They helped me get housing and income support. I see them often and it helps me a lot to meet with other women who have suffered like me, and to work out how to improve our situation.

Winning my immigration case was the most important thing. Everything else depended on that. It made me feel so much better, especially now that I am hoping my daughter will be able to join me here. Now I am like a human being – before I didn't feel human.

3.1.6 Testimony six

In 1989 I was raped by a man I met in a disco while backpacking in Australia. I was 19 and alone. I didn't handle it very well, not least because I had contracted an STD through the attack. I didn't report the attack because for the first 2 weeks afterwards I felt it was my fault; I also felt I could not face having to go through a trial. On returning to the UK I told no one except my best friend; but because it upset her so much, I decided there was no point in telling anyone else. Also at the same time there was a family crisis brewing and the last thing I wanted to do was add fuel to the fire. I did a year at college, where I began to drink heavily, got a boyfriend, with whom I had sex five times in 3 years, and got a job in the Midlands. After about a year of starting the job, I began behaving very strangely (e.g. sitting on the edge of my bed and rocking backwards and forwards) and my boyfriend sent me to the doctors, who sent me to Relate, which was the only service in the area that even vaguely came near to addressing problems such as mine. While well meaning, the person I saw at Relate was not qualified in any way to deal with my problems, though at least it gave me an outlet to talk.

Soon I got a new job, left the area and split up with my boyfriend. Six months later I went back to Australia to live in Sydney for a year. I felt fine about being back in Australia but on my return I continued to drink heavily and while out in clubs would, to my shame, tell people what had happened to me in 1989. I sought a counsellor, one of whom offered 'to re-enact the attack', but I declined and, despite her protestations, stopped seeing her.

In 2000 I started a new relationship with a man who was a big socialiser. My drinking and drug taking escalated and while I was doing very well in work, the pressure was growing and cracks were appearing. My partner told me I had to seek help, so I went to see a few more counsellors privately but none seemed able to help me. I stopped seeing them as they seemed to increase my despair at ever being able to find the right sort of help. While I was aware that my behaviour was destructive, I seemed unable to get out of the circle of depression and self-medication.

In May 2002, I was attacked at the top of my street. A man ran up behind me and brought me down to the floor. He threatened to rape me but eventually walked away leaving me physically unharmed. I reported the attack and the police were very good but they never caught the man. I had a leaflet from Victim Support but had no actual support to speak of. I took a week off sick and then returned to work, but a few weeks later my partner and my manager advised me to take more time off. During this two-month period, I visited my sister, where I broke down and became hysterical. My sister – a community psychiatric nurse – was very concerned and insisted that I visit my GP. My GP referred me to the local Traumatic Stress Clinic, where I saw a therapist who told me I was clinically depressed and had post-traumatic stress disorder and that it was likely that the latter was chronic, dating back to the first attack in Australia. He recommended antidepressants and for the first time in years, I felt I had hope.

While on a waiting list for psychological treatment I had my first alcohol-related blackout, during which I started a physical fight with my partner's family. I then stopped drinking for a month because I was afraid of what I might do. I was offered a choice of two treatments and chose exposure therapy, which started in January 2003. It was very hard work but my therapist was excellent – I could tell her everything about my habits, feelings and failures without feeling judged. The treatment sessions were an hour long and once we had gone through my thoughts and feelings about pretty much everything, we wrote out a narrative of the attack and then fine-tuned it. We also recorded it and I would read it through a number of times and we would note down the most stressful points and rate then in terms of anxiety. For 'homework' this would be repeated and there would be various other bits of relevant reading. I had one more alcohol-related blackout during this time.

The treatment ended successfully in June, but my relationship finished a month later (it had been breaking down since my first blackout). I moved out and stayed with a friend, while focusing on work as a way of avoiding the miserable reality of my life. When work stopped for a period, my drinking and blackouts increased. I felt anxious a lot of the time, and in November I took too many antidepressants (five as opposed to two) and talked openly about suicide. My housemate and mother took me to my GP and the following day I saw my psychiatrist at the Traumatic Stress Clinic. He increased my antidepressant dose and suggested I start a course of cognitive–behavioural therapy with my original therapist.

In January 2004 I started the treatment and it was a revelation to me. The literature I received plus the homework proved to be extremely illuminating; discovering what my 'trigger points' are, what core beliefs I hold, and where they come from, has been very helpful. I now understand why I behave the way I do. I believe it was a very important part of my recovery, as I have been given the tools to help myself and put them to use as soon as I could. I have learnt to recognise certain feelings, which I've discovered are triggers, and stop any negative behaviour. Throughout the treatment, I kept records of my thoughts and how much alcohol I had had, both of which were very useful as I could see my thoughts and actions written down in black and white, which made it easier to understand the thread that held them all together. I am now better than I have been for years, more confident, calmer, my anxiety has stopped and I can at last see a realistic future ahead of me – one I am looking forward to.

In the last year, I bought a house, stopped smoking, joined Weight Watchers and started to exercise regularly. Things are also going very well for me professionally. I feel incredibly lucky to have received effective treatment that helped me to break out of a miserable, vicious circle of depression, excessive drinking and anxiety that would only have got worse. I am in no doubt that the help of the staff and the treatment I received saved my life, or at least gave me back a life I think is worth living.

3.1.7 Testimony seven

I never told anyone what had happened to me until I was in my mid-40s. Until that point my partner and friends had no inkling of the secret that I had carried with me all my life. I had a successful career, a happy marriage and was, on the surface, outgoing and assertive. But on the inside I felt very differently. I was waiting, constantly on alert for my secret to be found out. I found it difficult to trust people and had sleep problems and other physical ailments now readily identified as being stress induced. My body, for decades, had lived on a knife-edge, on high alert.

I am one of five children, and was sexually abused by my father from the age of 10 until I was 15½ when I managed to leave home. In September 1994 I was devastated to discover that I was not the only family member to have been sexually abused. Even though our abuser was dead by that time, the impact on me was massive.

The enormity of what had happened to me overwhelmed me. I was swallowed up by a continuous stream of flashbacks replaying the ugliness of my childhood: the theft of innocence through escalating abuses with rapes on a daily basis towards the end; the physicality of the onslaught on my small, defenceless, body; the inevitability of pregnancy and, following a suicide attempt, the nightmare of the miscarriage (trying to ram the small foetus down the bath plughole before finally flushing it down the toilet).

I had panic attacks that felt like heart attacks, but I was unable to speak about the evilness that was my childhood. Saying it would make it real, and I had struggled all my life to not think about it.

I had always known that I had been sexually abused. That knowledge had never left me. But the enormity of that knowledge and the constant pressure of having to maintain my silence had created a legacy within my body. Headaches, irritable bowel, back pain, gynaecological problems, an irrational fear of thunderstorms, startle reaction, and sleeplessness were all clear indicators that something was wrong. But not one doctor ever asked me if I had ever been subjected to sexual abuse as a child. My body was crying out, saying that something was wrong. But because no one asked me the question, I knew, as the child had known, that it was not OK to talk about it.

Suicidal thoughts intruded once again and it felt like the only recourse I had – to escape the constant barrage of flashbacks. My life was a mess. I was off work sick. My husband could only look on, helplessly, as I shrivelled up before him, into the posture of a small child. I remember his hands hanging by his sides, unable to reach out to me because I recoiled at the mere thought of a man's hand touching my body. My father, though dead, was there. I could see him, smell him, taste him. I gagged on the memory it was so real. It was real. I was in a parallel universe, twinned with the past and present.

Eventually I gained the courage I needed to disclose my secret to my GP, which was a painful and shocking experience. She sat motionless, and months later told me that she had felt helpless, aware that her knowledge about such abuse and the long-term impact was inadequate. Notwithstanding her lack of experience, we made our way together down a pathway that could, so easily, have been the wrong one for me.

Given the state I was in, my GP could have had me admitted to hospital – and it is likely that I would have gone down that downward spiral of madness and the likelihood of misdiagnosis. But, she had enough about her to realise that I might be suffering something more readily identifiable as PTSD – and in doing so, she started me on the pathway that saved my life.

In 1994–95 I was able to gain immediate access to trauma counselling through my employer. During 16 sessions I worked in partnership with the counsellor to explore the memories that had so carefully been hidden (not all of them, though, for I am amnesic about large periods of my life prior to the age of 10). My counsellor worked gently with me and together we slowly unpeeled the onionskin of memories. She tried several approaches with me before she found the one that worked best for me. The approach was eclectic and focused on the trauma but in a way that was humane and minimised triggering further trauma. My counsellor used different techniques as the need arose and was able to hear what I needed rather than imposing theoretical models that would have been unworkable for me. It was a partnership, and was important because it meant that an early foundation of trust was laid. Gradually I came to understand the link between my fear of thunderstorms with my childhood experiences. I understood why I had avoided certain environments and why intimacy of any kind (including friendship) was so difficult.

My sexual relationship with my partner had taken a massive downward spiral – any touch evoked painful and intrusive memories. Initially I submitted to his sexual desires, because I felt guilty about saying 'no'. But in saying 'yes', it only made it worse. The flashbacks intensified and I felt that life was no longer worth living. It had been impossible to believe that I could ever escape from the world that my life had become.

I was able to find the will to live and my counsellor was instrumental in that, because she gave me the time to reflect on my experience and the feelings associated with it. But for me, sanity came through meeting others who had endured a similar childhood (I met these survivors through the group CISters). It gave me an insight that my counsellor had never achieved into the full impact on my life that the abuse had made. I was a workaholic, obese, with no real friends – and the only good thing I had going for me was that I had a determination in my heart that my abuser was NOT going to win.

Slowly I gained ground and as each new insight came I was able to see my symptoms diminish. The panic attacks tapered off, the intensity of the flashbacks dwindled, and my irritable bowel began to loosen some its hold on me. I was able to breathe again.

PTSD still walks beside me – the chronic impact of the abuse is not easily shaken off. At times of stress some of the symptoms return (such as startle reaction and insomnia) – but it is extremely rare for me to have flashbacks, which have only occurred twice in 7 years. I saw my counsellor again in 2001 for six sessions after a car accident and in 2003 for another six sessions after I was diagnosed with fibromyalgia. It was helpful to see the same person because she knew my history and was able to connect the feelings of helplessness I felt on both of these occasions to my feelings about my childhood. But life is easier and simpler, and my returning good health brought with it a return to work and the opportunity for a new way of living: finally being able to relax after years of living on the edge of my nerves and looking over my shoulder.

Anger was not an emotion I allowed myself as a child or as an adult. But anger is what I feel at times, and it is a powerful motivator and lifesaver. At times I wonder how my life would have been if someone had asked me decades ago whether I had ever been abused in my life. That question would have given me an opportunity to disclose my secret, and perhaps I would have gained a new quality of life, years earlier, rather than having to wait until I was nearly 50.

3.1.8 Testimony eight

It was November 2003 and I was on duty as a firefighter in South Wales, when I received notification that my wife and son had been involved in a car accident. I drove immediately to the scene of the accident not knowing how badly injured they were or even if they had been killed. When I arrived I saw several emergency vehicles on the scene and what looked like a bad accident from the amount of 999 personnel rushing around.

I remember seeing a paramedic carrying out resuscitation on a casualty, which I immediately thought was my wife. I felt tremendous anxiety and rushed over to see. However, it was not my wife but one of the young men in the other car. My wife did not require resuscitation, but had suffered multiple fractures and injuries and was trapped in her car. When she saw me she became very upset and begged me not to leave her while they cut her out. She looked in a bad way – I feared she might not be able to walk.

My son was also badly injured with a large head wound. I went to comfort him for a few minutes while the fire service cut my wife out. I helped put my son into an ambulance. In addition to the nasty laceration to his head my son was emotionally distraught, which caused tension between the ambulance staff and myself, as I believed he should go with his mother to the same hospital. I soon learnt that three of the four boys in the other car involved in the accident were killed instantly. I was sad for their parents but more concerned that my family would be OK and survive.

After their injuries were dealt with in the A&E units there was then the start of various out-patient appointments to attend. We have four children and the practical demands of coping with every day and family life, and the logistics of ensuring my wife's and son's attendance at the various hospital appointments, was therefore very demanding. After the crash I had mixed feelings; I would feel angry at the way the crash happened and that there was nothing I could do to stop it or help. I was physically exhausted, but was finding it hard to sleep. As soon as the bedroom light went out at night a light would come on in my head and all I could do was lie there and think. When I would eventually fall asleep, I would wake up with nightmares of the crash. I could not get away from it. It was all I could think about in the day and all I would dream about at night.

I had to try and be strong for the kids, but when I would get a moment to myself, I would just break down and cry. I didn't like feeling like this so I would just keep busy. Keeping on the move was stopping me getting upset, but was making me more run down. I wanted things back to normal; seeing my wife and son in pain every day was driving me mad – I just wanted to explode. I found myself getting even more angry and short-tempered. I was looking for confrontation, I wanted to take it out on someone, but I knew I couldn't as it would look as if I could not cope, so I kept it bottled up inside.

I was finding this a great strain and visited the brigade's medical adviser where we agreed that I should be referred to the local NHS traumatic stress service, with which South Wales Fire and Rescue have a partnership. I went to meet a cognitive–behavioural therapist with a special interest in post-traumatic stress disorder. After a few meetings with this therapist he diagnosed me as suffering from PTSD and depression. I was prescribed various antidepressants on his recommendation by my GP. My therapist then started my CBT treatment, which included breathing retraining to help control my anxiety symptoms when I had an intrusive image of the accident, and grounding techniques to help me with flashbacks of trauma and feelings of anger and frustration.

We then made an audiotape of what had happened that night in great detail, including what I saw, heard, smelt, touched, tasted and so on while at the scene of the accident, including all my thoughts and feelings, as though I were reliving it again. I took this tape home and listened to it for an hour a day, marking on a chart my anxiety feelings at the start, during and after approximately an hour. I also incorporated the breathing and grounding techniques to help me cope with the reliving with the tape. After a few weeks of this treatment the tape started to get boring, apart from a few incidents that my therapist referred to as 'hot spots'. We made a new tape with just these hot spots and added new information after them to emphasise what actually happened. For example to 'I thought my wife was dead' we added 'she is not dead but is still recovering from her injuries'. Once again, after a few weeks of listening to it every day it got boring as well and I was then able to think of events of that night and not get upset, angry or frustrated.

Before I met with my therapist for CBT I didn't think I needed help or that I was depressed, but after just a few meetings with him I could see that I did. I found my therapist very easy to talk to, understanding, a good listener and very helpful. The treatment he provided definitely helped me get over this traumatic time in my life. I am now back at work attending road traffic accidents as normal with no fear or reliving of my wife's accident. She is now seeing my therapist for CBT as she is suffering with PTSD. We are both hopeful that she can also recover with this therapy and that time heals her physical injuries.

3.1.9 Testimony nine

Working for the London Ambulance Service as an A&E paramedic, I expected a certain amount of trauma, but my experience with handling stress had been good and I believed nothing could affect me. For 4 years on the front line I was faced with many traumatic jobs, which I handled well. Although there was a counsellor on site, I usually talked to my fellow crewmates if something was troubling me. So I was not really expecting that I would ever feel traumatised by my job.

It all started in July 2001 without my really being aware of it, through a build-up of stressful situations. I was called to a job where we were verbally abused and physically threatened. I went home feeling upset but that it was nothing I couldn't handle – it was just an ordinary day. One week later a very similar situation occurred, but this time I felt slightly more anxious than the week before, vulnerable and what I can only describe as 'stressed out'. One week after that, while on the nightshift with a crewmate we were threatened again and this time I feared for my life. As we were running away from the man who had threatened us, I felt that I was running for my life: I seemed to float down the stairs from his flat, and the heavy medical response box that I was carrying felt weightless. When we were finally in a safe place we realised that the man did not actually leave the floor of his flat – we were both shaken up by this and went home. I went straight to bed when I got in, but was awoken suddenly by a major flashback from the night before. I was convinced that the man who I thought was going to kill me was in my bedroom – I could not breathe, my chest felt so tight, and my heart was racing. I was having a panic attack.

The next morning I called work. I was hysterical, but the station officer was very understanding; he told me to go my GP, take some time off from work, and offered me the opportunity to see the counsellor at work. I said I would probably like to see the counsellor but that I could not face it at that moment. I went to my GP, who was sympathetic and prescribed diazepam. I don't think this really made me feel much better, but it helped me to relax and made sleeping much easier. I did not stay on the tablets for very long.

In the following few weeks I felt hypervigilant (that is, highly aware of my surroundings and any slightest noise). It seemed like someone had turned up the volume in my head. I could not face going out of the house at first, and the thought of going to London, where I worked, seemed almost impossible. I was very tearful, anxious and could not sleep very well. I was scared most of the time and paranoid. I felt like a little person in a very big world. I had no confidence and my self-esteem was very low. What was hard for me to comprehend at the time was why was I feeling like this because my crewmate, who had also feared for her life, was not affected by this. I wondered how she was able to go back to work when my whole life was turned upside down. Other colleagues asked me why I was off work with stress when my crewmate was all right. This made me feel really low and totally worthless.

After about 4 weeks I contacted work to make an appointment with the counsellor because I knew that I needed help. Work arranged for someone to come and collect me and take me to London to see the counsellor as I could not manage this on my own. Over a period of 2 months I started to see the counsellor regularly. It was a task just getting into London for the meetings, but I could tell her how I was feeling and I knew she would not judge me or make me feel bad in any way – she was a tower of strength. She told me that I had symptoms consistent with PTSD (my GP, who was not so experienced in PTSD, agreed with this). I was aware of what other people thought of me, but after time I didn't really care about this. I knew that I had PTSD, that I had had a common reaction to very stressful events, and that I was not going mad.

My counsellor explained everything to me about PTSD and we worked together to set tasks: my goal was to go back to the place where I had feared for my life. But I was also given other tasks to perform, such as taking a walk, going shopping or visiting a friend, which don't even feel like tasks now, but at the time just thinking about going out would make my heart race and my chest tighten. Some of the tasks at the time made me feel really bad, bringing on feelings of fear and failure. I knew I had to be strong and not to give up – some days I was proud of myself for going shopping when the shops were full of people! In the end, though, the treatment I received from my counsellor was a great success.

Although at first I had wanted to resign from work because I felt that I would never be able to continue with the job that I loved so much, after about 6 months I started to cope with many tasks that I had been set, such as driving to London alone. I returned to work gradually and returned to full duties in February 2002. I was lucky to have a good station officer who realised that my returning to work slowly would be less stressful and manageable. Had it not been for him and my counsellor I feel that I would never have been able to get on with my life.

At first the fact that I had PTSD affected my whole family, especially my boyfriend, who I live with. I found it very difficult to socialise and we did not have a holiday for over a year. I was very dependent on my boyfriend to take me out, but he was very supportive and patient. I have got some really good friends who were also very understanding and supportive.

I am a very confident and outgoing person and feel that I am stronger now than I have been in my whole life. It is really strange how a bad situation, which almost destroyed you, can make you grow in character. I am on maternity leave at the moment after having a beautiful baby girl – I am still a paramedic and hopefully will be back on the road next year.

3.2 Understanding PTSD from the sufferer's perspective

The testimonies illustrate some of the traumatic events that can lead to the development of PTSD: being a survivor of a major disaster; combat (multiple trauma); sudden loss of a relative or friend; losing or fearing that one has lost relatives or friends in a major disaster; rape and childhood sexual abuse; and exposure to trauma in people who work for the emergency services. However, it should be emphasised that these testimonies do not represent all of the traumatic events that may culminate in PTSD.

3.2.1 Recognising and diagnosing PTSD

People with PTSD usually recognise all too painfully that there is something drastically wrong, but may not be able to put a name to their feelings and symptoms. Without a diagnosis, sufferers can feel as if they are losing their grip on the world around them, and even on a sense of who they are.

Sufferers can languish for years without a diagnosis. Disclosure may be a problem, particularly in cases of rape or sexual abuse both in the indigenous and refugee population, which can lead to significant delays in diagnosis. What is clear from many of the testimonies is that if the condition is unrecognised, left untreated or is poorly managed, then the symptoms can be prolonged or can worsen significantly over time. Sufferers may withdraw into themselves and be unable to communicate with their families.

The effect of a traumatic event on children not recognised or treated for PTSD can last a lifetime. The sufferer in the first testimony, who received no systematic treatment for PTSD, speaks of the 'psychological injuries' lasting for over 30 years. The sufferer in the seventh testimony who had been abused as a child felt that she could not speak about what happened to her because she was never encouraged to do so by healthcare professionals despite presenting with many physical complaints. She remained silent until she was middle-aged.

Once a diagnosis is made, the relief for some sufferers can be immense: professional recognition of a named and identifiable condition can make sufferers feel that someone understands and acknowledges how they might be feeling; as the sufferer in the second testimony puts it, he now knew that his problems 'were normal responses to abnormal occurrences'. However, the relief or emotional release can precipitate extreme distress. As the person in the third testimony puts it, it can make the sufferer refocus on what might be the reality of the situation: 'how could we survive feeling this way?'

3.2.2 Effect of PTSD on personal relationships and working life

For some people, PTSD can alter every aspect of their lives. The emotions generated by PTSD and the physical symptoms associated with it can have a profound effect on the sufferer's relationship with family and friends. Some sufferers might withdraw from people close to them, and coping strategies, such as drinking alcohol, can further distance sufferers from their social and familial circles, as can the symptoms themselves (mood swings, irritability, etc.). It is not uncommon for people with PTSD to feel that they can no longer relate to the world around them or to other people who have not experienced trauma. Ordinary events seem meaningless. The inability to share the traumatic experience with many people can, as the sufferer in the third testimony phrases it, put one 'into another category'. Other people's reactions to the events may seem invalid or untrustworthy. The sense of difference that PTSD might produce in the sufferer can further isolate these individuals. Protracted isolation can lead to a loss of self-confidence and self-esteem, culminating in periods of severe depression. Isolation was certainly experienced by the narrators of testimonies five and six, who felt that they could not talk to close family or other members of their community about being raped.

Some sufferers who have lost relatives in a disaster or other traumatic event can have overwhelming feelings of apprehension about losing other members of their family. This might result in overprotectiveness.

Post-traumatic stress disorder can also have a detrimental effect on employment. For some people the symptoms are so severe that they are unable to function properly in the workplace, although it can also be the case that some PTSD sufferers can perform very highly. Some sufferers attest to a lack of understanding from employers, even if the event or events have been job or service-related: for instance in combat or in the medical profession or emergency services.

For children, the memories of the event can have a significant impact on schooling and emotional development. Concentration might be poor, and educational performance affected as a result, although as in adults, it may also be that children can 'lose themselves' in schoolwork.

3.2.3 Sufferers' experience of services and treatment

The experiences described in this chapter cover a period of over 30 years. In the 1960s and 1970s there was often very limited knowledge on the part of many mental healthcare professionals of the nature and treatment of trauma-related psychological problems. However, as described in Chapter 2 and borne out by a number of the testimonies, there have been considerable improvements in the understanding of PTSD and in the provision of services in the UK. Nevertheless, the availability of effective services still varies considerably. It is a central aim of this guideline to address these variations in practice.

In the immediate aftermath of a traumatic event, people may want to talk to someone in a professional capacity (as did the authors of the second and fourth testimonies), which may mean nothing more than being listened to, shown understanding, and given some practical information about health issues and contact details for services and voluntary organisations.

In the first few months following a traumatic event, finding someone to work with who has appropriate training in the treatment of PTSD, with whom the sufferer can build up a relationship of trust and understanding, is crucial. It is important that these individuals are listened to and their symptoms taken seriously. Furthermore, the sufferer can be badly affected if doctors or therapists attempt treatments for which they have no competency or administer treatments that have no evidence for effectiveness. Such a situation could lead to a complete breakdown in the therapeutic relationship, especially if a lack of knowledge is coupled with an absence of trust.

It can also be detrimental if sufferers feel that they have to prove that 'there was something badly wrong', as was the case with the narrator of the third testimony. This struggle to prove the gravity of the condition may exacerbate the symptoms over time. It is also important that sufferers maintain sustained contact with one professional if this is required, otherwise they could feel that they are being passed from one professional to another.

If treatment is not working, this is not necessarily because the sufferer is a 'poor responder' or is 'resistant' to treatment, just that the right treatment, or the right combination of treatments, has not yet been found.

What is implicit in testimonies two and three is that the sufferers in general felt psychological therapy would have been the right form of treatment, had it been delivered by an appropriately trained professional. For the sufferer in the fourth testimony medication was prescribed to help manage sleep problems and to act as a sedative, but for the sufferer in the second testimony medication had a deleterious effect. The latter individual expressed some surprise that counselling or psychological therapy was not offered at the same time.

In contrast, in testimonies six, seven and eight, where the sufferers had received treatment more recently, there is a marked difference in the experience of services and provision of treatment (this includes the person with chronic PTSD). The sufferers in these testimonies praised a trusting and sympathetic relationship with healthcare professionals, well-delivered, effective psychological treatment and continuity of care.

3.2.4 Sufferers' perspective on coping and recovery

Although PTSD sufferers can recover naturally in the first few weeks or months – and even years – after a traumatic event without treatment, all of the sufferers above expressed a need for some form of support and treatment, and made the connection between lack of support and treatment and a worsening of their symptoms.

Some of the sufferers found a way through the disorder by founding support groups with other people affected by the traumatic event. The person in the fourth testimony accredits this with being the 'best intervention of all'. The person in the second testimony reduced and stopped his medication himself and started up a successful website dedicated to ex-service men and women suffering from PTSD. The person in the third testimony found her work helping others who had lost relatives in disasters enriching. The person in the first testimony speaks publicly about what happened to him, and finds that talking is the best means of coming to terms with the disorder. These strategies can be an important means of providing people with the self-confidence to return to work if they have lost their job as a result of PTSD.

These means of coping are also important milestones on the road to recovery. Testimonies six, seven and eight are stories of recovery, although some people will never completely come to terms with the trauma. They will learn to cope with it on a day-to-day basis, knowing that its effects will be with them for the rest of their life; others may find that with the passage of time and the right treatment they may be able to find some kind of equilibrium and quality of life returning; yet others may find that taking control of their own treatment and finding support from friends and family members will allow them to put some structure and meaning back into their life even if they still experience PTSD symptoms daily; others might be coping with the disorder but consider trying a different form of therapy.

As has already been suggested, PTSD can change a person irreversibly; and as the narrator of the second testimony understood it, recovery is a process, part of that process being learning to live with this change, moving to acceptance if that is possible.

3.3 Summary of PTSD sufferer concerns

The following concerns emerged from the personal testimonies above and the subsequent commentary. They emphasise the need for a listening and caring approach, backed by practical information and social support at the scene if needed. They also highlight the need for greater awareness and understanding on the part of healthcare professionals in both primary and secondary care. This requires improved training in the diagnosis and treatment of PTSD, the provision to sufferers and their families and carers of good written and verbal information about the nature, course and treatment of PTSD, and improved continuity between services when treating PTSD.

3.4 Carers' testimonies

3.4.1 Testimony one

I first met my husband in October 1998; at this time he was a serving police officer and had been in his job for about 14 years. The first thing I noticed about him was that he would drink to excess on a regular basis (I was very relieved when he stopped drinking suddenly about 3 months after we met). I remember him telling me about his experiences in the police and about some of the things he had seen and dealt with. I was horrified at what he told me. I had no idea what post-traumatic stress disorder was or that he was suffering from it until he told me in 1999 (it had been diagnosed by his GP in 1994).

When we moved in together I began to notice more about his condition. He became more withdrawn and tense, which resulted in outbursts of temper or uncontrollable sobbing, particularly after work. He became more and more stressed out and could not relax. This became apparent particularly at night, when he would be very restless and often wake himself up either screaming or shouting. He still does this today and suffers nightmares about the things he dealt with in the police.

The flashbacks he experiences are also very distressing for both of us. My husband just goes completely blank and it's as if he is not there, he's in a different place. He goes very pale and his breathing becomes erratic and he gets a pain in his chest and begins sweating. He feels embarrassed when this happens and usually disappears somewhere until it has passed. This makes him angry and frustrated and if I try to comfort or support him he more or less pushes me away, preferring to cope with it on his own. My husband has a very short fuse and is easily irritated at the slightest thing. Although he has never been physically violent towards me, I still find his outbursts of temper quite worrying.

Because of panic attacks and ever-increasing flashbacks my husband retired on ill-health grounds in 2002. The pressure of work, and the lack of support from his colleagues and supervisors, had also become too much for him. My husband feels complete and utter deep-rooted bitterness and hatred towards the people in the police force who had a duty of care towards him, but who failed him time after time, despite the fact that they knew about the PTSD. During 2½ years of sick leave he only received two sick visits and one phone call. It was only when the police set up a welfare department with trained counsellors that my husband received any care, but even then he had to ask to see someone and had to go in his own time.

Since he has retired he has no self-confidence and motivation, preferring to remain indoors most of the day, usually at his computer. He feels totally inadequate, as if he is on the scrap heap, and this makes him depressed. It causes an atmosphere at home and makes life unbearable at times. He has no interest in his hobbies any more and can't concentrate on anything for long. His short-term memory is terrible (he can't remember things I've told him the previous day), although he can recount things that happened years ago, things that he would ordinarily have forgotten about. He is smoking very heavily and his appetite is poor.

The antidepressants and sleeping tablets he has been taking for the past 3 years make him tired and lethargic and his personality has changed from an outgoing, fun-to-be-with person to the exact opposite. He very rarely socialises with anybody and doesn't really want to.

My husband has seen various psychiatrists and psychologists, attended therapy groups and has more recently tried behaviour therapy and a StressPac course. He has just begun a course of EMDR [eye movement desensitisation and reprogramming]. I think my husband is willing to try anything and everything to help himself, but given the nature of his police work he is very sceptical, and the majority of treatments he has received only seem to help in the short term. He feels he will be like this for the rest of his life because he has been suffering with these symptoms for over 10 years.

Despite his having treatment over the past 2 years, I haven't seen any improvement in him really. My husband's condition is in my view very debilitating for him and a strain on all of us, especially where the kids are concerned because they don't understand why he's the way he is.

3.4.2 Testimony two

When my husband joined the military he was army through and through and a secure, compassionate kind of guy. But things started going wrong for us when he was still in the army. He was diagnosed with PTSD, given a few brief counselling sessions at an army hospital in Germany and medically discharged. I was not involved in the treatment except in driving him to the hospital. Then we were out in the real world and neither of us had a clue of what was coming or how it would affect us.

With my husband I got the impression that when he first had PTSD it developed quite slowly, but that while he was fighting it, it crawled into all the nooks and crannies. It took him over, and before he knew it he didn't recognise himself (and neither did his loved ones nor his closest friends). He became confused, distant and scared of what happened and is happening. All his foundations that made him the person he was crumbled beneath his feet. The trust he had was shaken first by the trauma he suffered, then by the army rejecting him, and then by his spirit deserting him. He began to pull away from his closest family and friends, and became very unsure and lacking in confidence – a shadow of his former self.

When my husband first showed serious signs of PTSD we were concerned, but reassured by him that it was nothing. How ignorant we were! Then suddenly it changed my life, his and the children's lives. He left home and sent me a few messages saying that he didn't know who he was and where his life was going. He just walked away from our life without telling anyone, not even his brother, who he was very close to. I knew without a doubt something was seriously wrong because this was totally out of character.

I read what I could about PTSD in the library and on the internet but I really didn't know where to turn to for help, so I phoned the NHS helpline. The fellow who I spoke to was very nice and he gave me the number for Combat Stress (he told me that he was a sufferer and that there was light at the end of the tunnel). I phoned Combat Stress and was sent a standard information pack with a form for my husband to fill out. But when I contacted my husband he admitted that he was already in counselling via the SSAFA (Soldiers, Sailors, Airmen and Families Association – this is a volunteer-led charity that helps ex-service personnel deal with problems that they cannot cope with, among other things). This went on for 3 months.

Then my husband's psychiatrist told him he would have to see his own GP to get a referral in his local area, which he did, but the GP seemed more interested in starting him on a course of Prozac [fluoxetine]. My husband is very wary of drugs and this was not the best course of action for him. The GP did refer him but it took almost 2 months to get a reply from the local cognitive–behavioural therapist. The waiting list was a further 3 months long! It was suggested that in the meantime perhaps my husband would like to join a support group. I could not imagine my husband even considering this advice, and I was right.

By this time various personal things had happened that made an already difficult situation almost unbearable. My husband's brother died, and he [my husband] took on an air of hopelessness and refused help of any sort. This alienated him from me even further. All through this I was gently trying to persuade him that he needed help, but it was a losing battle.

I went to my own doctor for help for myself and was put on antidepressants to control the symptoms but was not offered counselling of any sort. I actually found counselling on my own through Relate. I went in to talk about my husband's PTSD and the breakdown of our marriage and the various problems connected with that. I found I was helping the counsellor understand PTSD because up till then she had never encountered a case like mine. I felt much better after taking antidepressants for a little over a year.

PTSD not only affects the individual suffering, it can have dreadful consequences for those nearest and dearest to the sufferer, breaking up marriages and affecting other close relationships. Fortunately I am a very capable person and I have, myself, experienced trauma first-hand, so I was able to realise that my husband was in trouble and phone anyone I could think of to help him. I am still trying to get through that wall he has built to defend himself. I am also involved in helping his parents understand what this is all about. I am still fighting to help my husband despite lack of help from outside sources.

I am not trying to blame one specific individual in all of this. It has been a catalogue of errors from the beginning and I do think that the military has a part to play in all of this. His treatment while in the army seemed too short – longer, more intensive sessions over a period of months rather than weeks might have been more beneficial. Discharging him did not help in any way – it only served to reinforce his lack of self-worth.

Doctors should have a clearer understanding of PTSD and the way men experience it and describe their feelings and reactions. Maybe they could include family members in the treatment sessions so they can get a different point of view – it has been my experience that men with PTSD play down what is actually happening because they are scared. I also think that things could improve in other areas, such as reducing the amount of time PTSD sufferers have to wait for psychological treatment. In addition, the family of the sufferer need help and information to understand PTSD and to help the sufferer. They also need to be aware of what is required of them and to be supported in their own right. Trying to help is much easier when you have a good support team in the background.

3.5 Understanding the impact of PTSD on carers

3.5.1 Emotional impact on carers

As both the above testimonies bear out, the experience of caring for someone with PTSD can be lonely, frustrating and frightening. It is not uncommon for the sufferer to feel that the carer can never truly understand the nature of the trauma, or to expect to know what the sufferer may be feeling. This may mean that sufferers do not disclose the full nature of their disorder and treatment. This acts to isolate the carers further, and make them feel unhelpful and helpless. Sometimes mood swings, irritability and anger felt by the sufferer can be alienating and difficult for the carer to deal with. This state of affairs can be exacerbated by a lack of professional help and support. Just as sufferers may feel permanently altered by the trauma, so carers may find that their relationship with the sufferer has changed irrevocably. It can take some time to adjust to this new situation. The diagnosis of PTSD can be a relief to the carer as well as to the sufferer, although as the carer in the second testimony suggests, coping with disorder on a day-to-day basis can still be very stressful and demanding.

3.5.2 Social implications of PTSD

As explained above, PTSD can have a profound effect on the sufferer's familial and social relationships. This can lead many carers to feel doubly isolated. The impact of the sufferer's difficulty in sustaining employment and social withdrawal can make family life difficult, as can the unpredictable nature of the condition. It is not uncommon for marriages to be put under considerable strain as a result of PTSD. However, with the right care and treatment both for the sufferer and the carer, this situation may improve.

3.5.3 The carer's experience of services and treatment

Because of the isolating effect of PTSD on carers and other family members, being able to access appropriate help and support is vital. This may include written and verbal information about the nature, course and treatment of PTSD, and information about voluntary organisations and support groups. The carer or family member may also require some counselling and pharmacological treatment.

3.6 Summary of carer needs

In many ways the need of family members and carers for care and support mirrors that of PTSD sufferers, but it can only be met if this need is first recognised. This means that healthcare professionals should be alert to the needs of families and carers and provide them with the right information and education about the nature, course and treatment of PTSD. Family members and carers bear the brunt of the impact of PTSD, but they also remain the most potent force for support and care for sufferers. They should be given the correct advice about the part they can play in supporting the family member with PTSD and support for themselves as carers, while also being fully informed about the effects of PTSD upon family life. They should receive information about possible treatment that they can themselves expect to receive, and details about support groups.

3.7 Clinical practice recommendations

Many of the recommendations in Chapter 2 reflect the concerns of both sufferers and carers as expressed in the testimonies and should be seen in that context. However, other recommendations that did not link clearly with the content of Chapter 2 or elsewhere in the guideline are included here.

3.7.1 PTSD sufferers

3.7.1.1   Healthcare professionals should treat PTSD sufferers with respect, trust and understanding, and keep technical language to a minimum. **GPP**

3.7.2 Relatives and carers

3.7.2.1   In addition to the provision of information, families and carers should be informed of self-help and support groups and encouraged to participate in such groups where they exist. **GPP**

4 Methods used to develop this guideline

4.1 Overview

The development of this guideline drew upon methods outlined by the National Institute for Clinical Excellence (2002; Eccles & Mason, 2001). A team of experts, professionals and PTSD sufferers, known as the Guideline Development Group, with support from the NCCMH staff, undertook the development of a PTSD sufferer-centred, evidence-based guideline. There are six basic steps in the process of developing a guideline:

(a)   define the scope, which sets the parameters of the guideline and provides a focus and steer for the development work

(b)   define clinical questions considered important for practitioners and PTSD sufferers

(c)   develop criteria for evidence searching, and search for evidence

(d)   design validated protocols for systematic review, and apply to the evidence recovered by the search

(e)   synthesise and (meta-)analyse data retrieved, guided by the clinical questions, and produce evidence statements

(f)   answer clinical questions with evidence-based recommendations for clinical practice.

The clinical practice recommendations made by the Guideline Development Group are therefore derived from the most up-to-date and robust evidence base for the clinical and cost-effectiveness of the treatments and services used in the management of PTSD. In addition, to ensure a sufferer and carer focus, the concerns of PTSD sufferers and carers regarding clinical practice have been highlighted and addressed by good practice points and recommendations agreed by the whole Group. The evidence-based recommendations and good practice points are the core of this guideline.

4.2 The Guideline Development Group

The Guideline Development Group consisted of professionals in psychiatry, clinical psychology, nursing, social work and general practice; academic experts in psychiatry and psychology; and PTSD sufferers. The guideline development process was supported by staff from the NCCMH, who undertook the clinical and health economics literature searches, reviewed and presented the evidence to the Group, managed the process, and contributed to the drafting of the guideline.

4.2.1 Guideline Development Group meetings

Seventeen Group meetings were held between February 2003 and June 2004. During each day-long meeting, in a plenary session, clinical questions and clinical evidence were reviewed and assessed, statements developed and recommendations formulated. At each meeting all Group members declared any potential conflict of interest, and PTSD sufferer and carer concerns were routinely discussed as part of a standing agenda.

4.2.2 Topic leads

The Group divided its workload along clinically relevant lines to simplify the guideline development process, and individual members took responsibility for advising on guideline work for particular areas of clinical practice (psychological interventions, pharmacological interventions, early intervention, risk factors and screening, and children).

4.2.3 PTSD sufferers and carers

Individuals with direct experience of services gave an integral PTSD sufferer focus to the Group and to the guideline. The Group included two PTSD sufferers, both of whom had contact with other

PTSD sufferers and carers. They contributed as full Group members to writing the clinical questions, helping to ensure that the evidence addressed their views and preferences, highlighting sensitive issues and terminology associated with PTSD, and bringing PTSD sufferer research to the attention of the Group. In drafting the guideline, they contributed to the editing of the introduction and Chapter 3, and identified good practice points from the PTSD sufferer and carer perspectives.

4.2.4 Special advisers

Special advisers who had specific expertise in one or more aspects of treatment and management relevant to the guideline assisted the Group, commenting on specific aspects of the developing guideline and making presentations to the Group. The Acknowledgements section at the beginning of this guideline lists those who agreed to act as special advisers.

4.2.5 National and international experts

National and international experts in the area under review were identified through the literature search and through the experience of the Group members. These experts were contacted to recommend unpublished or soon-to-be published studies in order to ensure up-to-date evidence was included in the development of the guideline. They informed the group about completed trials at the pre-publication stage, systematic reviews in the process of being published, studies relating to the cost-effectiveness of treatment, and trial data if the Group could be provided with full access to the complete trial report. Appendix 4 lists the researchers who were contacted.

4.3 Clinical questions

Clinical questions were used to guide the identification and interrogation of the evidence base relevant to the topic of the guideline. The questions were developed using a modified nominal group technique. The process began by asking each member of the Guideline Development Group to submit as many questions as possible. The questions were then collated and refined by the review team. At a subsequent meeting, the guideline chair facilitated a discussion to refine the questions further. At this point, the Group members were asked to rate each question for importance. The results of this process were then discussed and consensus reached about which questions would be of primary importance and which would be secondary. The Group aimed to address all primary questions; secondary questions would be covered only if time permitted. Appendix 5 lists the clinical questions.

4.4 Systematic clinical literature review

The aim of the clinical literature review was to systematically identify and synthesise relevant evidence from the literature in order to answer the specific clinical questions developed by the Group. Thus, clinical practice recommendations are evidence-based, where possible, and if evidence was not available, informal consensus methods were used (see section 4.4.10.1) and the need for future research was specified.

4.4.1 Methodology

A stepwise, hierarchical approach was taken to locating and presenting evidence to the Group. The NCCMH developed this process based on advice from the NICE National Guidelines Support and Research Unit and after considering recommendations from a range of other sources. These included:
- the Centre for Clinical Policy and Practice of the New South Wales Health Department (Australia)
- Clinical Evidence Online
- Cochrane Collaboration
- New Zealand Guideline Group
- NHS Centre for Reviews and Dissemination

- Oxford Centre for Evidence-Based Medicine
- Scottish Intercollegiate Guidelines Network
- United States Agency for Health Research and Quality
- Oxford Systematic Review Development Programme.

4.4.2 The review process

A brief search of the major bibliographic databases for recent systematic reviews and existing guidelines was first conducted to help inform the development of the scope. After the scope was finalised, a more extensive search for systematic reviews was undertaken. At this point, the review team, in conjunction with the Group, developed an evidence map that detailed all comparisons necessary to answer the clinical questions. The initial approach taken to locating primary-level studies depended on the type of clinical question and availability of evidence.

After consulting the Group, the review team decided which questions were likely to have a good evidence base and which questions were likely to have little or no directly relevant evidence. For questions in the latter category, a brief descriptive review was initially undertaken by a member of the Group (see section 4.4.10). For questions with a good evidence base, the review process depended on the type of clinical question.

4.4.2.1 Search process for questions concerning interventions

For questions related to interventions, the initial evidence base was formed from well-conducted randomised controlled trials (RCTs) that addressed at least one of the clinical questions. Although there are a number of difficulties with the use of RCTs in the evaluation of interventions in mental health, the RCT remains the most important method for establishing treatment efficacy.

The initial search for RCTs involved searching the standard mental health bibliographic databases (EMBASE, Medline, PsycINFO, Cochrane Library) for all RCTs potentially relevant to the guideline.

After the initial search results were scanned liberally to exclude irrelevant papers, the review team used a purpose-built 'study information' database to manage both the included and the excluded studies (eligibility criteria were developed after consultation with the Group). For questions without good-quality evidence (after the initial search), a decision was made by the Group about whether to repeat the search using subject-specific databases, such as CINAHL, the Allied and Complementary Medicine Database (AMED), the System for Information on Grey Literature in Europe (SIGLE) and the Publishers International Literature on Traumatic Stress (PILOTS); conduct a new search for lower levels of evidence; or adopt a consensus process (see section 4.4.10.1). Future guidelines will be able to update and extend the usable evidence base starting from the evidence collected, synthesised and analysed for this guideline.

Data from unpublished pharmacological trials held by the Medical and Healthcare Products Regulatory Agency were routinely requested, and where these data were available and could be released they are considered within the review.

Recent high-quality English-language systematic reviews were used primarily as a source of RCTs (see Appendix 7 for quality criteria). However, where existing data-sets were available from appropriate reviews, they were cross-checked for accuracy before use. New RCTs meeting inclusion criteria set by the Group were incorporated into the existing reviews and fresh analyses performed. The review process is illustrated in Fig. 4.1.

Additional searches were made of the reference lists of all eligible systematic reviews and RCTs, and the list of evidence submitted by stakeholders. Known experts in the field (see Appendix 2), based both on the references identified in early steps and on advice from Group members, were sent letters requesting systematic reviews or RCTs that were in the process of being published (unpublished full trial reports were also accepted where sufficient information was available to judge eligibility and quality). In addition, the standard mental health bibliographic databases were periodically checked for relevant studies.

4.4.2.2 Search process for questions of screening and risk factors

For questions related to screening and risk factors, the search process was the same as described above, except that the initial evidence base was formed by identifying recent high-quality

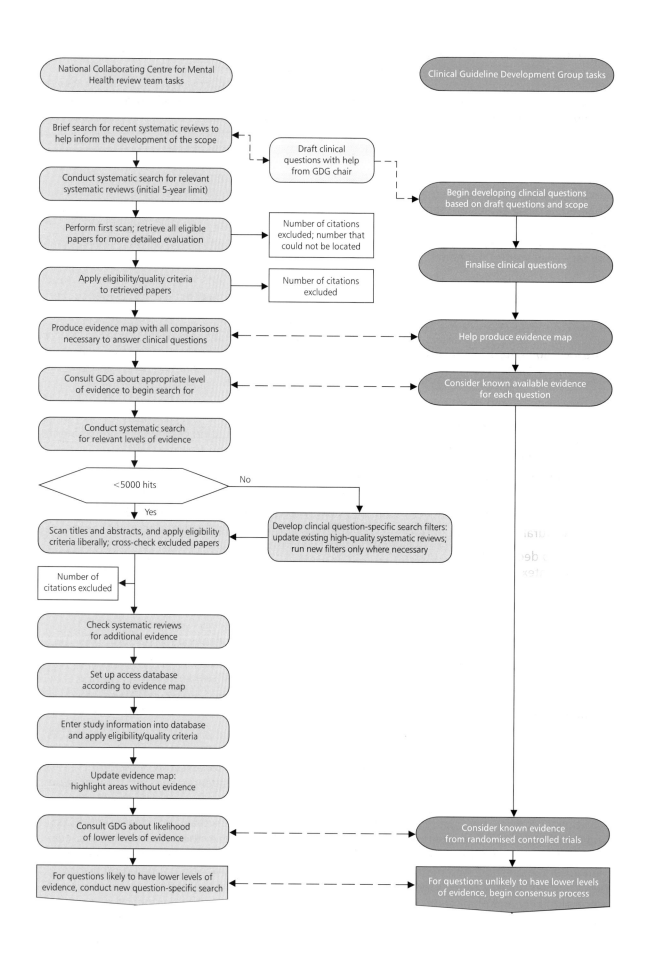

National Collaborating Centre for Mental Health review team tasks

Clinical Guideline Development Group tasks

Brief search for recent systematic reviews to help inform the development of the scope

Draft clinical questions with help from GDG chair

Begin developing clincial questions based on draft questions and scope

Conduct systematic search for relevant systematic reviews (initial 5-year limit)

Perform first scan; retrieve all eligible papers for more detailed evaluation

Number of citations excluded; number that could not be located

Finalise clinical questions

Apply eligibility/quality criteria to retrieved papers

Number of citations excluded

Produce evidence map with all comparisons necessary to answer clinical questions

Help produce evidence map

Consult GDG about appropriate level of evidence to begin search for

Consider known available evidence for each question

Conduct systematic search for relevant levels of evidence

<5000 hits — No

Yes

Scan titles and abstracts, and apply eligibility criteria liberally; cross-check excluded papers

Develop clincial question-specific search filters: update existing high-quality systematic reviews; run new filters only where necessary

Number of citations excluded

Check systematic reviews for additional evidence

Set up access database according to evidence map

Enter study information into database and apply eligibility/quality criteria

Update evidence map: highlight areas without evidence

Consult GDG about likelihood of lower levels of evidence

Consider known evidence from randomised controlled trials

For questions likely to have lower levels of evidence, conduct new question-specific search

For questions unlikely to have lower levels of evidence, begin consensus process

Fig. 4.1 Guideline review process (GDG, Guideline Development Group)

systematic reviews and updating the searches for these systematic reviews. Additional searches were run to cover aspects of screening and risk factors that the Group felt had not been comprehensively covered by these earlier systematic reviews. (Separate searches were run for screening tools and risk factors of injury, compensation and litigation, and all studies of risk factors with a longitudinal prospective design.) In situations in which it was not possible to identify a substantial body of appropriately designed studies that directly addressed each clinical question, a consensus process was adopted (see section 4.4.10.1).

4.4.3 Search filters

Search filters developed by the review team consisted of a combination of subject heading and free-text phrases. Specific filters were developed for the guideline topic, and where necessary, for each clinical question. In addition, the review team used filters developed for systematic reviews, RCTs and other appropriate research designs (Appendix 6).

4.4.4 Study selection

All primary-level studies included after the first scan of citations were acquired in full and re-evaluated for eligibility at the time they were being entered into the study information database. The inclusion criteria for RCTs are listed below (see section 4.4.8). For certain clinical questions these inclusion criteria were amended (see Chapter 9). All eligible papers were then critically appraised for methodological quality (see Appendix 8). The eligibility of each study was confirmed by at least one member of the Group.

For some clinical questions, it was necessary to prioritise the evidence with respect to the UK context. To make this process explicit, the Group took into account the following factors when assessing the evidence:

- participant factors (e.g. gender, age, ethnicity)
- provider factors (e.g. model fidelity, the conditions under which the intervention was performed, the availability of experienced staff to undertake the procedure)
- cultural factors (e.g. differences in standard care, differences in the welfare system).

The Group decided which prioritisation factors were relevant to each clinical question in light of the UK context, and then how they should modify the recommendations.

4.4.5 Synthesising the evidence

Where possible, outcome data were extracted directly from all eligible studies, which met the quality criteria, into Review Manager 4.2 (Cochrane Collaboration, 2003). Meta-analysis was then used, where appropriate, to synthesise the evidence using Review Manager. If necessary, re-analyses of the data or sensitivity analyses were used to answer clinical questions not addressed in the original studies or reviews. For continuous outcomes, where more than 50% of the total number randomised in a particular study were not accounted for, the data were excluded from the analysis because of the risk of bias (as outlined within the inclusion criteria in section 4.4.8).

Included/excluded studies tables, generated automatically from the study information database, were used to summarise general information about each study (see Appendix 14). Where meta-analysis was not appropriate and/or possible, the reported results from each primary-level study were also presented in the included studies table.

Consultation was used to overcome difficulties with coding. Data from studies included in existing systematic reviews were extracted independently by one reviewer directly into Review Manager and cross-checked with the existing data-set. Two independent reviewers extracted data from new studies, and disagreements were resolved with discussion. Where consensus could not be reached, a third reviewer resolved the disagreement. Masked assessment (i.e. masked to the journal from which the paper came, the authors, the institution and the magnitude of the effect) was not used, since it is unclear that doing so reduces bias (Jadad *et al*, 1996; Berlin, 1997).

4.4.6 Presenting the data to the Guideline Development Group

Where possible, meta-analysis was used to synthesise data. If necessary, sub-analyses were used to answer clinical questions not addressed in the original studies or reviews. The Group was given a graphical presentation of the results using forest plots generated with the Review Manager software. Each forest plot displayed the effect size and confidence interval (CI) for each study as well as the overall summary statistic. The graphs were organised so that the display of data in the area to the left of the 'line of no effect' indicated a 'favourable' outcome for the treatment in question. Dichotomous outcomes were presented as relative risks (RR) with the associated 95% CI (for an example, see Fig. 4.2). A relative risk (or risk ratio) is the ratio of the treatment event rate to the control event rate. An RR of 1 indicates no difference between treatment and control. In Figure 4.2, the overall RR of 0.73 indicates that the event rate (i.e. non-remission rate) associated with intervention A is about three-quarters of that with the control intervention, or in other words, the relative risk reduction is 27%.

The confidence interval shows with 95% certainty the range within which the true treatment effect should lie and can be used to determine statistical significance. If the CI does not cross the 'line of no effect', the effect is statistically significant.

All dichotomous outcomes were calculated on an intention-to-treat basis (i.e. a 'once randomised always analyse' basis). This assumes that participants who ceased to engage in the study – from whatever group – had an unfavourable outcome (with the exception of the outcomes of death and certain adverse events). Continuous outcomes were analysed as standardised mean differences (SMDs) to allow for ease of comparison across studies (Fig. 4.3). If provided, intention-to-treat data, using a method such as 'last observation carried forward', were preferred over data from completers.

To check for heterogeneity between studies, both the I^2 and χ^2 tests of heterogeneity ($P<0.10$), as well as visual inspection of the forest plots, were used. The I^2 statistic describes the proportion of total variation in study estimates that is due to heterogeneity (Higgins & Thompson, 2002). An I^2 of less than 30% was taken to indicate mild heterogeneity and a fixed effects model was used to synthesise the results. An I^2 of more than 50% was taken as notable heterogeneity. In this case, an attempt was made to explain the variation. If studies with heterogeneous results were found to be comparable, a random effects model was used to summarise the results (DerSimonian & Laird, 1986). In the random effects analysis, heterogeneity is accounted for both in the width of CIs and in the estimate of the treatment effect. With decreasing heterogeneity the random effects

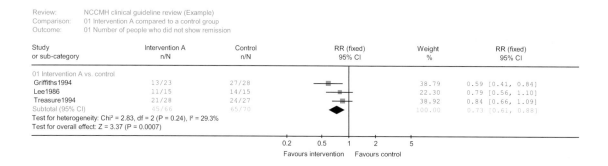

Fig. 4.2 Example of a forest plot displaying dichotomous data (RR, relative risk)

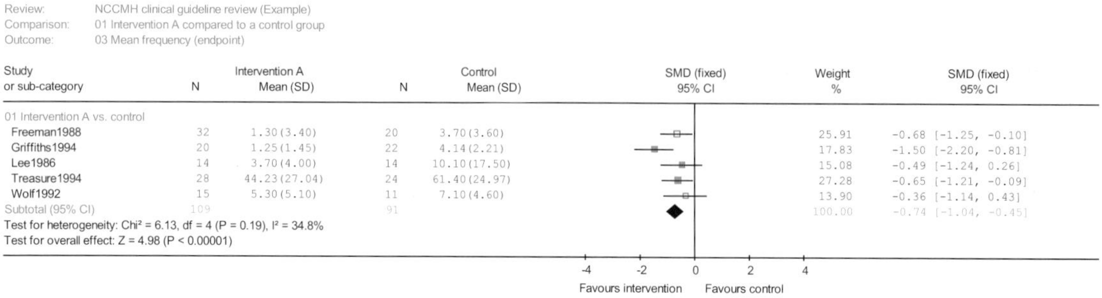

Fig. 4.3 Example of a forest plot displaying continuous data (SMD, standardised mean difference)

approach moves asymptotically towards a fixed effects model. An I^2 of 30–50% was taken to indicate moderate heterogeneity. In this case, both the χ^2 test of heterogeneity and a visual inspection of the forest plot were used to decide between a fixed and random effects model.

4.4.7 Forming and grading the statements and recommendations

The evidence tables and forest plots formed the basis for developing clinical statements and recommendations.

4.4.7.1 Developing statements

For each outcome a clinical statement describing the evidence found was developed. To assess clinical importance where a statistically significant summary was obtained (after controlling for heterogeneity) the Group set thresholds for determining clinical importance, in addition to taking into account the trial population and nature of the outcome.

Two separate thresholds for determining clinical importance were set. For comparisons of one active treatment against waiting list or non-active interventions, a higher threshold was applied than for comparisons of active treatments against one another.

For comparisons of one active treatment against another treatment the following thresholds were applied: for dichotomous outcomes an RR of 0.80 or less was considered clinically important and for continuous outcomes an effect size of approximately 0.5 (a 'medium' effect size; Cohen, 1988) or less was considered clinically important.

For comparisons of active treatment against waiting list the following thresholds were applied: for dichotomous outcomes a RR of 0.65 or less was considered clinically important and for continuous outcomes an effect size of approximately 0.8 (a 'large' effect size; Cohen, 1988) or less was considered clinically important.

In order to facilitate consistency in generating and drafting the clinical statements the Group used a statement decision tree (Fig. 4.4). This flow chart was designed to assist with decision-making, not to replace clinical judgement. Using this procedure, the Group classified each effect size as clinically important or not (i.e. whether or not the treatment is likely to benefit PTSD sufferers), taking into account both the comparison group and the outcome.

Where heterogeneity between studies was judged problematic, in the first instance an attempt was made to explain the cause of the heterogeneity (e.g. outliers were removed from the analysis, or sub-analyses were conducted to examine the possibility of moderators). Where homogeneity could not be achieved, a random effects model was used.

In cases where the point estimate of the effect was judged clinically important, a further consideration was made about the precision of the evidence by examining the range of estimates defined by the CI. For level I evidence, where the effect size was judged clinically important for the full range of plausible estimates, the result was described as *evidence* favouring intervention *x* over intervention *y* (i.e. statement 1, or S1). For non-level-I evidence or in situations where the point estimate was clinically important but the CI included clinically unimportant effects, the result was described as *limited evidence* favouring intervention *x* over intervention *y* (i.e. S2). Where a point estimate was judged as *not* clinically important and the CI did not include any clinically important effects, the result was described as *unlikely to be clinically important* (i.e. S3). Alternatively, if the range of estimates defined by the CI included clinically important benefits as well as no effect or harmful effects, the result was described as *inconclusive* (i.e. S4).

Where for a particular review very few trials meet the threshold for clinical importance, further criteria are required to differentiate the relative efficacy of treatments considered. In this case treatments are evaluated according to whether they are both statistically significant and reasonably well tolerated. Specifically, the most effective treatments are identified as those for which, for the principal outcome measures, the effect sizes are statistically significant (95% CI to the left of the line of no effect).

4.4.7.2 Developing and grading the recommendations

Once all evidence statements relating to a particular clinical question were finalised and agreed by the Group, the associated recommendations were produced and graded. Grading allowed

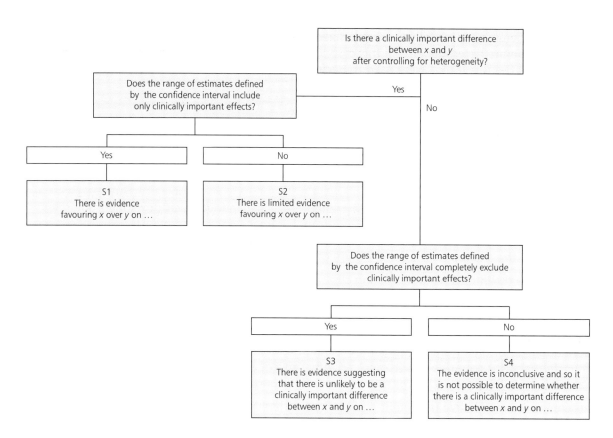

Fig. 4.4　Guideline statement decision tree

the Group to distinguish between the level of evidence and the strength of the associated recommendation. This allowed the Group to moderate recommendations based on factors other than the strength of evidence. Such considerations include the applicability of the evidence to the people in question, economic considerations, values of the development group and society, and the group's awareness of practical issues (Eccles *et al*, 1998).

Each clinical evidence statement was classified according to a hierarchy. Recommendations were then graded A to C based on the level of associated evidence (Table 4.1), or as a good practice point (GPP). All evidence statements and associated forest plots are presented in Appendices 16 and 15 respectively, while a subset of the key evidence statements are presented in the relevant chapters for ease of reference.

4.4.8 Inclusion criteria

The review used the following inclusion criteria:

- the study used a randomised controlled design
- at least 70% of participants needed to have a diagnosis of PTSD, other participants must have PTSD symptoms following a traumatic event
- the main target of treatment was PTSD
- PTSD symptoms were measured
- pre- and post-treatment data were reported
- for continuous data at least 50% of the intent-to-treat sample were assessed at the relevant time point
- double-blind administration of treatment (for pharmacological treatments only).

Table 4.1   Hierarchy of evidence and recommendations grading scheme

Level	Type of evidence	Grade	Evidence
I	Evidence obtained from a single randomised controlled trial or a meta-analysis of randomised controlled trials	A	At least one randomised controlled trial as part of a body of literature of overall good quality and consistency addressing the specific recommendation (evidence level I) without extrapolation
IIa	Evidence obtained from at least one well-designed controlled study without randomisation	B	Well-conducted clinical studies but no randomised clinical trial on the topic of recommendation (evidence levels II or III); or extrapolated from level I evidence
IIb	Evidence obtained from at least one other well-designed quasi-experimental study		
III	Evidence obtained from well-designed, non-experimental descriptive studies, such as comparative studies, correlation studies and case studies		
IV	Evidence obtained from expert committee reports or opinions and/or clinical experiences of respected authorities	C	Expert committee reports or opinions and/or clinical experiences of respected authorities (evidence level IV) or extrapolated from level I or II evidence. This grading indicates that directly applicable clinical studies of good quality are absent or not readily available
		GPP	Recommended good practice based on the clinical experience of the Guideline Development Group

Adapted from Eccles & Mason (2001); Department of Health (1996).

4.4.9 Measures of outcome

The main criterion for treatment effectiveness was its effect on PTSD symptoms. These were assessed either by independent assessors or by self-report. The instruments included in the analysis were as follows:

● assessor-rated PTSD symptoms: the Clinician-Administered PTSD Scale for DSM–IV (CAPS), the PTSD Symptom Scale – Interview Version (PSS–I), or the number of symptoms on the Structured Clinical Interview for DSM–IV (SCID)

● self-report instruments of PTSD symptoms: the Davidson Trauma Scale (DTS), or the Post-traumatic Diagnostic Scale (PDS), or the PTSD Checklist (PCL), or the Impact of Event Scale (IES) or Impact of Event Scale – Revised (IES–R).

If more than one self-report scale (for example, PCL and IES) was used, the instrument that mapped onto the DSM–IV criteria was included (in the example, PCL). Both continuous data (outcome measures scores and changes) and dichotomous data (PTSD remission) based on these scores were considered.

A number of scales have been developed for the measurement of PTSD and other outcomes for children and young people and these are discussed in Chapter 9.

4.4.10 Method used to answer a clinical question in the absence of appropriately designed, high-quality research

In the absence of level I evidence (or a level that is appropriate to the question), or where the Group members were of the opinion (on the basis of previous searches or their knowledge of the literature) that there was unlikely to be such evidence, either an informal or a formal consensus process was adopted. This process focused on questions that the Group considered a priority.

4.4.10.1 Informal consensus

The starting point for this process of informal consensus was that a member of the topic group identified, with help from the systematic reviewer, a narrative review that most directly addressed the clinical question. Where this was not possible, a brief review of the recent literature was initiated. This existing narrative review (or new review) was used as a basis for beginning an iterative process to identify lower levels of evidence relevant to the clinical question and to lead to written statements for the guideline. The process involved a number of steps:

1   A description of what was known about the issues concerning the clinical question was written by one of the topic group members.

2   Evidence from the existing review or new review was then presented in narrative form to the Group and further comments were sought about the evidence and its perceived relevance to the clinical question.

3   Based on the feedback from the Group, additional information was sought and added to the information collected. This might include studies that did not directly address the clinical question but were thought to contain relevant data.

4   If, during the course of preparing the report, a significant body of primary-level studies (of appropriate design to answer the question) was identified, a full systematic review was done.

5   At this time, subject possibly to further reviews of the evidence, a series of statements that directly addressed the clinical question was developed.

6   Following this, on occasions and as deemed appropriate by the Guideline Development Group, the report was then sent to appointed experts outside the Group for peer review and comment. The information from this process was then fed back to the Group for further discussion of the statements.

7   Recommendations were then developed and could also be sent for further external peer review.

8   After this final stage of comment, the statements and recommendations were again reviewed and agreed upon by the Group.

4.4.10.2 Primary care focus group

The Guideline Development Group (GDG) was concerned about the lack of primary care representation among its members. Therefore, in an attempt to address this issue, a general practitioner with extensive experience in primary-care service development in mental health and experience of running focus groups was commissioned by the GDG to run a focus group on the clinical practice recommendations developed for this guideline. A focus group, comprising six general practitioners, two clinical psychologists and a primary-care-based nurse with special experience in mental health, was recruited.

All the focus group members were supplied with the guideline introductory chapters and a final draft of the short form of the NICE clinical guideline before they met. In addition, two members of the GDG also attended the focus group to present relevant summaries of the methods adopted by the GDG and the evidence underpinning the recommendations, and to respond to any specific queries raised by the primary care practitioners. The specific aims of the focus group were to review the appropriateness and wording of the clinical practice recommendations for primary care. The discussions in the group were structured around individual patient pathways. All discussions were recorded and summarised by the GDG project manager; these were reviewed first by the general practitioner consultant and then by all focus group members.

The general practitioner consultant then presented the outcome of the focus group to the GDG, who used the presentation and subsequent discussion to amend the clinical practice recommendations relevant to primary care.

4.5 Health economics review strategies

A systematic review for health economic evidence was conducted. The aim was threefold:

- to identify all publications with information about the economic burden of PTSD in the UK
- to identify existing economic evaluations of any psychological or pharmacological interventions for the treatment of PTSD undertaken in the UK
- to find studies with health state utility evidence generalisable to the UK context to facilitate a possible cost–utility modelling process.

Although no attempt was made to review systematically studies with only resource use or cost data, relevant UK-based information was extracted for future modelling exercises if it was considered appropriate.

4.5.1 Search strategy

In January 2004, bibliographic electronic databases – Medline, PreMedline, EMBASE, CINAHL, PsycINFO, the Cochrane Database of Systematic Reviews (CDSR), Cochrane Controlled Trials Reports (CCTR), Database of Abstracts of Reviews of Effectiveness (DARE) and the NHS Health Technology Assessment (HTA) – and specific health economic databases, the NHS Economic Evaluation Database (NHS EED) and the Office of Health Economics Health Economic Evaluation Database (OHE HEED), were searched for economic studies. For Medline, PreMedline, EMBASE, CINAHL, PsycINFO, CDSR, CCTR and DARE, a combination of a specially developed health economics search filter already tested in earlier NCCMH guidelines and a general filter for post-traumatic stress disorder was used. A combination of subject headings and free-text searches was used. The HTA, NHS EED and OHE HEED databases were searched using shorter, database-specific strategies.

In addition to searches of electronic databases, reference lists of eligible studies and relevant reviews were searched by hand. Studies included in the clinical evidence review were also screened for economic evidence.

4.5.2 Review process

The database searches for general health economic evidence for PTSD resulted in a total of 345 references. Of these, 27 were identified as potentially relevant. Secondary searches for additional pharmaco-economic papers resulted in a further 46 references, of which 8 were initially considered relevant to criteria for health economic appraisal. A further 6 potentially eligible references were found by hand-searching. Full texts of all potentially eligible studies (including those for which relevance or eligibility was not clear from the abstract) were obtained: a total of 41 papers. (At this stage inclusion was not limited to papers only from the UK.) These publications were then assessed against a set of standard inclusion criteria by the health economist, and papers eligible for inclusion as economic evaluations were subsequently assessed for internal validity. The quality assessment was based on the 32-point checklist used by the *British Medical Journal* to assist referees in appraising economic analyses (Drummond & Jefferson, 1996) (Appendix 12).

4.5.3 Selection criteria

Cost-of-illness/economic burden studies:
- no restriction was placed on language or publication status of the papers
- studies published between 1980 and 2003 were included (this date restriction was imposed in order to obtain data relevant to current healthcare settings and costs)
- only studies from the UK were included, as the aim of the review was to identify economic burden information relevant to the national context

- selection criteria based on types of clinical conditions and patients were identical to the clinical literature review (see Appendix 7)
- studies were included provided sufficient details regarding methods and results were available to enable the methodological quality of the study to be assessed and provided the study's data and results were extractable.

Economic evaluations:
- studies were included provided they had used cost-minimisation analysis, cost-effectiveness analysis, cost–utility analysis or cost–benefit analysis
- only clinical evidence from a meta-analysis, a randomised controlled trial, a quasi-experimental trial or a cohort study was used
- no restriction was placed on language or publication status of the papers
- studies published between 1980 and 2003 were included (this date restriction was imposed in order to obtain data relevant to current healthcare settings and costs)
- only studies from the UK were considered, as the aim of the review was to identify economic evaluation information relevant to the national context
- selection criteria based on types of clinical conditions, patients, treatments and settings were identical to the clinical literature review (see Appendix 7)
- studies were included provided sufficient details regarding methods and results were available to enable the methodological quality of the study to be assessed and provided the study's data and results were extractable.

Health state utility studies:
- studies reporting health state utilities for PTSD were considered for inclusion
- no restriction was placed on language or publication status of the papers
- studies published between 1980 and 2003 were included
- only studies from Organization for Economic Cooperation and Development countries were considered, to assure the generalisability of the results to the UK context
- selection criteria based on types of clinical conditions, patients, treatments and settings were identical to the clinical literature review (see Appendix 7).

4.5.4 Data extraction

Data were extracted by the health economist. Masked assessment, whereby data extractors are masked to the details of journal, authors and so on was not undertaken, because the evidence does not support the claim that this minimises bias (Alderson *et al*, 2004).

4.6 Stakeholder contributions

Professionals, PTSD sufferers and companies have contributed to and commented on the guideline at key stages in its development. Stakeholders for this guideline include:
- PTSD sufferer/carer stakeholders: the national PTSD sufferer and carer organisations that represent people whose care is described in this guideline
- professional stakeholders: the national organisations that represent healthcare professionals who are providing services to PTSD sufferers
- commercial stakeholders: the companies that manufacture medicines used in the treatment of PTSD
- primary care trusts
- Department of Health and Welsh Assembly Government.

Stakeholders have been involved in the guideline's development at the following points:
- commenting on the initial scope of the guideline and attending a briefing meeting held by NICE
- contributing lists of evidence to the Guideline Development Group
- commenting on the first and second drafts of the guideline.

4.7 Validation of this guideline

This guideline has been validated through two consultation exercises. Drafts of the full and NICE versions of the guideline were submitted to the NICE Guidelines Review Panel and posted on the NICE website (http://www.nice.org.uk). Stakeholders and other reviewers nominated by the Guideline Development Group were then informed that the documents were available.

The Group reviewed comments from stakeholders, the NICE Guidelines Review Panel, a number of health authority and trust representatives and a wide range of national and international experts from the first round of consultation. The Group then responded to all comments and prepared final consultation drafts of all three versions of the guideline – the full guideline, the NICE guideline, and the information for the public. These were made available on the NICE website, and stakeholders were informed. Following consultation, the drafts were amended and responses to any comments were made. The final drafts were then submitted to NICE to be signed off after review by the Guidelines Review Panel.

5 Psychological treatment of PTSD in adults

5.1 Introduction

A range of psychological treatments is currently used in the NHS to treat PTSD sufferers. They vary from generic psychological treatments, such as supportive and psychodynamic therapy, to treatments that are specifically designed for PTSD, linked to specific theories or treatment techniques. The focus of these guidelines is on those approaches for which there is some evidence for efficacy from randomised controlled trials.

It is important to note that the term 'psychological treatment' is meant to define a group of treatments that use psychological methods to help PTSD sufferers. The term is not meant to denote the profession of the person delivering the treatment. However, this guideline considers it necessary that mental health professionals who deliver these treatments receive appropriate training and supervision. In the NHS and in the non-statutory sector, psychological treatments are currently delivered by a range of mental health professionals, including clinical and counselling psychologists, mental health nurses, occupational therapists, psychiatrists, psychotherapists, counsellors and social workers.

5.2 Definitions

5.2.1 Cognitive–behavioural therapies

Cognitive–behavioural therapies (CBT) draw on psychological models describing the relationship between thoughts, emotions and behaviour. Examples include learning theories that explain how emotions, beliefs and behaviours are acquired and can be changed, and models of information processing (for example, memory and attention). Cognitive–behavioural therapy employs a range of therapeutic techniques that aim to change people's distressing emotions by changing their thoughts, beliefs and/or behaviour. These approaches have been shown to be effective for a range of anxiety disorders (e.g. Barlow & Lehman, 1996), and in recent years specific programmes for particular disorders have been developed.

All CBT programmes for PTSD include an element of psycho-education about common reactions to trauma that normalises the PTSD sufferer's symptoms, and a rationale for the interventions. Cognitive–behavioural therapy programmes for PTSD include one or more of the following groups of treatment techniques: exposure, cognitive therapy and stress management (see sections 5.2.1.1 to 5.2.1.4).

5.2.1.1 Exposure

During exposure, the therapist helps PTSD sufferers to confront their trauma memories and specific situations, people or objects that have become associated with the traumatic stressor and evoke what is now an unrealistically intense emotional or physical response. Exposure is a common therapeutic technique of effective behaviour therapies for anxiety disorders that have been developed since the 1960s (e.g. Wolpe, 1958; Marks, 1969; Rachman, 1978; Rachman & Hodgson, 1980). Keane (Keane & Kaloupek, 1982; Keane et al, 1989) and Foa (Foa et al, 1991) were the first to develop exposure therapies for PTSD sufferers, and these approaches have since been refined with a trend for increases in efficacy. A treatment manual for prolonged exposure, the best-evaluated treatment programme for PTSD focusing on exposure, is available (Foa & Rothbaum, 1998).

In the treatment of PTSD, exposure is usually done in two ways:

- Imaginal exposure or narrative writing: the emotional and detailed recounting of the traumatic memory in the temporal order in which the events unfolded, including one's thoughts and feelings, either in one's imagination while giving a running commentary on what one visualises, or in writing. This is usually repeated until the recounting no longer evokes high levels of distress, and until the trauma memories are experienced as memories rather than something happening all over again.
- *In vivo* exposure: confrontation with now safe situations that the person avoids because they are associated with the trauma and evoke strong emotions or physical reactions (e.g. driving a car again after being involved in an accident; using lifts again after being assaulted in a lift). Repeated exposures help the person realise that the feared situation is no longer dangerous and that the anxiety about it does not persist for ever (Foa & Kozak, 1986).

5.2.1.2 Cognitive therapy

Cognitive therapy was developed by Beck (1976), originally with an emphasis on the treatment of depression. Effective versions of cognitive therapy for a range of anxiety disorders have been developed since the 1980s (e.g. Clark, 1999). In cognitive therapy, the therapist helps patients to identify and modify their excessively negative cognitions (thoughts and beliefs) that lead to disturbing emotions and impaired functioning. Cognitive treatments of anxiety disorders and PTSD focus on the identification and modification of misinterpretations that lead the patient to overestimate threat. In PTSD, this threat stems from interpretations of the trauma and its aftermath. For example, PTSD sufferers may feel strong guilt or shame related to the trauma: rape victims may blame themselves for the rape; war veterans may feel it was their fault that a best friend was killed. Others overestimate the current danger they are encountering in everyday life. Accident survivors may become convinced that they are at great risk of having a further trauma. Others may take the intrusive re-experiencing symptoms as a sign that they are losing a sense of reality.

By discussing the evidence for and against the interpretations, and by testing out the predictions derived from the interpretations with the help of the therapist, the patient arrives at more adaptive conclusions. The patient is encouraged to drop behaviours and cognitive strategies that prevent a disconfirmation of the negative interpretations, e.g. excessive precautions to prevent further trauma or excessive rumination about what one could have done differently during the event.

Treatment manuals that describe the use of cognitive techniques in the treatment of PTSD include those by Resick & Schnicke (1993), Blanchard & Hickling (2004) and Foa & Rothbaum (1998).

5.2.1.3 Stress management

Teaching people a set of skills that they can use to cope with stress has a long tradition in CBT. Examples of the skills that help people manage their anxiety include:
- relaxation training: teaching techniques for relaxation, for example, relaxing major muscle groups, in a way that decreases anxiety
- breathing retraining: teaching techniques of slow, abdominal breathing to avoid hyperventilation and the unpleasant physical sensations that accompany it
- positive thinking and self-talk: positive statements (e.g. 'I did it before and I can do it again') are written on cards and rehearsed so that they can be used to replace the negative thoughts that often occur during stressful experiences
- assertiveness training: teaching the person how to express wishes, opinions and emotions appropriately and without alienating others
- thought stopping: teaching the person distraction techniques to overcome distressing thoughts by inwardly shouting 'stop'.

The most widely used stress management programme for trauma survivors is the stress inoculation training developed by Meichenbaum (1985). It aims to provide patients with a sense of mastery over their stress by teaching them a variety of coping skills and then providing an opportunity to practise those skills in a graduated ('inoculation') fashion. It has been adapted for the treatment of survivors of sexual assault by Kilpatrick and colleagues (e.g. Veronen & Kilpatrick, 1983).

The CBT programmes tested in the available RCTs differ in several ways. First, whereas in most studies treatment was on an individual basis, a few studies used group treatments. Group cognitive–behavioural therapy was considered separately from individual therapies in the meta-analysis. The focus of the group treatment programmes that were tested in the RCTs was on education about trauma reactions, exposure to reminders of the event, stress management and problem-solving. Schnurr *et al* (2003) compared a trauma-focused group CBT programme with a control group treatment that did not focus on the traumatic event. The latter included education about trauma reactions and discussion of present difficulties with relationships or problem-solving.

Among the studies that delivered CBT on an individual basis, the main difference was the extent to which the memory of the traumatic event and its meaning were the focus of treatment. In most CBT studies, the focus was on the trauma. For the purpose of the meta-analysis, these treatment programmes were labelled 'trauma-focused CBT'. Programmes included in this category differ in whether the emphasis in treatment techniques is on exposure or on cognitive interventions. Some programmes place their main emphasis on exposure (e.g. Keane *et al*, 1989; Foa & Rothbaum, 1998), others on cognitive techniques (e.g. Resick & Schnicke, 1993; Kubany *et al*, 2003; Ehlers *et al*, 2005), and most use a combination (e.g. Devilly & Spence, 1999; Fecteau & Nicki, 1999; Power *et al*, 2002; Blanchard *et al*, 2003*b*). There is considerable overlap in the proposed mechanisms underlying the effectiveness of the various versions of trauma-focused CBT. For example, a prominent theory of exposure treatment (Foa & Kozak, 1986) suggests that exposure changes problematic meanings. In the same vein, nearly all trauma-focused CBT treatments that include cognitive therapy use some form of exposure (e.g. narrative writing, imaginal exposure) to access problematic meanings. Two studies (Marks *et al*, 1998; Tarrier *et al*, 1999) included cognitive therapy conditions without exposure. The following treatment programmes were included in the category of trauma-focused CBT: prolonged exposure (Foa *et al*, 1991, 1999; Marks *et al*, 1998), image habituation training (Vaughan *et al*, 1994), imaginal flooding (implosive flooding) therapy (Keane *et al*, 1989), imaginal exposure and biofeedback-assisted desensitisation treatment (Peniston & Kulkosky, 1991), cognitive reprocessing therapy (Resick *et al*, 2002), cognitive–behavioural treatment (Fecteau & Nicki, 1999; Paunovic & Ost, 2001; Blanchard *et al*, 2003*b*), cognitive therapy for PTSD (Ehlers *et al*, 2005), cognitive restructuring plus exposure (Marks *et al*, 1998; Bryant *et al*, 2003), cognitive restructuring (Marks *et al*, 1998; Tarrier *et al*, 1999), cognitive trauma therapy (Kubany *et al*, 2003, 2004) and brief eclectic psychotherapy (Gersons *et al*, 2000). The last also included some elements of psychodynamic therapy, but the main treatment components overlapped with those of other trauma-focused cognitive–behavioural therapies.

Trauma-focused CBT was distinguished from CBT programmes that focus on stress management. For the purposes of the meta-analysis, the following treatment programmes were grouped as stress management: stress inoculation training (Foa *et al*, 1991, 1999) and progressive muscle relaxation (Marks *et al*, 1998; Taylor *et al*, 2003).

There is some overlap in treatment techniques between trauma-focused CBT and stress management. In trauma-focused CBT, patients with PTSD sometimes receive training in stress management strategies, for example, breathing retraining or relaxation training to make exposure to the trauma memory or reminders more tolerable. Similarly, the stress inoculation training programme tested in the studies by Foa *et al* (1991, 1999) studies involved discussion of the meaning of the traumatic event in the later sessions, overlapping with the cognitive elements of trauma-focused CBT.

The relevant consideration for the classification was whether or not the treatment *mainly* focused on the trauma memory and its meaning. Thus, the combination of prolonged exposure with stress inoculation training was classified as 'trauma-focused CBT', whereas stress inoculation training alone was classified as 'stress management'.

In summary, the review classified CBT programmes into three groups:

- trauma-focused CBT (individual treatment)
- stress management (individual treatment)
- group CBT.

A few recent RCTs investigated new forms of delivering CBT for PTSD, internet-based therapy (Lange *et al*, 2003) and delivery through interpreters in refugee settlements (Neuner *et al*, 2004).

These could not be included in the meta-analysis because treatment setting and method of delivery were too different from other studies. These studies are reviewed separately in section 5.6.2.

5.2.2 Eye movement desensitisation and reprocessing

Eye movement desensitisation and reprocessing (EMDR) was developed by Shapiro (1989). It is based on a theoretical model which posits that the dysfunctional intrusions, emotions and physical sensations experienced by trauma victims are due to the improper storage of the traumatic event in implicit memory. The EMDR procedures are based on stimulating the patient's own information processing in order to help integrate the targeted event as an adaptive contextualised memory (Shapiro, 2001).

Therapy with EMDR involves eliciting specific targets to represent the traumatic event, the current triggers and future templates for appropriate future action. Standardised procedures are used to process the targets to resolution. Patients are prepared to attend to the memory and associations while their attention is also engaged by a bilateral physical stimulation (eye movements, taps or tones). Each target is accessed individually according to procedures that bring together all the relevant cognitive, emotional and sensory aspects of the traumatic memory. Then, the patient is guided into a receptive state of awareness regarding aspects of the targeted event, and any concomitant memory associations. Guided by standardised procedures, the clinician elicits sets of dual attention stimuli, basing the length of the set and the focus of attention on the patient's response.

Desensitisation, de-arousal, insights and changes in belief are viewed as by-products of this direct processing, which is posited to move the targeted event from implicit memory to explicit memory, which no longer contains the disturbing affects, thoughts and sensations. It is postulated, first, that what is useful is learned, stored with appropriate affects and is able to guide the person in the future, and second, that what is not useful (the negative emotions, thoughts and sensations) is progressively discarded as part of the transformation of the memory. The EMDR procedures are also used to elicit and strengthen positive affects, cognitions and future behaviours. The eye movement element of EMDR has attracted the most attention; however, Shapiro has emphasised in her recent writing (e.g. Shapiro, 1996, 2001) that EMDR is a multiple-stage therapy that is meant to be integrated into a comprehensive plan for the treatment of trauma. Furthermore, eye movements are not the only treatment technique, and others such as 'sequential exposure, desensitisation, cognitive restructuring, and classical conditioning' (Shapiro, 1996: p. 209) are also used.

Many of the procedures used in EMDR overlap with those used in trauma-focused CBT; for example, holding an image of the trauma in mind resembles imaginal exposure, although the exposure is much briefer and the patient does not verbalise the content of the image. Replacing negative cognitions associated with the trauma with positive cognitions overlaps with cognitive interventions. The associative techniques resemble those used in psychodynamic approaches. This has led several recent reviews to conclude that the effectiveness of EMDR may be due to these common treatment components, rather than the eye movements (e.g. Davidson & Parker, 2001). Several empirical studies have suggested that the eye movements might not be necessary in producing the therapeutic effects observed with EMDR (reviewed by Davidson & Parker, 2001). However, the treatment originator and other authors maintain that rhythmic bilateral stimulation is an important therapeutic element (e.g. Shapiro, 1996; Welch & Beere, 2002).

Despite the similarity in many treatment procedures, EMDR was considered separately from CBT approaches for the purposes of the meta-analysis, as its originator considers it a distinct treatment (Shapiro, 2001), and specific training programmes are required.

5.2.3 Other therapies

A range of other psychological treatments are currently used in the NHS to treat trauma survivors. As the empirical evidence base for each of these treatments is sparse, they were combined for the purposes of the review. It is important to note, however, that the different treatments have different rationales and procedures.

5.2.3.1 Supportive therapy and non-directive counselling

Supportive therapy builds on the concept of client-centred therapy by Rogers (1951). It is defined here as equivalent to non-directive counselling and as a way for the individual to explore how they relate and respond to another person. In supportive therapy individuals are helped to focus on their thoughts, feelings and behaviour; reach clearer self-understanding; and to find and use their strengths so that they cope more effectively with their lives by making appropriate decisions, or by taking relevant action. Essentially, supportive therapy is a purposeful relationship in which one person helps another to help themselves.

Supportive therapy is primarily non-directive and non-advisory, but recognises that some situations require positive guidance by means of information and advice (Hoxter, 1998, cited by Bond, 2000). In the review, the RCTs of supportive therapy for PTSD included psycho-education about stress reactions and the normalisation of PTSD symptoms. One RCT also encouraged patients to explore coping strategies that they had used to cope with earlier life events (Blanchard *et al*, 2003*b*).

5.2.3.2 Psychodynamic therapies

Psychodynamic therapies build on psychoanalytic theories of trauma (Breuer & Freud, 1895; Janet, 1889; Freud, 1920; see also van der Hart *et al*, 1989). Several different forms of psychodynamic treatments for PTSD have been described (see Garland, 1998; Kudler *et al*, 2000, for an overview;). The emphasis in psychodynamic therapies lies on resolving the unconscious conflicts provoked by the stressful event. 'Psychodynamic treatment seeks to re-engage normal mechanisms of adaptation by addressing what is unconscious, and in tolerable doses, making it conscious' (Kudler *et al*, 2000: p. 339). The goal of treatment is to understand the meaning of the stressful event in the context of the individual's personality, attitudes and early experiences (Levy & Lemma, 2004). The psychological meaning of the event is explored by a range of methods such as 'sifting and sorting through wishes, fantasies, fears, and defences stirred up by the event' (Kudler *et al*, 2000: p. 339). Treatment strategies include exploratory insight-oriented, supportive or directive activity. It may also include working with transference, but with the therapist using a less strict technique than that used in psychoanalysis.

Despite the long history of psychodynamic therapies and numerous case reports of successful treatments, the review only identified one RCT testing its efficacy in PTSD (BROM 1989) and one trial using elements of psychodynamic therapy in combination with cognitive–behavioural treatment (GERSONS 2000).

5.2.3.3 Hypnotherapy

Hypnotherapy involves giving the patient instructions (e.g. 'focus on your right arm and on the sensation that it is getting lighter and lighter') to induce a state of highly focused attention, a reduced awareness of peripheral stimuli and a heightened responsiveness to social cues (suggestibility). The goal is to enhance control over trauma-related emotional distress and hyperarousal symptoms and to facilitate the recollection of details of the traumatic event. It is often considered as an adjunct to psychodynamic, cognitive–behavioural or other therapies rather than as a therapy *per se* (see Cardeòa *et al*, 2000).

The meta-analysis only identified one RCT testing the efficacy of hypotherapy in PTSD (BROM 1989). Data from the hypnotherapy condition in this study were combined with data from the psychodynamic therapy condition to form an 'other therapies' comparator in the meta-analysis.

5.2.4 Overview of classification of psychological treatments

In summary, the systematic review classified the psychological treatment programmes as follows. Two of the treatment categories – trauma-focused CBT and EMDR – focus on the memory for the traumatic event and its meaning; these are referred to as trauma-focused psychological treatments throughout this guideline. Two other treatment categories do not place the main focus of treatment on the trauma: these are stress management and relaxation, and other therapies, including supportive therapy/non-directive counselling, psychodynamic therapies and hypnotherapy. The above four categories refer to treatments that are delivered on an individual basis; the final category was group cognitive–behavioural therapies.

5.3 Previous systematic reviews

Several previous systematic reviews of psychological treatments have been conducted. Van Etten & Taylor (1998) concluded that cognitive–behavioural therapy and EMDR are both effective in the treatment of PTSD. The practice guidelines from the International Society for Traumatic Stress Studies (Foa *et al*, 2000) came to similar conclusions. Several systematic reviews highlight the exposure to the memory of the traumatic event and reminders of the trauma as common elements of effective trauma treatments (Paunovic, 1997; Rothbaum *et al*, 2000).

5.4 Studies considered for review

Previous meta-analyses included both controlled and uncontrolled studies. This review, in line with the procedure set out in Chapter 4, only included RCTs.

5.4.1 Inclusion criteria

In addition to the generic inclusion criteria listed in Chapter 4, further inclusion criteria were that the intervention did not occur less than 3 months after the trauma (earlier interventions are considered in Chapter 7), and that treatment entailed more than one intervention session.

5.4.2 Measures of outcome

Unfortunately, for continuous measures of outcome such as the Clinician-Administered PTSD Scale for DSM–IV, few studies reported intent-to-treat analyses (i.e. included all patients originally assigned to the treatment condition). Therefore, the analysis of the continuous assessor-rated and self-reported symptom scores is a completer analysis. This type of analysis may overestimate treatment effectiveness, as one may expect that people who withdraw from treatment may on average respond less well than those who complete the treatment.

To compensate for this potential bias, the percentage of people who still met diagnostic criteria for PTSD at the end of treatment was calculated as an intent-to-treat analysis. This analysis made the conservative assumption that people who did not complete the treatment still met diagnostic criteria.

When making recommendations, we considered completer analyses for self-reported and clinician-rated PTSD symptoms, and intent-to-treat analyses for the number of the people still suffering from PTSD, together to form an overall estimate of treatment effectiveness.

Three further types of treatment outcome were considered as additional criteria. First, in order to evaluate the acceptability of the treatments, the percentage of people who did not complete treatment or any comparable active intervention was recorded. Second, we reviewed whether the treatment of PTSD also led to significant improvement in symptoms of depression and anxiety. The most commonly used standard measures were the Beck Depression Inventory (Beck *et al*, 1961) and the Beck Anxiety Inventory (Beck & Steer, 1993) or State–Trait Anxiety Inventory (STAI, trait version; Spielberger *et al*, 1973). Last – but not least – we considered whether the treatments had a measurable effect on the PTSD sufferer's overall social and occupational functioning and quality of life. Few studies included relevant measures such as the Sheehan Disability Scale (American Psychiatric Association, 2000), the Global Assessment of Functioning Scale (Endicott *et al*, 1976) or the Social Adjustment Scale (Weissman & Paykel, 1974). However, in general, these measures focused on impairment in functioning rather than positive aspects of quality of life.

5.5 Evidence statements

The review team conducted a new systematic research for RCTs of each of the five therapy groupings outlined above (trauma-focused CBT, EMDR, stress management, group CBT and other therapies) that compared these treatments against waiting list or usual care or against another psychological treatment. The following studies were identified by the Guideline Development Group as meeting the inclusion criteria. (Full details of the search strategy for this and other reviews of the guideline are given in Appendix 6. Information about each study along with an assessment of methodological quality is given in Appendix 14, which also contains a list of excluded studies with reasons for exclusions.)

- 24 studies compared trauma-focused CBT with waiting list or other psychological interventions (BLANCHARD 2003, BROM 1989, BRYANT 2003A, CLOITRE 2002, COOPER 1989, DEVILLY 1999, ECHEBURUA 1997, EHLERS, FECTEAU 1999, FOA 1991, FOA 1999, GERSONS 2000, IRONSON 2002, KEANE 1989, KUBANY 2003, KUBANY 2004, LEE 2002B , MARKS 1998, PAUNOVIC 2001, PENISTON 1991, POWER 2002, RESICK 2002, TAYLOR 2003, VAUGHAN 1994)

- 11 studies compared EMDR with waiting list or other psychological interventions (CARLSON 1998, DEVILLY 1999, IRONSON 2002, JENSEN 1994, LEE 2002B, MARCUS 1997, POWER 2002, ROTHBAUM 1997, SCHECK 1998, TAYLOR 2003, VAUGHAN 1994)

- 7 studies compared stress management with waiting list or other psychological interventions (CARLSON 1998, ECHEBURUA 1997, FOA 1991, FOA 1999, MARKS 1998, TAYLOR 2003, VAUGHAN 1994)

- 6 studies compared other therapies with waiting list or other psychological interventions (BLANCHARD 2003, BROM 1989, BRYANT 2003A, FOA 1991, MARCUS 1997, SCHECK 1998)

- 4 studies compared group CBT with waiting list or other psychological interventions (CLASSEN 2001, KRAKOW 2001, SCHNURR 2003, ZLOTNICK 1997).

Two additional RCTs met inclusion criteria, but differed in mode of delivery and are discussed separately in section 5.6.2 (LANGE 2003, NEUNER 2004). One further RCT compared two versions of trauma-focused CBT (exposure and cognitive therapy) with each other (data for this RCT are reported in two papers: TARRIER 1999 and TARRIER 1999B).

5.5.1 Comparing intervention against waiting list

The comparisons against waiting list are summarised in the following order: trauma-focused CBT, EMDR, stress management, other therapies and group CBT. The full list of evidence statements is given in Appendix 16.

5.5.1.1 Trauma-focused CBT versus waiting list

There is evidence favouring trauma-focused CBT over waiting list on reducing the likelihood of having a PTSD diagnosis after treatment (k=14; n=716; RR=0.47, 95% CI 0.37 to 0.59). |

There is evidence favouring trauma-focused CBT over waiting list on reducing the severity of PTSD symptoms (self-report measures) (k=8; n=388; SMD=−1.7, 95% CI −2.21 to −1.18). |

There is evidence favouring trauma-focused CBT over waiting list on reducing the severity of PTSD symptoms (clinician-rated measures) (k=13; n=609; SMD=−1.36, 95% CI −1.88 to −0.84). |

There is limited evidence favouring trauma-focused CBT over waiting list on reducing depression symptoms (k=13; n=585; SMD=−1.2, 95% CI −1.65 to −0.75). |

There is limited evidence favouring trauma-focused CBT over waiting list on reducing anxiety symptoms (self-report measures) (k=10; n=375; SMD=−0.94; 95% CI −1.16 to −0.72). |

5.5.1.2 EMDR versus waiting list

There is limited evidence favouring EMDR over waiting list on reducing the likelihood of having a PTSD diagnosis after treatment (k=5; n=169; RR= 0.51; 95% CI 0.28 to 0.95). |

There is limited evidence favouring EMDR over waiting list on reducing the severity of PTSD symptoms (self-report measures) (k=4; n=116; SMD=−1.1; 95% CI −2.42 to 0.23). |

There is evidence favouring EMDR over waiting list on reducing the severity of PTSD symptoms (clinician-rated measures) (k=4; n=122; SMD=−1.54, 95% CI, −1.96 to −1.12). |

There is evidence favouring EMDR over waiting list on reducing depression symptoms (k=4; n=120; SMD=−1.67, 95% CI −2.1 to −1.25). |

There is limited evidence favouring EMDR over waiting list on reducing anxiety symptoms (k=4; n=116; SMD=−1.18, 95% CI −1.58 to −0.78). I

5.5.1.3 Stress management versus waiting list

There is limited evidence favouring stress management therapy over waiting list on reducing the likelihood of having a PTSD diagnosis after treatment (k=4; n=121; RR=0.64, 95% CI 0.47 to 0.87). I

The evidence is inconclusive and so it is not possible to determine if there is a clinically important difference between stress management therapy and waiting list on reducing the severity of PTSD symptoms (self-report measures) (k=1; n=24; SMD=0.33, 95% CI −0.47 to 1.14). I

There is limited evidence favouring stress management therapy over waiting list on reducing the severity of PTSD symptoms (clinician-rated measures) (k=3; n=86; SMD=−1.14, 95% CI −1.62 to −0.67). I

The evidence is inconclusive and so it is not possible to determine if there is a clinically important difference between stress management therapy and waiting list on reducing depression symptoms (k=4; n=109; SMD=−0.73, 95% CI −1.12 to −0.33). I

The evidence is inconclusive and so it is not possible to determine if there is a clinically important difference between stress management therapy and waiting list on reducing anxiety symptoms (k=3; n=82; SMD=−0.77, 95% CI −1.23 to −0.32). I

5.5.1.4 Other therapies versus waiting list

The evidence is inconclusive and so it is not possible to determine if there is a clinically important difference between other therapies and waiting list on reducing the likelihood of having a PTSD diagnosis after treatment (k=2; n=85; RR=0.79, 95% CI 0.53 to 1.18). I

The evidence is inconclusive and so it is not possible to determine if there is a clinically important difference between other therapies and waiting list on reducing the severity of PTSD symptoms (self-report measures) (k=2; n=132; SMD=−0.61, 95% CI −0.98 to −0.24). I

The evidence is inconclusive and so it is not possible to determine if there is a clinically important difference between other therapies and waiting list on reducing the severity of PTSD symptoms (clinician-rated measures) (k=2; n=72; SMD=−0.43, 95% CI −0.9 to 0.04). I

There is evidence suggesting there is unlikely to be a clinically important difference between other therapies and waiting list on reducing depression symptoms (k=2; n=72; SMD=−0.25, 95% CI −0.71 to 0.22). I

The evidence is inconclusive and so it is not possible to determine if there is a clinically important difference between other therapies and waiting list on reducing anxiety symptoms (k=3; n=153; SMD=−0.48, 95% CI −0.82 to −0.14). I

5.5.1.5 Group CBT versus waiting list

The full range of outcome measures was not provided in the three studies of group CBT.

There is limited evidence favouring group CBT over waiting list on reducing the likelihood of having a PTSD diagnosis after treatment (k=1; n=48; RR=0.56, 95% CI 0.31 to 1.01). I

The evidence is inconclusive and so it is not possible to determine if there is a clinically important difference between group CBT and waiting list/usual care on reducing the severity of PTSD symptoms (self-report measures) (k=2; n=71; SMD=−0.71, 95% CI −1.2 to −0.22). I

5.5.2 Intervention versus intervention

Although many of the included studies compared active treatments against waiting list, there were fewer studies available for direct comparisons of each of the active treatments against one another. The comparisons are set out in the following order. Each treatment is considered in turn in the same order as in the preceding section (trauma-focused CBT, EMDR, stress management and other therapies). So the first treatment considered in the review, trauma-focused CBT, is compared against each of the other classifications of treatments in turn (except group CBT, for which no study provided a direct comparison). Next, EMDR is compared against each of the remaining treatments for which a direct comparison has not already been provided (therefore the comparison against trauma-focused CBT is not repeated). Hence for stress management only one comparison is listed directly (against other therapies), as all other comparisons have already been listed. Where available, three outcome measures are reported for each comparison in the following section: a self-report measure of the severity of PTSD symptoms (or where this is not reported, the clinician-rated measure), likelihood of having a PTSD diagnosis, and leaving treatment early. The full list of evidence statements is given in Appendix 16.

5.5.2.1 Trauma-focused CBT versus EMDR

The evidence is inconclusive and so it is not possible to determine if there is a clinically important difference between EMDR and trauma-focused CBT on reducing the likelihood of having a PTSD diagnosis after treatment (k=6; n=220; RR=1.03, 95% CI 0.64 to 1.66). ▌

The evidence is inconclusive and so it is not possible to determine if there is a clinically important difference between EMDR and trauma-focused CBT on reducing the severity of PTSD symptoms (self-report) (k=6; n=166; SMD=−0.31, 95% CI −0.62 to 0). ▌

The evidence is inconclusive and so it is not possible to determine if there is a clinically important difference between EMDR and trauma-focused CBT on reducing the likelihood of leaving treatment early for any reason (k=7; n=240; RR=0.83, 95% CI 0.54 to 1.27). ▌

5.5.2.2 Trauma-focused CBT versus stress management therapies

There is limited evidence favouring trauma-focused CBT over stress management therapy on reducing the likelihood of having a PTSD diagnosis after treatment (k=6; n=284; RR=0.78, 95% CI 0.61 to 0.99). ▌

The evidence is inconclusive and so it is not possible to determine if there is a clinically important difference between trauma-focused CBT and stress management therapy on reducing the severity of PTSD symptoms (self-report measures) (k=3; n=127; SMD=−0.37, 95% CI −0.74 to 0.01). ▌

The evidence is inconclusive and so it is not possible to determine if there is a clinically important difference between trauma-focused CBT and stress management therapy on reducing the likelihood of leaving treatment early for any reason (k=6; n=284; RR=1.17, 95% CI 0.69 to 2). ▌

5.5.2.3 Trauma-focused CBT versus other therapies

There is limited evidence favouring trauma-focused CBT over other therapies on reducing the likelihood of having a PTSD diagnosis after treatment (k=5; n=286; RR=0.71, 95% CI 0.56 to 0.89). ▌

There is limited evidence favouring trauma-focused CBT over other therapies on reducing the severity of PTSD symptoms (self-report measures) (k=3; n=176; SMD=−1.18, 95% CI −2.32 to −0.03). ▌

The evidence is inconclusive and so it is not possible to determine if there is a clinically important difference between trauma-focused CBT and other therapies on reducing the likelihood of leaving treatment early for any reason (k=5; n=290; RR=1.14, 95% CI 0.68 to 1.9). ▌

5.5.2.4 EMDR versus stress management therapies

There is limited evidence favouring EMDR over stress management on reducing the likelihood of having a PTSD diagnosis after treatment (k=3; n=84; RR=0.69, 95% CI 0.46 to 1.04). ▌

The evidence is inconclusive and so it is not possible to determine if there is a clinically important difference between EMDR and stress management therapy on reducing the severity of PTSD symptoms (self-report measures) (k=3; n=75; SMD=−0.4, 95% CI −0.86 to 0.06). ▌

The evidence is inconclusive and so it is not possible to determine if there is a clinically important difference between EMDR and stress management therapy on reducing the likelihood of leaving treatment early for any reason (k=3; n=84; RR=1.03, 95% CI 0.37 to 2.88). ▌

5.5.2.5 EMDR versus other therapies

There is limited evidence favouring EMDR over other therapies on reducing the likelihood of having a PTSD diagnosis after treatment (k=1; *n*=67; RR=0.4, 95% CI 0.19 to 0.84). ∎

There is limited evidence favouring EMDR over other therapies on reducing the severity of PTSD symptoms (self-report measures) (k=2; *n*=124; SMD=−0.84, 95% CI −1.21 to −0.47). ∎

There is limited evidence favouring other therapies over EMDR on reducing the likelihood of leaving treatment early for any reason (k=2; *n*=127; RR=1.48, 95% CI 0.26 to 8.54). ∎

5.5.2.6 Stress management versus other therapies

The evidence is inconclusive and so it is not possible to determine if there is a clinically important difference between stress management therapy and other therapies on reducing the likelihood of having a PTSD diagnosis after treatment (k=1; *n*=31; RR=0.58, 95% CI 0.3 to 1.11). ∎

There is limited evidence favouring stress management therapy over other therapies on reducing the severity of PTSD symptoms (clinician-rated measures) (k=1; *n*=25; SMD=−1.22, 95% CI −2.09 to −0.35). ∎

The evidence is inconclusive and so it is not possible to determine if there is a clinically important difference between stress management therapy and other therapies on reducing the likelihood of leaving treatment early for any reason (k=1; *n*=31; RR=0.82, 95% CI 0.2 to 3.46). ∎

5.5.2.7 Group CBT (trauma-focused) versus group CBT (non-trauma-focused)

There is evidence suggesting there is unlikely to be a clinically important difference between group CBT (trauma-focused) and group CBT (non-trauma-focused) on reducing the likelihood of having a PTSD diagnosis after treatment (k=1; *n*=360; RR=0.98, 95% CI 0.83 to 1.16). ∎

There is evidence suggesting there is unlikely to be a clinically important difference between group CBT (trauma-focused) and group CBT (non-trauma-focused) on reducing the severity of PTSD symptoms (k=1; *n*=325; SMD=0.12, 95% CI −0.34 to 0.1). ∎

There is limited evidence suggesting a difference favouring group CBT (non-trauma-focused) over group CBT (trauma-focused) on reducing the likelihood of leaving treatment early for any reason (k=1; *n*=360; RR=1.38, 95% CI 1 to 1.9). ∎

5.6 Clinical summary for psychological treatments

5.6.1 Summary of meta-analysis

Trauma-focused CBT showed clinically important benefits over waiting list on all measures of PTSD symptoms. In addition, there was limited evidence that this therapy also has clinically important effects on depression and anxiety. Trauma-focused CBT had the largest empirical database (16 RCTs with 857 participants compared trauma-focused CBT with waiting lists). The studies included survivors of a range of different traumas, including accidents, assault, sexual assault (including childhood sexual assault), domestic violence, military combat, 'mixed' trauma groups and refugees with multiple traumatic events. Treatment duration ranged between 4 and 18 sessions, and the duration of sessions was between 50 min and 120 min. Furthermore, there was limited evidence that trauma-focused CBT was superior to supportive/non-directive therapies, hence it is highly unlikely that the effectiveness of this group of treatments is due to non-specific factors such as attention.

The effectiveness of EMDR was also generally supported by the meta-analysis, but the evidence base was not as strong as that for trauma-focused CBT, both in terms of the number of RCTs available and the certainty with which clinical benefit was established. The EMDR treatments showed clinically important benefits on clinician-rated PTSD symptom criteria compared with waiting lists, and there was limited evidence for its effectiveness in self-report measures of PTSD symptoms and PTSD diagnosis (5 studies, *n*=169). In addition, there was evidence or limited evidence for clinically important effects on anxiety and depression. There was limited evidence that EMDR was superior to supportive/non-directive therapy, suggesting that it is unlikely that its effectiveness is due to non-specific factors such as attention. The studies included survivors of a range of different traumas, including accidents, sexual assault (including childhood sexual assault) and military combat, and 'mixed' trauma groups. Treatment duration ranged between 2 and 12 sessions, and the duration of sessions was between 50 min and 97 min.

The treatments supported by the review (trauma-focused CBT and EMDR) are both trauma-focused psychological treatments that specifically address the PTSD sufferers' troubling memories of the traumatic event and the personal meanings of the event and its consequences. Direct comparisons of these two approaches did not reveal any significant advantages for one over the other, with respect to either treatment outcome or the speed of therapeutic change (Taylor et al, 2001). Similarly, studies comparing different versions of trauma-focused CBT did not find differences (MARKS 1998; TARRIER 1999; RESICK 2002).

Other therapies (supportive/non-directive therapy, psychodynamic therapies and hypnotherapies) that focus on current or past aspects of the patient's life other than the trauma or general support did not show clinically important effects on PTSD symptoms, depression or anxiety. However, there were very few studies of the latter two approaches. Thus the review did not find support for any clinically important benefits of these treatments, although this does not mean that these treatments were shown to be ineffective.

For stress management and relaxation there was limited evidence for clinical effects on some measures when compared with waiting lists, but no consistent differences in effectiveness compared with other treatments. This may be due to the overlap of stress inoculation training with the cognitive components of trauma-focused CBT. The RCTs that compared trauma-focused CBT or EMDR with relaxation training only, found clearer differences favouring the trauma-focused psychological treatments (VAUGHAN 1994; CARLSON 1998; MARKS 1998; TAYLOR 2003).

Psychological group treatments have rarely been investigated. Three RCTs compared group CBT with waiting lists (n=271) and did not find convincing evidence for its effectiveness, in contrast to clinically important effects observed with individual trauma-focused CBT. Similarly, a large RCT (n=360) did not find that trauma-focused group CBT had larger clinical benefits than non-trauma focused group treatment in US military veterans, using the strict intent-to-treat analyses which included everyone who was randomised (SCHNURR 2003). However, a sub-analysis of participants who received an adequate amount of therapy showed some evidence that trauma-focused group CBT had advantages over non-trauma-focused group treatment.

5.6.2 Delivering effective treatments

Considerable concern is often expressed about whether the results of clinical trials can generalise to routine clinical practice in the NHS. Two aspects of RCTs are often highlighted in this discussion, specifically that therapists in RCTs usually have considerable expertise in delivering the respective treatments, and that patients are not representative because they have to meet certain inclusion and exclusion criteria for the trial. It is therefore encouraging to note that two recent studies demonstrated that treatment effects comparable with those found in RCTs of cognitive therapy for PTSD (EHLERS 2005), and of prolonged exposure (FOA 1991; FOA 1999; Foa & Rothbaum, 1998), can be achieved by training and providing regular supervision to healthcare professionals who are not experts in CBT or to individuals working in the non-statutory sector (Gillespie et al, 2002; Cahill et al, 2005) and under routine NHS conditions without any exclusion criteria (Gillespie et al, 2002).

A further problem with the generalisability of RCTs of psychological treatments for PTSD is that not all PTSD sufferers are able to attend treatment in the usual clinical settings. It is therefore encouraging that several groups have presented treatment innovations that may help deliver effective PTSD treatments to PTSD sufferers in remote locations. This includes studies in traumatised communities affected by disaster (Basoglu et al, 2003, 2005) and studies in non-Western societies (NEUNER 2004). These innovations build on trauma-focused CBT programmes.

Neuner (NEUNER 2004) developed 'narrative exposure therapy' for traumatised survivors of war or torture. The four-session programme builds on exposure therapy and testimony therapy. With the help of interpreters, PTSD sufferers are asked to give a narrative account of their lives with special emphasis on a detailed description of traumatic events. They are asked to relive the emotions they experienced during the traumatic events while reporting them. The narratives are read back to the sufferer repeatedly and details are added. Neuner and colleagues randomly assigned 43 Sudanese refugees who lived in a refugee settlement to one of the following: narrative exposure therapy, supportive therapy or psychoeducation. At 12-month follow-up, but not at the post-treatment assessment, there was limited evidence for clinically important benefits of narrative exposure therapy compared with both supportive therapy and psychoeducation on measures of PTSD symptoms (NEUNER 2004).

Lange (LANGE 2003) developed and tested 'interapy', a form of therapy delivered over the internet. It involves writing about the traumatic event, similar to some trauma-focused CBT programmes (e.g. BLANCHARD 2003; RESICK 2002). An RCT involving 101 trauma survivors showed clinically important effects of the internet therapy on self-reported PTSD symptoms compared with a waiting list, and limited evidence for effect on depression and anxiety.

Basoglu *et al* (2003, 2005) developed a short, trauma-focused cognitive–behavioural treatment for earthquake survivors. The main emphasis of the treatment was on encouraging self-exposure to reminders of the traumatic event. The treatment rationale emphasised the enhancement of a sense of control over one's fear. An open trial of 231 earthquake survivors with chronic PTSD (Basoglu *et al*, 2003) found that the majority of participants experienced a reduction in PTSD symptoms after one or two sessions. In an RCT (Basoglu *et al*, 2005), 53 earthquake survivors with PTSD were identified among a community sample and randomly assigned to either treatment (1 hour, plus 30 min follow-up) or waiting list. (Participants who did not attend the post-treatment assessment were replaced by other participants.) The treatment group showed greater changes on measures of PTSD symptoms and depression than the waiting list group.

5.6.3 Predictors of response to trauma-focused psychological treatment

A number of studies have investigated whether response to trauma-focused CBT can be predicted from patient or trauma characteristics. Overall, few predictors have been found. Some clinically important findings from these analyses were:

- The time that had passed since the trauma was not related to treatment effectiveness (Gillespie *et al*, 2002; RESICK 2002; EHLERS 2005).
- Comorbidity was not associated with outcome, but patients with comorbid disorders needed more treatment sessions (Gillespie *et al*, 2002).
- People who were physically injured during the trauma had poorer outcome than those without physical injuries (Gillespie *et al*, 2002). The same applied to people with chronic pain as a result of the trauma (Taylor *et al*, 2001).
- People with greater PTSD symptom severity at the beginning of treatment have greater symptom severity at the end of treatment (van Minnen *et al*, 2002; Blanchard *et al*, 2003*b*), but the degree of improvement does not differ (EHLERS 2005).

Pitman *et al* (1991) presented a case series suggesting that exposure treatment may not be suitable for perpetrators of harm, especially those in whom guilt is the primary emotion. However, for other PTSD sufferers the presence of guilt does not seem to predict response to exposure (van Minnen *et al*, 2002).

5.7 Recommendations for psychological treatments for chronic PTSD

5.7.1.1   All PTSD sufferers should be offered a course of trauma-focused psychological treatment (trauma-focused cognitive–behavioural therapy or eye movement desensitisation and reprocessing). These treatments should normally be provided on an individual out-patient basis. **A**

5.7.1.2   Trauma-focused psychological treatment should be offered to PTSD sufferers regardless of the time that has elapsed since the trauma. **B**

5.7.1.3   The duration of trauma-focused psychological treatment should normally be 8–12 sessions when the PTSD results from a single event. When the trauma is discussed in the treatment session, longer sessions than usual are generally necessary (for example

90 min). Treatment should be regular and continuous (usually at least once a week) and should be delivered by the same person. **B**

5.7.1.4   Healthcare professionals should consider extending the duration of treatment beyond 12 sessions if several problems need to be addressed in the treatment of PTSD sufferers, particularly after multiple traumatic events, traumatic bereavement or where chronic disability resulting from the trauma, significant comorbid disorders or social problems are present. Trauma-focused treatment needs to be integrated into an overall plan of care. **C**

5.7.1.5   Treatment should be delivered by competent individuals who have received appropriate training. These individuals should receive appropriate supervision. **C**

5.7.1.6   Some PTSD sufferers may initially find it difficult and overwhelming to disclose details of their traumatic events. In these cases, healthcare professionals should consider devoting several sessions to establishing a trusting therapeutic relationship and emotional stabilisation before addressing the traumatic event. **C**

5.7.1.7   When PTSD sufferers request other forms of psychological treatment (for example, supportive therapy/non-directive therapy, hypnotherapy, psychodynamic therapy or systemic psychotherapy), they should be informed that there is as yet no convincing evidence for a clinically important effect of these treatments on PTSD. **GPP**

5.7.1.8   Non-trauma-focused interventions such as relaxation or non-directive therapy, which do not address traumatic memories, should *not* routinely be offered to people who present with chronic PTSD. **B**

5.7.1.9   For PTSD sufferers who have no or only limited improvement with a specific trauma-focused psychological treatment, healthcare professionals should consider the following options:

- an alternative form of trauma-focused psychological treatment
- the augmentation of trauma-focused psychological treatment with a course of pharmacological treatment. **C**

5.8 Research recommendations

5.8.1 Guided self-help

5.8.1.1   A randomised controlled trial, using newly developed guided self-help materials based on trauma-focused psychological interventions, should be conducted to assess the efficacy and cost-effectiveness of guided self-help compared with trauma-focused psychological interventions for mild and moderate PTSD.

Rationale

Post-traumatic stress disorder is a common and potentially disabling condition; it has a 1-month prevalence of between 1.5% and 3% (Stein *et al*, 1997; Andrews *et al*, 1999). Many individuals may recover without specific intervention, but a significant proportion go on to develop a chronic disorder with associated psychological and social handicaps (Kessler *et al*, 1995). Trauma-focused psychological interventions are generally effective for the treatment of PTSD, with brief interventions appearing to be effective for acute PTSD (Van Etten & Taylor, 1998). In contrast to many other anxiety and depressive disorders, where there is good evidence for the efficacy of self-help-based interventions (Lewis *et al*, 2003), no such evidence exists for PTSD and to date only one trial of guided self-help has been conducted, which failed to show any benefit from this intervention (Ehlers *et al*, 2003). However, if the benefits that have been demonstrated in other anxiety and depressive disorders were to be demonstrated in PTSD, it would offer the possibility of increasing the availability of cost-effective treatments and reducing the burden of illness through speeding the process of recovery. The research programme would first need to develop a suitable guided self-help programme in a series of smaller-scale pilot studies. The final programme would then need to be tested in an RCT.

5.8.2 Trauma-focused psychological interventions in adults

5.8.2.1   Adequately powered effectiveness trials of trauma-focused psychological interventions for the treatment of PTSD (trauma-focused CBT and EMDR) should be conducted. They should provide evidence on the comparative effectiveness and cost-effectiveness of these interventions and consider the format of treatment (type and duration) and the specific populations who might benefit.

Rationale

Post-traumatic stress disorder is a common and potentially disabling condition; it has a 1-month prevalence of between 1.5% and 3% (Stein *et al*, 1997; Andrews *et al*, 1999). Many individuals may recover without specific intervention, but a significant proportion go on to develop a chronic disorder with associated psychological and social handicaps (Kessler *et al*, 1995). Good evidence for the efficacy of trauma-focused psychological interventions is available (Van Etten & Taylor, 1998), but less is known about the effectiveness of these treatments in routine practice, although some recent trials suggest that it may be possible to replicate the findings of RCTs in more routine clinical settings (e.g. Gillespie *et al*, 2002). Effectiveness trials should use established measures of PTSD severity and quality of life, and also provide information not only about the value of such interventions in routine clinical practice but also about the type and duration of intervention (CBT or EMDR) and the training requirements of the different types of intervention. Particular populations may also derive differential benefit from different interventions in routine clinical practice, and the characteristics of those who do and do not respond to the interventions should be a focus of these trials (e.g. Taylor *et al*, 2001; Gillespie *et al*, 2002).

6 Pharmacological and physical interventions for PTSD in adults

6.1 Introduction

Drug treatments currently have an important place in the management of PTSD. This is supported by reviews, which suggest that they are effective (e.g. Van Etten & Taylor, 1998; Friedman et al, 2000). Drug treatments have been shown to achieve statistically significant (positive) effects on each of the three main elements of PTSD (re-experiencing, avoidance and hyperarousal). However, other reviews, for example Stein et al (2004), have suggested that the efficacy of drug treatments may be less strong (they estimated an SMD for drug treatments against placebo of –0.46 (k=4; n=327; 95% CI –0.71 to –0.2). This more modest view was based on a rigorous systematic review of relevant studies, including only randomised controlled trials and applying more strenuous inclusion criteria (in particular those for trial quality). As with this review, Stein et al (2004) used between-group rather than within-group effect sizes, thereby reducing the likelihood of artificially inflating the effect size (as is acknowledged by Van Etten & Taylor, 1998).

Given issues concerning the lack of wide-scale availability of psychological interventions and the desire to provide increased patient choice, it is important to establish the relative efficacy of drug treatments in PTSD. If there are drugs with comparable efficacies to the psychological treatments, for which there is currently the strongest evidence base (see Chapter 5), these would allow rapid access to an effective intervention, especially in primary care settings. They would be available as adjunctive or alternative treatments in case of treatment failure and would allow individuals with PTSD to make a choice as to the approach they favour. Even if the efficacy were less good, these drugs would still be available as a second-line intervention.

In the UK, only two drugs are currently licensed for the treatment of PTSD, paroxetine and sertraline (the latter being licensed only for women). However, other drugs that are not licensed for use in the UK have been subjected to randomised clinical trial for the treatment of PTSD and are considered within this review.

6.2 Current clinical practice

Robust evidence on the pattern of drug usage for the treatment of PTSD in the UK is not available. However, it is widely accepted that many patients in the UK are treated with drugs: predominantly selective serotonin reuptake inhibitors (SSRIs) and newer antidepressants, although to a lesser extent tricyclic antidepressants and atypical antipsychotic agents are also prescribed. The major uses of these drugs are for the treatment of PTSD symptoms, related sleep disturbance and agitation and comorbid depression. Low-dose amitriptyline may also be used in the treatment of chronic pain syndromes. In one major UK centre for the treatment of PTSD it was estimated that around 30% of patients at point of assessment are taking some form of psychotropic medication and a further 30% are prescribed medication during their attendance at the clinic (C. Freeman, 2004, personal communication).

Mellman et al (2003) have reported on a survey of drug treatments in the USA in a community-based sample of mental health clinic attenders with PTSD. They compared drug prescribing for patients with PTSD alone, depression alone and PTSD comorbid with depression. Of the PTSD alone group, 77% were prescribed medication, compared with 89% of the comorbid group and 82% of the depression alone group. Patients with PTSD alone were prescribed a range of antidepressant medication, but 17% were taking atypical antipsychotics and 41% were taking benzodiazepines and related drugs. Mellman et al (2003) point out that the use of the latter two drug types is likely not to conform to international guidelines (Friedman et al, 2000).

6.3 Limitations of the literature: comparing RCTs of pharmacological and psychological treatment

There are some important differences between drug treatment and psychological treatment clinical trials. Drug trials use a double-blind method, often with a placebo arm. What this means is that the effect of the drug treatment can, in principle, be separated from the non-specific effects of being in a trial. There are a number of non-specific effects that may occur. The most prominent of these is the placebo effect, which can account for a significant component of a drug treatment effect, and in the case of mild depression this may be as much as 80% (Kirsch, 2000). In addition, in any trial – and in particular in drug trials – much attention is paid to measurement, and the assessment interviews are likely to be mutative (i.e. they may in themselves have a therapeutic effect). It is therefore no surprise to find that the total effect of drug intervention is greater than the chemical effect of the drug treatment alone.

In trials of active drug versus placebo, the control for non-specific attentional effects is greater than is the case in a psychological therapy trial when a waiting list control is used (see intervention *v.* waiting list comparisons in Chapter 5), as opposed to a trial in which some form of attentional control has been used (see intervention *v.* intervention comparisons in Chapter 5). Further, in drug trials, researchers are masked to the treatments being evaluated. In psychological therapy trials there is greater potential for the degree of enthusiasm of the researcher for a particular treatment to affect the outcomes. There may therefore be both a less effective control for the placebo effect and also the potential for inflation of the estimated active treatment effect. What this means is that when comparing the results of meta-analyses of drug treatment and psychological treatment trials (particularly where these are intervention *v.* waiting list comparisons) caution is required, especially in drawing conclusions from simple comparisons of effect sizes. The design of the drug trial may lead to a lower effect size for the active drug than for an equivalent psychological therapy when a comparison is made against no other active intervention. Unfortunately, direct comparisons between pharmacological and psychological treatments are largely lacking.

We have attempted to respond to this problem in comparability by assuming that the placebo arm of a drug trial, with its significant clinical input and enhanced measurement strategies, constitutes an active intervention and therefore we have adopted the lower of the two thresholds for effect size used in the psychological treatment comparisons. This means that we have regarded, on *a priori* grounds, a standardised mean difference (SMD) of −0.5 as indicative of a clinically meaningful difference between active drug and placebo. It may be helpful at this point to explain this process in more detail. What we set out to achieve was a recommendation based not on statistical difference alone but on the sort of change in symptom score likely to be experienced as beneficial by clinicians and PTSD sufferers. Selecting an SMD of −0.5 was a decision taken before the statistical analyses were undertaken. The evidence statements derive not only from the SMD but also from the confidence intervals in the meta-analysis (see Chapter 4).

We have been faced with data from smaller, older trials and larger, more recent trials. There are some limitations that should be pointed out in any comparison of these studies, because the more recent trials have tended to be more robust, using intention-to-treat analyses. They may also have included more patients in primary care, who would have been less severely affected. These differences might have influenced the effect sizes found in the different studies, to the disadvantage of some of the newer drugs.

Before leaving the general issue of differences between study designs, there is another factor to take into account. In drug treatment trials it is common to offer a flexible dosage regimen. This allows the clinician (masked to the allocation of placebo and active drug) to increase the number of tablets taken within an approved range. Trial designs may therefore encourage early increases in dosage in the absence of a marked treatment response. This may lead to somewhat elevated mean dosages in drug treatment trials as opposed to clinical practice, where experience suggests a more cautious use of dosage escalation.

6.4 Issues and topics covered by this review

In broad terms we have tried to address the issues of comparative efficacy, acceptability and tolerability of pharmacological treatments most commonly prescribed in the UK both for acute phase treatment and continuation/relapse prevention treatments in adults. (There is a separate review of treatments of all types in children and young people.)

For the purposes of this review the following drug treatments were considered: paroxetine and sertraline (the only two drugs licensed in the UK for PTSD), including a small comparison trial of paroxetine versus trauma-focused CBT, fluoxetine (another SSRI antidepressant), amitriptyline, imipramine (a tricyclic antidepressant), phenelzine and brofaromine (monoamine oxidase inhibitors), mirtazapine and venlafaxine (other antidepressants), olanzapine and risperidone (atypical antipsychotics) and combined drug and therapy interventions (phenelzine and psychotherapy, and imipramine and psychotherapy). There are a number of other drugs that are not licensed for the treatment of PTSD in the UK but may be prescribed with some frequency for this condition (based on advice from the Guideline Development Group). These include the SSRIs citalopram, escitalopram and fluvoxamine, the atypical antipsychotic quetiapine and the reversible monoamine oxidase inhibitor moclobemide. However, for these latter drugs no study met the inclusion criteria, and so these drugs could not be assessed within the meta-analysis.

Finally, we have included one non-pharmacological but biological intervention (repetitive transcranial magnetic stimulation of the right dorsolateral prefrontal cortex) in this chapter.

6.4.1 Measures of outcome

When making recommendations, two primary outcomes were considered: completer data for self-reported symptoms and completer data for clinician-rated PTSD symptoms. In contrast to the reviews of psychological interventions, for this review of drug treatments few studies reported data for PTSD diagnosis and so this outcome measure was of less use in forming an overall assessment of effectiveness.

6.5 Studies included

Full details of the search strategy for this and other reviews in the guideline are given in Appendix 6. From the main search for RCTs, 26 separate studies were identified by the Guideline Development Group as meeting the inclusion criteria. These include 23 studies of drug treatments against placebo (BRADY 2000A, BUTTERFIELD 2001, CONNOR 1999B, DAVIDSON 1990, DAVIDSON 2001, DAVIDSON 2001C, DAVIDSON 2003, DAVIDSON 2004, DAVIDSON, ELI LILLY, HERTZBERG 2000, KATZ 1994, KOSTEN 1991, MARSHALL 2001, MARTENYI 2002, MARTENYI 2002A, PFIZER 588, PFIZER 589, SKB 627, SKB 650, STEIN 2002, TUCKER 2001, ZOHAR 2002) and three studies of combined drug and or therapy interventions (FROMMBERGER 2004, HAMNER 2003A, KOSTEN 1992). (References given in shortened format are listed in Appendix 14.) In addition, one study of repeated transcranial magnetic stimulation (rTMS) against placebo (sham treatment) was identified (COHEN 2004B). The report by SAYGIN 2002 is not considered further in this review, because one of the drugs involved has now been withdrawn in the UK. (Details of the search for RCT studies are given in Appendix 6 and summary characteristics of individual included trials are given in Appendix 14.)

In the meta-analysis, a number of crossover studies were excluded owing to the non-availability of pre-crossover point data. (In crossover trials all participants receive all interventions (or control or other non-active intervention) in sequence and hence participants act as their own control. At present, methods for interpreting and using crossover data are not sufficiently developed to allow integration of complete (post-crossover point) data from such trials with standard RCT trials within the same meta-analysis.)

6.6 Study characteristics

In contrast to the reports of psychological interventions, the studies included did not typically provide data on remission of PTSD diagnosis, but instead reported response rate in terms of a percentage decrease in symptoms from baseline score. Response rate data were not used within the meta-analysis because of the inconsistency in reporting (thresholds for reported response rates typically vary from 30% to 50%). This decision was taken because it is known that relatively small differences in mean scores (which are not clinically significant) between two comparison groups can produce statistically significant differences when presented as response rates (Kirsch et al, 2002). Remission rates have the advantage of being clinically determined in advance (diagnosis v. no diagnosis). Recent research in depression suggests that remission is a more reliable indicator of a stable return to normal mood states than response rates (Keller, 2003). The most consistent evidence reported for tolerability was the number of participants leaving the treatment early and this is reported within the review.

6.6.1 SSRI drugs

Before proceeding to review the SSRI drugs individually, we wish to draw attention to the recent guidance issued by the Committee on Safety of Medicines concerning the use of these drugs in people of all ages, but especially in children and young adults (Committee on Safety of Medicines, 2004). This draws attention to the increased risks of self-harm and suicidal thoughts in children and young people. In the treatment of children and young people under the age of 18 years with depression, the balance of risks and benefits is favourable only for fluoxetine on current data. Careful and frequent monitoring is also important in the use of SSRIs in young adults of 18 years of age or over, all adults in the early stages of treatment (particularly if they experience a worsening or new symptoms after starting treatment), and at the time of dosage changes. If a PTSD sufferer is not doing well after starting treatment, the possibility of an adverse reaction to the drug should be considered. For the majority of SSRIs in the treatment of depressive illness, clinical trial data do not show an increasing benefit from increasing the dosage above the recommended daily amount. Increasing the dosage in the presence of agitation or restlessness, particularly at the beginning of treatment, may be detrimental. To minimise withdrawal reactions on stopping SSRIs, the dosage should be tapered gradually over a period of several weeks. This guidance is regularly updated and practitioners are advised to consult the Department of Health website (http://www.dh.gov.uk) for further developments.

6.6.2 Paroxetine

Four studies of paroxetine were identified that met the inclusion criteria (MARSHALL 2001, SKB 627, SKB 650, TUCKER 2001) and this included one continuation/relapse prevention study. In these trials patients with depression were admitted provided PTSD was considered to be the primary diagnosis. All four trials were of mixed-trauma populations.

6.6.2.1 Paroxetine versus placebo (acute phase)
Efficacy of treatment
There is evidence suggesting there is unlikely to be a clinically important difference between paroxetine and placebo on reducing the severity of PTSD symptoms as measured by the Davidson Trauma Scale (self-report measure) (k=3; n=1065; SMD=−0.37, 95% CI −0.49 to −0.24) I

The evidence is inconclusive and so it is not possible to determine if there is a clinically important difference between paroxetine and placebo on reducing the severity of PTSD symptoms as measured by CAPS (clinician-rated measure) (k=3; n=1070; SMD=−0.42, 95% CI −0.55 to −0.3) I

The evidence is inconclusive and so it is not possible to determine if there is a clinically important difference between paroxetine and placebo on reducing depression symptoms as measured by the Montgomery–Åsberg Depression Rating Scale (MADRS) (clinician-rated measure) (k=3; n=1069; SMD=−0.34, 95% CI −0.61 to −0.07). I

Tolerability of treatment

The evidence is inconclusive and so it is not possible to determine if there is a clinically important difference between paroxetine and placebo on reducing the likelihood of leaving treatment early (k=3; *n*=1196; RR=0.95, 95% CI 0.79 to 1.15). ▌

6.6.2.2 Paroxetine versus placebo (continuation/relapse prevention)
Efficacy of treatment

There are some continuation/relapse prevention data for paroxetine from an unpublished trial (SKB 650). This trial consisted of 12 weeks of single-blind acute phase treatment, followed by a further 24 weeks of double-blind administered treatment for those assessed as having responded to treatment within the acute phase. In the continuation phase responders were allocated either to placebo or paroxetine (dose range 20–50 mg).

There is evidence suggesting there is unlikely to be a clinically important difference between paroxetine and placebo on reducing the severity of PTSD symptoms as measured by the Davidson Trauma Scale (self-report measure) for continuation/relapse prevention treatments (k=1; *n*=127; SMD=0.06, 95% CI –0.28 to 0.41). ▌

The evidence is inconclusive and so it is not possible to determine if there is a clinically important difference between paroxetine and placebo on reducing the severity of PTSD symptoms as measured by CAPS (clinician-rated measure) for continuation/relapse prevention treatments (k=1; *n*=129; SMD=0.19, 95% CI –0.15 to 0.54). ▌

The evidence is inconclusive and so it is not possible to determine if there is a clinically important difference between paroxetine and placebo on reducing the likelihood of having a diagnosis of PTSD for continuation/relapse prevention treatments (k=1; *n*=173; RR=0.81, 95% CI 0.55 to 1.19). ▌

Tolerability of treatment

The evidence is inconclusive and so it is not possible to determine if there is a clinically important difference between paroxetine and placebo on reducing the likelihood of leaving treatment early for continuation/relapse prevention treatments (k=1; *n*=176; RR=0.84, 95% CI 0.51 to 1.38). ▌

6.6.2.3 Dosage levels
There is one study comparing paroxetine at dosages of 20 mg and 40 mg. There was no difference between these groups (MARSHALL 2001), suggesting that in general the dosage of 20 mg is appropriate.

6.6.2.4 Paroxetine 20 mg versus paroxetine 40 mg (acute phase)
The evidence is inconclusive and so it is not possible to determine if there is a clinically important difference between paroxetine (20 mg) and paroxetine (40 mg) on reducing the severity of PTSD symptoms as measured by the Davidson Trauma Scale (k=1; *n*=365; SMD=–0.08, 95% CI –0.29 to 1.2). ▌

6.6.2.5 Paroxetine versus trauma-focused CBT
Efficacy of treatment

One small study (FROMMBERGER 2004) compared 12 weeks of paroxetine (10–50 mg) with 12 weekly sessions of trauma-focused CBT. In studies comprising both drug and psychological intervention treatment arms individuals are not masked to treatment allocation, and in this study neither were the rating assessors. Further, given the lack of placebo control it is not possible to isolate specific effects. It is noteworthy that the measures that provide limited evidence favouring CBT are based on self-ratings. These effects were not replicated in the clinician ratings. The withdrawal rates were also based on a very small difference (early withdrawal of 3 of 11 in the paroxetine group versus 2 of 11 in the trauma-focused CBT group). This study is the only one to compare directly drug and psychological interventions, but it should be interpreted cautiously.

There is limited evidence favouring trauma-focused CBT over paroxetine on reducing PTSD severity as measured by the Posttraumatic Stress Scale (self-rated measure) post-treatment (k=1; *n*=16; SMD=1.06, 95% CI –0.01 to 2.13). ▌

The evidence is inconclusive and so it is not possible to determine if there is a clinically important difference between paroxetine and trauma-focused CBT on reducing PTSD severity as measured by CAPS (clinician-rated measure) post-treatment (k=1; *n*=16; SMD=0.09, 95% CI –0.89 to 1.07). ▌

There is limited evidence favouring trauma-focused CBT over paroxetine on reducing depression symptoms post-treatment as measured by the Beck Depression Inventory (self-rated measure) (k=1; *n*=16; SMD=0.55, 95% CI –0.46 to 1.55). ▌

The evidence is inconclusive and so it is not possible to determine if there is a clinically important difference between paroxetine and trauma-focused CBT on reducing post-treatment depression symptoms as measured by the MADRS (clinician-rated measure) (k=1; n=16; SMD=−0.37, 95% CI −1.36 to 0.62). ▌

Tolerability of treatment
There is limited evidence favouring trauma-focused CBT over paroxetine on reducing the likelihood of leaving the study early due to any reason prior to treatment end-point (k=1; n=21; RR=1.36, 95% CI 0.28 to 6.56). ▌

6.6.3 Sertraline

Six published studies of sertraline were identified for this review as meeting the inclusion criteria (BRADY 2000A, DAVIDSON 2001, DAVIDSON 2001C, DAVIDSON 2004, DAVIDSON and ZOHAR 2002), one of which (DAVIDSON 2001) was a continuation/relapse prevention study covering the same population as DAVIDSON 2001C. Four trials were of mixed trauma populations and one was of military veterans. Full data for two large unpublished trials (PFIZER 588, PFIZER 589) held by the manufacturers were unavailable (n=166 for a trial with combat veterans, n=188 for a mixed trauma population trial) despite repeated requests to the manufacturer. In order to incorporate these substantial trials within the meta-analysis, estimates for missing standard deviation data are included (standard deviations were estimated as the highest standard deviation for each outcome measure as derived from the other published drug trials).

6.6.3.1 Sertraline versus placebo (acute phase)

Efficacy of treatment
There is evidence suggesting there is unlikely to be a clinically important difference between sertraline and placebo on PTSD diagnosis (k=2; n=747; RR=0.91, 95% CI 0.85 to 0.98). ▌

There is evidence suggesting there is unlikely to be a clinically important difference between sertraline and placebo on reducing the severity of PTSD symptoms as measured by the Davidson Trauma Scale (self-report measure) (k=5; n=1091; SMD=−0.18, 95% CI −0.41 to 0.06). ▌

The evidence is inconclusive and so it is not possible to determine if there is a clinically important difference between sertraline and placebo on reducing the severity of PTSD symptoms as measured by CAPS (clinician-rated measure) k=6; n=1123; SMD=−0.26, 95% CI −0.51 to 0.00). ▌

There is evidence suggesting there is unlikely to be a clinically important difference between sertraline and placebo on reducing the severity of PTSD symptoms as measured by the Impact of Event Scale (self-report measure) (k=4; n=739; SMD=−0.06, 95% CI −0.39 to 0.26). ▌

There is evidence suggesting there is unlikely to be a clinically important difference between sertraline and placebo on reducing the severity of depression as measured by pooled clinician-rated measures (k=3; n=417; SMD=−0.27, 95% CI −0.46 to −0.07). ▌

Tolerability of treatment
The evidence is inconclusive and so it is not possible to determine if there is a clinically important difference between sertraline and placebo on reducing the likelihood of leaving treatment early (k=6; n=1148; RR=1.10, 95% CI 0.90 to 1.33). ▌

6.6.3.2 Sertraline versus placebo (continuation/relapse prevention)

Efficacy of treatment
The evidence is inconclusive and so it is not possible to determine if there is a clinically important difference between sertraline and placebo on reducing the severity of PTSD symptoms as measured by CAPS (clinician-rated measure) for continuation/relapse prevention treatments (k=1; n=42; SMD=−0.14, 95% CI −0.75 to 0.47). ▌

6.6.4 Fluoxetine

Five studies of fluoxetine met the inclusion criteria (CONNOR 1999B, ELI LILLY, HERTZBERG 2000, MARTENYI 2002, MARTENYI 2002A), one of which was a continuation/relapse prevention study. The studies were of mixed trauma populations with the exception of one small study (HERTZBERG 2000) of male military veterans.

Efficacy of treatment

The evidence is inconclusive and so it is not possible to determine if there is a clinically important difference between fluoxetine and placebo on reducing the severity of PTSD symptoms as measured by the Davidson Trauma Scale (self-report measure) (k=3; *n*=363; SMD=−0.41, 95% CI −0.98 to 0.15). I

The evidence is inconclusive and so it is not possible to determine if there is a clinically important difference between fluoxetine and placebo on reducing the severity of PTSD symptoms as measured by CAPS (clinician-rated measure) (k=1; *n*=301; SMD=−0.28, 95% CI −0.54 to −0.02). I

There is evidence suggesting there is unlikely to be a clinically important difference between fluoxetine and placebo on reducing the severity of PTSD symptoms as measured by the 8-item Treatment Outcome PTSD Scale (TOP8) (self-report measure) (k=1; *n*=411, SMD=0.02, 95% CI −0.21 to 0.26). I

There is limited evidence favouring fluoxetine over placebo on enhancing quality of life (k=2; *n*=61; SMD=−0.62, 95% CI −1.13 to −0.1). I

Tolerability of treatment

There is limited evidence favouring fluoxetine over placebo on reducing the likelihood of leaving treatment early (k=2; *n*=66; RR=0.6, 95% CI 0.28 to 1.3). I

6.6.4.2 Fluoxetine versus placebo (continuation/relapse prevention)

Efficacy of treatment

The evidence is inconclusive and so it is not possible to determine if there is a clinically important difference between fluoxetine and placebo on reducing the severity of PTSD symptoms as measured by the Davidson Trauma Scale (self-report measure) (k=1; *n*=98; SMD=−0.19, 95% CI −0.59 to 0.21). I

The evidence is inconclusive and so it is not possible to determine if there is a clinically important difference between fluoxetine and placebo on reducing the severity of PTSD symptoms as measured by CAPS (clinician-rated measure) (k=1; *n*=98; SMD=−0.28, 95% CI −0.68 to 0.12). I

Tolerability of treatment

There is limited evidence favouring fluoxetine over placebo on reducing the likelihood of leaving treatment early (k=1; *n*=131; RR=0.51, 95% CI 0.28 to 0.96). I

6.6.5 Tricyclic antidepressants

Although they are not licensed for PTSD, tricyclic antidepressants have been in use for much longer than the SSRI drugs. The trials of tricyclic antidepressants are of older design and this needs to be borne in mind as these results are considered.

6.6.5.1 Amitriptyline versus placebo (acute phase)

One trial (in combat veterans) of amitriptyline met the study criteria (DAVIDSON 1990).

Efficacy of treatment

There is limited evidence favouring amitriptyline over placebo on reducing the severity of PTSD symptoms as measured by the Impact of Event Scale (self-report measure) (k=1; *n*=33; SMD=−0.90, 95% CI −1.62 to −0.18). I

There is limited evidence favouring amitriptyline over placebo on reducing depression symptoms as measured by the Hamilton Rating Scale for Depression (k=1; *n*=33; SMD=−1.16, 95% CI −1.90 to −0.41). I

There is limited evidence favouring amitriptyline over placebo on reducing anxiety symptoms as measured by the Hamilton Rating Scale for Anxiety (k=1; *n*=33; SMD=−0.99, 95% CI −1.72 to −0.26). I

Tolerability of treatment

There is limited evidence favouring placebo over amitriptyline on reducing the likelihood of leaving treatment early (k=1; *n*=46; RR=1.34, 95% CI 0.52 to 3.49). I

6.6.5.2 Imipramine versus placebo (acute phase)

Two trials (both in combat veterans) of imipramine met the inclusion criteria – one of imipramine alone (KOSTEN 1991) and one of combined imipramine and psychodynamic therapy (KOSTEN 1992).

Efficacy of treatment
The evidence is inconclusive and so it is not possible to determine if there is a clinically important difference between imipramine and placebo on reducing the severity of PTSD symptoms as measured by the Impact of Event Scale (self-report measure) (k=1; *n*=41; SMD=−0.24, 95% CI −0.86 to 0.38). I

The evidence is inconclusive and so it is not possible to determine if there is a clinically important difference between imipramine and placebo on reducing depression symptoms as measured by the Hamilton Rating Scale for Depression (k=1; *n*=41; SMD=−0.22, 95% CI −0.84 to 0.40). I

The evidence is inconclusive and so it is not possible to determine if there is a clinically important difference between imipramine and placebo on reducing anxiety symptoms as measured by Covi Anxiety (k=1; *n*=41; SMD=−0.46, 95% CI −1.08 to 0.17). I

Tolerability of treatment
There is limited evidence favouring imipramine over placebo on reducing the likelihood of leaving treatment early (k=1; *n*=41; RR=0.78, 95% CI 0.47 to 1.3). I

6.6.5.3 Imipramine and psychodynamic therapy versus placebo (acute phase)

The evidence is inconclusive and so it is not possible to determine if there is a clinically important difference between imipramine and psychodynamic therapy and placebo on reducing the severity of PTSD symptoms as measured by Impact of Event Scale (self-report) (k=1; *n*=39; SMD=−0.16, 95% CI −0.8 to 0.48). I

6.6.6 Monoamine oxidase inhibitors

The use of traditional monoamine oxidase inhibitors (MAOIs) such as phenelzine has been limited by the need to impose dietary restrictions. However, there has been research into this group of drugs in PTSD with trials of phenelzine and brofaromine.

6.6.6.1 Brofaromine versus placebo (acute phase)

Brofaromine is a reversible MAOI with fewer side-effects than the more traditional MAOIs; although investigated for the treatment of depression, it has never been marketed in the UK. One trial (in a mixed trauma population) met the inclusion criteria (KATZ 1994).

Efficacy of treatment
There is limited evidence favouring brofaromine over placebo on reducing the severity of PTSD symptoms as measured by CAPS (clinician-rated measure) (k=1; *n*=45; SMD=−0.58, 95% CI −1.18 to 0.02). I

Tolerability of treatment
There is limited evidence favouring placebo over brofaromine on reducing the likelihood of leaving treatment early (k=1; *n*=66; RR=1.44, 95% CI 0.69 to 3.01). I

6.6.6.2 Phenelzine versus placebo (acute phase)

A trial of phenelzine alone (KOSTEN 1991) and a trial of combined phenelzine and psychodynamic therapy (KOSTEN 1992) met the inclusion criteria. Both trials were in combat veterans.

Efficacy of treatment
There is limited evidence favouring phenelzine over placebo on reducing the severity of PTSD symptoms as measured by the Impact of Event Scale (self-report measure) (k=1; *n*=37; SMD=−1.06, 95% CI −1.75 to −0.36). I

The evidence is inconclusive and so it is not possible to determine if there is a clinically important difference between phenelzine and placebo on reducing depression symptoms as measured by the Hamilton Rating Scale for Depression (k=1; *n*=37; SMD=−0.4, 95% CI −1.06 to 0.25). I

There is evidence favouring phenelzine over placebo on reducing the likelihood of leaving treatment early (k=1; *n*=37; RR=0.32, 95% CI 0.12 to 0.80). ▌

6.6.6.3 Phenelzine and psychodynamic therapy versus placebo (acute phase)

There is limited evidence favouring phenelzine and psychodynamic therapy over placebo on reducing the severity of PTSD symptoms as measured by the Impact of Event Scale (k=1; *n*=34; SMD=−1.01, 95% CI −1.73 to −0.29). ▌

6.6.7 Mirtazapine

One study of mirtazapine (DAVIDSON 2003) for a mixed trauma population met the inclusion criteria.

6.6.7.1 Mirtazapine versus placebo (acute phase)

Efficacy of treatment

There is evidence favouring mirtazapine over placebo on reducing the severity of PTSD symptoms as measured by the Structured Interview for PTSD (k=1; *n*=21; SMD=−1.89, 95% CI −3 to −0.78). ▌

There is limited evidence favouring mirtazapine over placebo on reducing the severity of PTSD symptoms as measured by the Davidson Trauma Scale (k=1; *n*=26; SMD=−0.76, 95% CI −1.6 to 0.08). ▌

There is limited evidence favouring mirtazapine over placebo on reducing depression symptoms as measured by the depression sub-scale of the Hospital Anxiety and Depression Scale (k=1; *n*=25; SMD=−0.92, 95% CI −1.81 to −0.04). ▌

There is limited evidence favouring mirtazapine over placebo on reducing anxiety symptoms as measured by the anxiety sub-scale of the Hospital Anxiety and Depression Scale (k=1; *n*=25; SMD=−0.88, 95% CI −1.77 to 0). ▌

Tolerability of treatment

The evidence is inconclusive and so it is not possible to determine if there is a clinically important difference between mirtazapine and placebo on reducing the likelihood of leaving treatment early (k=1; *n*=29; RR=0.9, 95% CI 0.29 to 2.82). ▌

6.6.8 Venlafaxine

The Committee on Safety of Medicines has recently recommended that treatment with venlafaxine should only be initiated by mental health specialists because of concerns about cardiotoxicity and toxicity in overdose (Committee on Safety of Medicines, 2004).

There is one unpublished study of venlafaxine that met the inclusion criteria (DAVIDSON); the trauma population was unspecified.

6.6.8.1 Venlafaxine versus placebo (acute phase)

Efficacy of treatment

There is evidence suggesting there is unlikely to be a clinically important difference between venlafaxine and placebo on reducing the severity of PTSD symptoms as measured by the Davidson Trauma Scale (k=1; *n*=358; SMD=−0.19, 95% CI −0.4 to 0.01). ▌

There is evidence suggesting there is unlikely to be a clinically important difference between venlafaxine and placebo on reducing the severity of PTSD symptoms as measured by CAPS (k=1; *n*=358; SMD=−0.14, 95% CI −0.35 to 0.06). ▌

Tolerability of treatment

There is evidence suggesting there is unlikely to be a clinically important difference between venlafaxine and placebo on increasing the likelihood of leaving treatment early (k=1; *n*=358; RR=0.83, 95% CI 0.62 to 1.12). ▌

6.6.9 Olanzapine

Two trials met the inclusion criteria. One study (BUTTERFIELD 2001) was of olanzapine alone versus placebo for a mixed-trauma population (predominantly female rape victims). There was one study (STEIN 2002) of adjunctive olanzapine (taken in conjunction with SSRIs) for male combat veterans.

6.6.9.1 Olanzapine versus placebo (acute phase)

Efficacy of treatment
The evidence is inconclusive and so it is not possible to determine if there is a clinically important difference between olanzapine and placebo on reducing the severity of PTSD symptoms as measured by the Davidson Trauma Scale (self-report measure) (k=1; n=11; SMD=0.04, 95% CI –1.19 to 1.26). ▮

Tolerability of treatment
There is limited evidence favouring placebo over olanzapine on the likelihood of leaving treatment early (k=1; n=15; RR=1.5, 95% CI 0.2 to 11). ▮

6.6.9.2 Adjunctive olanzapine (acute phase)

One study (STEIN 2002) examined the efficacy of olanzapine for people already receiving but not responsive to SSRI treatment within the first 12 weeks of SSRI treatment. During the trial, of the total of 19 participants 5 were taking fluoxetine, 7 were taking paroxetine and 7 were taking sertraline.

Efficacy of treatment
There is limited evidence favouring adjunctive olanzapine (to SSRI) over placebo on reducing the severity of PTSD symptoms (clinician-rated measure) (k=1; n=19; SMD=–0.92, 95% CI –1.88 to 0.04). ▮

There is limited evidence favouring adjunctive olanzapine (to SSRI) over placebo on reducing depression symptoms (k=1; n=19; SMD=–1.2, 95% CI –2.2 to –0.21). ▮

6.6.10 Risperidone

One study of adjunctive risperidone (HAMNER 2003A) met the inclusion criteria. In this study, participants (all combat veterans) continued taking their previously prescribed antipsychotic, antidepressant, benzodiazepine or sleep medications. Given the variability in the other (non-risperidone) medications being taken by participants, some caution is required in interpreting the effect sizes from the review of this study.

6.6.10.1 Adjunctive risperidone (acute phase)

Efficacy of treatment
The evidence is inconclusive and so it is not possible to determine if there is a clinically important difference between adjunctive risperidone (combined with miscellaneous medication) and placebo on reducing the severity of PTSD symptoms as measured by CAPS (k=1; n=37; SMD=0.1, 95% CI –0.55 to 0.74). ▮

Tolerability of treatment
There is limited evidence favouring adjunctive risperidone (combined with miscellaneous medication) over placebo on reducing the likelihood of leaving treatment early (k=1; n=40; RR=0.5, 95% CI 0.05 to 5.08). ▮

6.7 General issues arising in the management of antidepressant medication

This guideline has been developed in parallel with a set of guidelines applicable to the treatment of depressive disorders. There is a certain amount of common ground arising from the use of antidepressant drugs in both settings. This section draws heavily on the forthcoming NICE guideline on the treatment of depression (National Collaborating Centre for Mental Health, 2005).

Common concerns in PTSD sufferers about taking medication, such as fears of addiction or that taking medication will be seen as a weakness, should be addressed in an early discussion about prescribing options. Discontinuation/withdrawal symptoms can occur after stopping many drugs (that are not drugs of dependence), including antidepressants, and may be explained in the context of 'receptor rebound': for example, an antidepressant with potent anticholinergic side-effects may be associated with diarrhoea on withdrawal. Discontinuation/withdrawal symptoms may be new or hard to distinguish from some of the original symptoms of the underlying illness. They are experienced by at least a third of patients (Lejoyeux et al, 1996).

All patients who are prescribed antidepressants should be informed, at the time that treatment is initiated, of potential side-effects and of the risk of discontinuation/withdrawal symptoms (particularly with paroxetine and venlafaxine). Patients started on antidepressants should be informed about the delay in onset of effect, the time course of treatment and the need to take medication as prescribed. Written information appropriate to the patient's needs should be made available.

The onset of discontinuation/withdrawal symptoms is usually within 5 days of stopping treatment, or occasionally during taper or after missed doses (Rosenbaum et al, 1998; Michelson et al, 2000). Symptoms can vary in form and intensity and occur in any combination.

Discontinuation/withdrawal symptoms may be mistaken for a relapse of illness or the emergence of a new physical illness (Haddad, 2001), leading to unnecessary investigations or reintroduction of the antidepressant. It is important to counsel patients before, during and after antidepressant therapy about the nature of this syndrome.

Generally, the antidepressant drugs recommended for use in PTSD should be discontinued over at least a 4-week period (Rosenbaum et al, 1998). (A shorter period may be appropriate for fluoxetine because of its long half-life.) The end of the taper may need to be slower as symptoms may not appear until the reduction in the total daily dosage of the antidepressant is substantial.

If discontinuation/withdrawal symptoms do emerge and are mild, the clinician may reassure the patient that these symptoms are not uncommon after discontinuing an antidepressant and will pass in a few days. If symptoms are severe, reintroduction of the original antidepressant (or another with a longer half-life from the same class) and gradual tapering are advised (Lejoyeux & Ades, 1997; Haddad, 2001).

During treatment with antidepressant medication, it is important to consider the risk of self-harm. Adult PTSD sufferers started on antidepressants who are considered to present an increased suicide risk, and all those aged 18–29 years (because of the potentially increased risk of suicidal thoughts associated with the use of antidepressants in this age group), should normally be seen after 1 week and frequently thereafter until the risk is no longer considered significant.

For PTSD sufferers at high risk of suicide, consideration should be given to prescribing an appropriate quantity of antidepressants and providing additional support for administering medication. Toxicity in overdose should also be considered when choosing an antidepressant for patients at significant risk of suicide. Practitioners should be aware that SSRIs and mirtazapine are safer in overdose than other tricyclic antidepressants.

Patients with PTSD started on antidepressants who are not considered to be at increased risk of suicide should normally be seen after 2 weeks and thereafter on an appropriate and regular basis: for example, at intervals of 2–4 weeks in the first 3 months, and at greater intervals thereafter if response is good.

There are specific issues relating to the use of SSRI medication. Particularly in the initial stages of SSRI treatment, healthcare professionals should actively seek out signs of akathisia, suicidal ideation and increased anxiety and agitation. They should also advise PTSD sufferers of the risk of these symptoms in the early stages of treatment and advise them to seek help promptly if these are at all distressing. If a PTSD sufferer develops marked and/or prolonged akathisia while taking an antidepressant, the use of the drug should be reviewed. In the treatment of PTSD, where this is not an uncommon issue anyway, it is also important to consider the impact of sexual side-effects.

Similarly, there are specific issues relating to the use of the monoamine oxidase inhibitor phenelzine. All patients receiving phenelzine require careful monitoring (including blood pressure measurement) and advice on interactions with other medicines and foodstuffs, and should have their attention drawn to the product information leaflet.

Administration of some drugs to nursing mothers may lead to effects in the infant if the drug passes into breast milk. It is therefore important to exercise additional care. In any individual case, a decision to prescribe should only be made after full and open discussion with the PTSD sufferer, reference to the appendix on breast-feeding in the *British National Formulary* and full consideration of the risks and benefit of this action. In general, this is likely to be an additional factor pointing strongly to the advantages of a psychological treatment.

It is likely that guidance on the use of antidepressant drugs will be further updated during the life of this guideline and practitioners should maintain an awareness of current guidance set out by the Committee on Safety of Medicines and available on the Department of Health website (http://www.info.doh.gov.uk/doh/embroadcast.nsf/vwDiscussionAll/ 9AA9EC56B07B3B4F80256F61004BAA88).

6.8 Repetitive transcranial magnetic stimulation

Repetitive transcranial magnetic stimulation (rTMS) is a new technique under investigation in a range of conditions, such as depression and stroke. It involves placing an electromagnetic coil on the scalp and rapidly turning on and off a high-intensity current through the discharge of a capacitor. The magnetic pulse induces electrical effects in the underlying brain cortex. These pulses vary in frequency. If the stimulation occurs faster than once per second (1 Hz), it is referred to as fast or high-frequency rTMS and may result in excitatory physiological changes. On the other hand, low-frequency or slow rTMS may have an inhibitory effect on brain excitability. There is a low risk of seizure and certain exclusion criteria apply. In the study by Cohen (COHEN 2004) investigators administered rTMS over the right dorsolateral prefrontal cortex of the brain for 20 min per day over 10 working days. The sham treatment group also underwent the same procedure but the positioning of the coil was such that it did not have an effect (it was held vertically to the scalp rather than being placed on the scalp). There were two treatment groups: one receiving fast rTMS (10 Hz) and the other slow rTMS (1 Hz).

6.8.1 High-frequency rTMS versus control

Efficacy of treatment
There is limited evidence favouring high-frequency rTMS over control on reducing the severity of PTSD symptoms as measured by clinician-rated CAPS at 14 days' follow-up (k=1; n=16; SMD=−0.72, 95% CI −1.77 to 0.33). I

There is limited evidence favouring high-frequency rTMS over control on reducing the severity of PTSD symptoms at 14 days' follow-up as measured by self-report PTSD checklist (k=1; n=16; SMD=−0.68, 95% CI −1.73 to 0.36). I

The evidence is inconclusive and so it is not possible to determine if there is a clinically important difference between high-frequency rTMS and control on reducing depression symptoms at 14 days' follow-up as measured by the clinician-rated Hamilton Rating Scale for Depression (k=1; n=16; SMD=−0.13, 95% CI −1.14 to 0.89). I

Tolerability of treatment
There is limited evidence favouring high-frequency rTMS over control on reducing the likelihood of leaving the study early for any reason prior to 14 days' follow-up (k=1; n=19; RR=0.36, 95% CI 0.04 to 3.35). I

6.8.2 Low-frequency rTMS versus control

Efficacy of treatment
There is limited evidence favouring control over low-frequency rTMS on reducing the severity of PTSD symptoms as measured by CAPS (clinician-rated measure) at 14 days' follow-up (k=1; n=14; SMD=0.82, 95% CI −0.25 to 1.88). I

There is limited evidence favouring control over low-frequency rTMS on reducing the severity of PTSD symptoms at 14 days' follow-up as measured by the PTSD Checklist (self-report measure) (k=1; n=14; SMD=0.67, 95% CI −0.43 to 1.77). I

The evidence is inconclusive and so it is not possible to determine if there is a clinically important difference between low-frequency rTMS and control on reducing depression symptoms at 14 days' follow-up as measured by the Hamilton Rating Scale for Depression (clinician-rated measure) (k=1; n=14; SMD=0.36, 95% CI –0.71 to 1.43). ▌

Tolerability of treatment

There is limited evidence favouring low-frequency rTMS over control on reducing the likelihood of leaving the study early for any reason prior to 14 days' follow-up (k=1; n=18; RR=0.8, 95% CI 0.14 to 4.49). ▌

6.9 Clinical summary

We have drawn attention to the important difficulties of comparing drug treatment trials with psychological therapy trials. The tough design of the drug trial is likely to produce a lower effect size than a comparable psychological treatment trial.

However, using an *a priori* criterion for a clinically important effect, the drug treatments were disappointing. For paroxetine, there is a reliable, positive but small effect, which (although statistically significant) fell short of the target effect size of 0.5 for a clinically important intervention. Once we included additional unpublished data, we were able to demonstrate neither clinically important nor statistically significant effects in the meta-analysis for sertraline, the other drug licensed in the UK.

There are a number of other randomised controlled trials that met the inclusion criteria, although these tended to be based on relatively small samples and therefore need to be interpreted with some caution. These suggest that there may be a clinically important effect for mirtazapine, amitriptyline and the MAOI antidepressants phenelzine and brofaromine.

The difficulties arising from simple comparisons of recent large trials and older small trials have already been identified. It would be incorrect to conclude that an older drug with an apparently larger effect size in a small trial is preferable. It is likely that none of the drug treatments has a very large effect size using current robust trial methodology. Current policy is to favour the use of licensed drugs in preference to unlicensed drugs. However, prescribers should be aware of other positive trial data in reaching a clinical decision. The use of unlicensed drugs is the responsibility of the prescriber.

This review includes one RCT using a non-pharmacological treatment (rTMS). This report is encouraging (for high-frequency rTMS) but further research is required to determine the place of interventions like this in the management of PTSD.

In the event that few trials for a review had effect sizes that met the thresholds for clinical significance, as was the case for this review of drug treatments, statistical significance in the meta-analysis was also taken into account in reaching a recommendation (see Chapter 4).

A specific drug is recommended here if it meets the threshold for clinical effect as outlined above and is currently available in the UK. Thus, mirtazapine, amitriptyline and phenelzine have been included (brofaromine not being currently available), although we do recognise that in each case, this recommendation is made on the basis of data from single trials.

We have concluded that we should recommend paroxetine on the basis of its robust statistically significant effect based on large-trial data, even though it did not meet the threshold for a clinically significant effect as we have defined it in the list of recommended drugs. This is the only drug in the list of recommendations with a current UK product licence for PTSD.

We have also made a recommendation about the use of adjunctive olanzapine in people who are non-responsive to initial drug treatment. In this case, the recommendation is based on limited evidence of a clinically important effect on comorbid depression symptoms. Although the meta-analysis shows a limited evidence of effect on PTSD symptoms as well, this does not reach statistical significance and needs to be interpreted with caution.

We have also examined tolerability data and side-effect profiles. On this basis, we recommend that paroxetine and mirtazapine should be the drugs of choice for use in primary care.

Phenelzine, amitriptyline (and adjunctive olanzapine) should be recommended as additional drug treatments for use under supervision of mental health specialists.

6.10 Clinical practice recommendations

6.10.1 Recommendations specific to PTSD

6.10.1.1   Drug treatments for PTSD should not be used as a routine first-line treatment for adults (in general use or by specialist mental health professionals) in preference to a trauma-focused psychological therapy. A

6.10.1.2   Drug treatments (paroxetine or mirtazapine for general use, and amitriptyline or phenelzine for initiation only by mental health specialists) should be considered for the treatment of PTSD in adults when a sufferer expresses a preference not to engage in a trauma-focused psychological treatment. B

6.10.1.3   Drug treatments (paroxetine or mirtazapine for general use and amitriptyline or phenelzine for initiation only by mental health specialists) should be offered to adult PTSD sufferers who cannot start a psychological therapy because of serious ongoing threat of further trauma (for example, where there is ongoing domestic violence). C

6.10.1.4   Drug treatments (paroxetine or mirtazapine for general use and amitriptyline or phenelzine for initiation only by mental health specialists) should be considered for adult PTSD sufferers who have gained little or no benefit from a course of trauma-focused psychological treatment. C

6.10.1.5   Where sleep is a major problem for an adult PTSD sufferer, hypnotic medication may be appropriate for short-term use but, if longer-term drug treatment is required, consideration should also be given to the use of suitable antidepressants at an early stage in order to reduce the later risk of dependence. C

6.10.1.6   Drug treatments (paroxetine or mirtazapine for general use and amitriptyline or phenelzine for initiation only by mental health specialists) for PTSD should be considered as an adjunct to psychological treatment in adults when there is significant comorbid depression or severe hyperarousal that significantly impacts on a sufferer's ability to benefit from psychological treatment. C

6.10.1.7   When an adult sufferer with PTSD has not responded to a drug treatment, consideration should be given to increasing the dosage within approved limits. If further drug treatment is considered, this should generally be with a different class of antidepressant or involve the use of adjunctive olanzapine. C

6.10.1.8   When an adult sufferer with PTSD has responded to drug treatment, it should be continued for at least 12 months before gradual withdrawal. C

6.10.2 General recommendations

6.10.2.1   All PTSD sufferers who are prescribed antidepressants should be informed, at the time that treatment is initiated, of potential side-effects and of the risk of discontinuation/ withdrawal symptoms (particularly with paroxetine). C

6.10.2.2.   Discontinuation/withdrawal symptoms are usually mild and self-limiting but occasionally can be severe. Prescribers should normally gradually reduce the doses of antidepressants over a 4-week period, although some people may require longer periods. C

6.10.2.3   If discontinuation/withdrawal symptoms are mild, practitioners should reassure the PTSD sufferer and arrange for monitoring. If symptoms are severe, the practitioner should consider reintroducing the original antidepressant (or another with a longer half-life from the same class) and reducing it gradually while monitoring symptoms. C

6.10.2.4   Adult PTSD sufferers started on antidepressants who are considered to present an increased suicide risk and all patients aged between 18 and 29 years (because of the potential increased risk of suicidal thoughts associated with the use of antidepressants in this age group) should normally be seen after 1 week and frequently thereafter until the risk is no longer considered significant. **GPP**

6.10.2.5   Particularly in the initial stages of SSRI treatment, practitioners should actively seek out signs of akathisia, suicidal ideation and increased anxiety and agitation. They should also advise PTSD sufferers of the risk of these symptoms in the early stages of treatment and advise them to seek help promptly if these are at all distressing. **GPP**

6.10.2.6   If a PTSD sufferer develops marked and/or prolonged akathisia while taking an antidepressant, the use of the drug should be reviewed. **GPP**

6.10.2.7   Adult PTSD sufferers started on antidepressants who are not considered to be at increased risk of suicide should normally be seen after 2 weeks and thereafter on an appropriate and regular basis, for example, at intervals of 2–4 weeks in the first 3 months, and at greater intervals thereafter, if response is good. **GPP**

6.11 Research recommendations

6.11.1 Trauma-focused psychological treatment versus pharmacological treatment

6.11.1.1   Adequately powered, appropriately designed trials should be conducted to determine if trauma-focused psychological treatments are superior in terms of efficacy and cost-effectiveness to pharmacological treatments in the treatment of PTSD and whether they are efficacious and cost-effective in combination.

Rationale

Post-traumatic stress disorder is a common and potentially disabling condition. It has been shown that trauma-focused psychological treatments are effective for this disorder (Van Etten & Taylor, 1998). At the moment, these interventions (done properly) are often hard to access. Drug treatments have the advantage of accessibility, although the evidence for the efficacy of pharmacological treatment is less strong (Stein *et al*, 2004). Currently there is no large, well-designed trial that directly compares these two approaches (Stein *et al*, 2004). There is one small trial comparing paroxetine and cognitive–behavioural therapy (Frommberger *et al*, 2004), but this lacks adequate power. Therefore, the only real comparison between these two approaches relies on indirect methods of limited validity, further hampered by high withdrawal rates in many trials. Large, well-designed trials would allow direct comparisons and should help to determine the relative places of trauma-focused psychological treatment and pharmacological treatment in PTSD, both individually and in combination. There is also an opportunity for the NHS to use this as a case example for forging a real partnership between itself, the pharmaceutical industry and other major research funders in undertaking this investigation.

7 Early interventions for PTSD in adults

7.1 Introduction

The incentive to identify and develop effective early interventions for post-traumatic stress disorder comes from three sources. First, PTSD is a distressing and disabling condition from which a great number of sufferers do not spontaneously recover. Therefore, early and effective treatment might reduce the burden of PTSD on both the individual and society. Second, now that studies have identified the post-incident prevalence rates of PTSD from large-scale disasters and combat, there is concern to ameliorate the impact of PTSD by responding in the early days and weeks following such incidents. Third, occupational groups such as firefighters have campaigned to have the psychological impact of their work recognised and support services delivered as part of their conditions of employment. In addition, in military organisations, there exists a specific drive to early interventions – that of enabling traumatised combatants to return to front-line duties as soon as possible.

However, given that the prevalence of initial distress following a traumatic event is far greater than that of either acute stress disorder or PTSD, the potential exists to deliver interventions to people whose problems would spontaneously remit. As well as the time commitment required of the traumatised individual, interventions for traumatic stress generally involve confronting aspects of distressing experiences, the emotional cost of which might not warrant early intervention. This potential for diluting the cost-effectiveness of early interventions is a significant factor in service planning, particularly disaster planning and employee support. There is a vigorous debate between those who would provide some intervention for all victims and survivors of traumatic incidents, and those who advocate waiting and targeting interventions at people likely to develop the disabling symptoms of chronic PTSD (Litz *et al*, 2002).

7.2 Current practice

Several interventions often referred to generically as 'debriefing', such as crisis intervention (Raphael, 1986) and critical incident stress debriefing (CISD; Mitchell, 1983), have been developed since the 1980s to help deal with the immediate psychological aftermath of severe trauma. In particular, CISD – defined as a meeting of those involved in a traumatic event, which aims to diminish the impact of the event by promoting support and encouraging processing of traumatic experiences in a group setting (Richards, 2001) – gained widespread initial popularity. Subsequently, Mitchell & Everly (1997) coined the term 'critical incident stress management' (CISM) to differentiate the single-session, stand-alone debriefing meeting from a broader, multicomponent programme including pre-trauma training, CISD, follow-up and case management. Both CISD and CISM were designed to try to accelerate recovery before harmful stress reactions have had a chance to damage the performance, career, health and families of victims. However, there is no agreement on the best way to deliver early interventions or indeed whether it is possible to reduce the incidence of PTSD through this route (Litz *et al*, 2002). Indeed, the area is hotly contested. The efficacy of debriefing has been called into question in systematic reviews (e.g. van Emmerik *et al*, 2002; Rose *et al*, 2004), which have suggested that single-session CISD produced either no improvement compared with controls or had the potential to cause significant harm to those debriefed. It has been suggested that single-session debriefing might sensitise traumatised individuals further or might persuade people not to use the necessary natural social support networks likely to assist with recovery (van Emmerik *et al*, 2002). These studies led to claims that CISD was an ineffective technique and that it should not be routinely used in supporting people after traumatic incidents (Avery & Orner, 1998; Wessely *et al*, 1998). Other reviews, however, came to the conclusion that CISD is a useful technique as part of an overall CISM programme (Everly *et al*, 1999) and that the studies included in the negative reviews sacrifice internal validity for experimental control, use self-selected participants, misapply these techniques to individuals rather than to the groups for which they were originally designed, use CISD outside the time scale recommended and have debriefers who appear inadequately trained (Mitchell & Everly, 1997). Indeed, negative reviews such as that by van Emmerick *et al* (2002) do include the caveat that CISD was never designed to be a stand-alone intervention. Some have suggested that early intervention and debriefing should be directed at community or group support rather than individual treatment and have called for new research methods to investigate this approach (British Psychological Society, 2002).

Indeed, the lack of non-intervention controls in studies of 'pure' debriefing is a problem for clinicians and policy-makers alike, a problem compounded by the ethical difficulty of designing non-intervention conditions in sensitive post-incident or workplace environments where offering no support may be unacceptable to employees and employers alike. The provision of psychological debriefing as a community support and cohesion strategy (British Psychological Society, 2002) rather than a treatment intervention to prevent PTSD is beyond the scope of this guidance.

More recently, there has been significant interest in replicating some of the findings from the treatment of chronic PTSD in an early intervention format with populations identified as at risk of developing chronic PTSD. The belief that cognitive–behavioural therapy is effective for PTSD, the disquiet over debriefing and the desire referred to earlier to limit the duration of disability for sufferers has led to either the adaptation of routine CBT into shorter variants delivered close to the time of the incident or the application of more standard CBT within a few months of the incident. Given that the efficacy of CBT for PTSD was only established in the late 1990s, early interventions of this kind are a new development and have only recently been the subject of research.

7.3 Studies included

The review team conducted a new systematic search for RCTs that assessed the efficacy of treatments delivered in any of the two areas described above. From the main search for RCTs (see Appendix 6), 21 studies in all were identified that met the inclusion criteria. The retrieved studies were divided into three groups:

- treatment for all – studies that investigated treatments delivered to all traumatic incident survivors, normally within the first month after the incident
- early psychological interventions for acute PTSD and acute stress disorder – studies that investigated treatments delivered to people who were assessed as having a high risk of chronic PTSD, initiated within 3 months of the incident
- early pharmacological interventions – studies using drug treatments for people in the acute phase of the disorder.

Ten studies were identified as falling within the 'treatment for all' category: BISSON 1997, BROM 1993, CAMPFIELD 2001, CONLON 1999, DOLAN, HOBBS 1996, LEE 1996, MAYOU 2000, ROSE 1999 and ZATZICK 2001. Nine studies, comprising five different types of intervention, were identified as falling within the category of early interventions for acute PTSD and acute stress disorder: BISSON 2004, BRYANT 1998, BRYANT 1999, BRYANT 2003, BRYANT A, BRYANT B, ECHEBURA 1996, EHLERS 2003A and OST 2003. (In EHLERS 2003A the self-monitoring period was taken to be part of the active intervention and as occurring within 3 months of the trauma.) Two studies were identified as falling in the pharmacological category: PITMAN 2002 and SCHELLING 2001. References given in shortened format and summary characteristics of individual included trials are given in Appendix 14.

7.4 Treatment for all

Four different types of early intervention for all were identified in the RCTs that met the inclusion criteria. These were education, collaborative care, trauma-focused counselling and debriefing.

7.4.1 Education

One study (ROSE 1999, *n*=157) included a 30 min educational intervention in its randomised design, comparing it with debriefing and an assessment-only control group. Individuals were assault victims and the intervention was delivered to them 9–31 days after the assault. Education consisted of a 30 min session related to the individual's experiences and information on when and where to find help, and included a specially written leaflet. Education was delivered by a therapist whose qualifications were not described. Outcomes were reported at 6 months post-intervention.

7.4.1.1 Education versus control

The evidence is inconclusive and so it is not possible to determine if there is a clinically important difference between education and control on reducing the likelihood of having a PTSD diagnosis at 6 months' follow-up (k=1; n=103; RR=0.69, 95% CI 0.37 to 1.3). I

There is evidence suggesting there is unlikely to be a clinically important difference between education and control on reducing the severity of PTSD symptoms (self-reported) at 6 months' follow-up (k=1; n=91; SMD=−0.18, 95% CI −0.59 to 0.24). I

7.4.2 Collaborative care

One study (ZATZICK 2001, n=34) compared a collaborative care programme delivered by a trauma support specialist for road traffic accident survivors with usual care. Collaborative care involved eliciting and monitoring patients' post-traumatic concerns and joint provider–patient treatment planning. Monitoring was undertaken by consultation liaison psychiatrists and a trauma clinical nurse specialist. The intervention was delivered from 1 month after the accident for 4 months and involved trauma support specialists monitoring psychological health, reviewing the traumatic event, providing education on coping strategies, jointly developing problem definitions and plans with individuals, and liaison with a multidisciplinary trauma team. Outcomes were reported at 4 months post-intervention.

7.4.2.1 Collaborative care versus control

The evidence is inconclusive and so it is not possible to determine if there is a clinically important difference between collaborative care and control on reducing the severity of PTSD symptoms (self-report measures) at 1 month's follow-up (k=1; n=29; SMD=−0.5, 95% CI −1.24 to 0.24). I

The evidence is inconclusive and so it is not possible to determine if there is a clinically important difference between collaborative care and control in severity of PTSD symptoms (self-report measures) at 4 months' follow-up (k=1; n=26; SMD=0.4, 95% CI −0.38 to 1.18). I

7.4.3 Trauma-focused counselling

One study (BROM 1993, n=151) compared a three- to six-session counselling programme with a monitoring control. Counselling was delivered 1–3 months after the traumatic incident to road traffic accident survivors. Counselling included practical help, education, support, reality testing and confrontation with the traumatic experience. Outcomes were reported at 6 months following the accident.

7.4.3.1 Trauma-focused counselling versus control

There is evidence suggesting there is unlikely to be a clinically important difference between trauma-focused counselling and control on reducing the severity of PTSD symptoms (self-report measures) at 6 months' follow-up (k=1; n=151; SMD=0.17, 95% CI −0.15 to 0.49). I

7.4.4 Debriefing

Seven RCTs of individual psychological debriefing were identified: BISSON 1997, CONLON 1999, DOLAN, HOBBS 1996, LEE 1996, MAYOU 2000 and ROSE 1999; n=629. Studies involved individuals who had experienced a range of traumatic events including road traffic incidents, assaults, miscarriages, fires and unspecified other incidents. Psychological debriefing was delivered between 10 hours and 31 days after the incident, with a duration of 30–120 min. Five studies were of individual treatment only, one study included some debriefing of groups of two to five PTSD sufferers and another included family members in some debriefing sessions. All debriefing interventions were single sessions and included education about traumatic stress, expression of emotions and planning for the future. Debriefing was delivered by a range of professionals, including nurses, mental health nurses, psychiatrists and psychologists. The training and qualifications of the debriefers was not comprehensively described in any of the studies. Five studies reported post-intervention outcomes up to 4 months; three studies reported outcomes from 6 months to 13 months and one study reported outcomes to 3 years. There was no randomised study of critical incident debriefing, the group-focused approach advocated by Mitchell & Everly (1997), in contrast to the single-session, typically individually focused debriefing interventions considered in this section.

7.4.4.1 Delayed versus immediate debriefing

One study of delayed versus immediate debriefing for victims of robbery was included (CAMPFIELD 2001). Debriefing lasted 1–2 hours and was conducted individually or in small groups. There was evidence favouring immediate debriefing (occurring within 10 hours of the trauma) to delayed debriefing (occurring within 48 hours of the trauma) for reducing PTSD severity at 2 weeks post-trauma. However, the study provided no data to indicate how sustained this relative improvement was, and in the absence of a control group it is not possible to determine whether both treatments led to an improvement relative to natural recovery at 2 weeks.

7.4.4.2 Debriefing versus control

The evidence is inconclusive and so it is not possible to determine if there is a clinically important difference between debriefing and control on reducing the likelihood of having a PTSD diagnosis at 3–6 months' follow-up (k=2; n=238; RR=1.2, 95% CI 0.84 to 1.71). ▮

There is limited evidence suggesting a difference favouring control over debriefing on reducing the likelihood of having a PTSD diagnosis at 13 months' follow-up (k=1; n=133; RR=1.87, 95% CI 1.12 to 3.12). ▮

There is evidence suggesting there is unlikely to be a clinically important difference between debriefing and control on reducing the severity of PTSD symptoms (self-report measures) at 1–4 months' follow-up (k= 5; n=356; SMD=0.11, 95% CI –0.1 to 0.32). ▮

There is evidence suggesting there is unlikely to be a clinically important difference between debriefing and control on reducing depression symptoms at 1–4 months' follow-up (k= 3; n=225; SMD=0, 95% CI –0.27 to 0.26). ▮

7.5 Treatment for all – clinical summary

When brief, single-session interventions of debriefing or education are offered as an individually structured intervention to any person involved in a traumatic incident, there is evidence suggesting that there is unlikely to be a clinically important effect on subsequent PTSD and across a range of self-report measures. However, one study (BISSON 1997) suggested that there is limited evidence of harmful effects of debriefing at 13 months' post-injury for PTSD diagnosis. On current evidence, therefore, single-session debriefing may be at best ineffective.

An important reservation in interpreting the evidence for early interventions for all is that all the studies were of survivors who had experienced individual traumas and who in the main received an individual intervention. No trial on critical incident stress debriefing as it was originally conceived by Mitchell and colleagues (i.e. as a group intervention for teams of emergency workers, military personnel or others who are used to working together) or critical incident stress management (i.e. a multicomponent programme of debriefing, follow-up and case management) met our methodological inclusion criteria. As a consequence we have a lack of evidence for practice in these situations. Furthermore, there is a paucity of methodologically sound early intervention studies, containing detailed descriptions of training and fidelity checks on interventions used.

Notwithstanding these methodological reservations, given the evidence that there is unlikely to be a clinically important effect on subsequent PTSD, we do not recommend that systematic, brief, single-session interventions focusing on the traumatic incident are provided individually to everyone who has been exposed to such an incident. However, we do recommend the good practice of providing general practical and social support and guidance to anyone following a traumatic incident. Acknowledgement of the psychological impact of traumatic incidents should be part of healthcare and social service workers' responses to incidents. Support and guidance are likely to cover reassurance about immediate distress, information about the likely course of symptoms, and practical and emotional support in the first month after the incident.

7.6 Early psychological interventions for acute PTSD and acute stress disorder

Five different types of early intervention for all were identified in the RCTs that met the inclusion criteria: trauma-focused cognitive–behavioural therapy (as defined in Chapter 5), trauma-focused CBT supplemented with hypnosis or anxiety management, relaxation techniques and a self-help booklet.

7.6.1 Cognitive–behavioural therapy

All nine studies identified for 'early intervention for acute PTSD' had one treatment group that underwent some form of CBT (see Chapter 5 for descriptions of the treatments that fall within this category): BISSON 2004, BRYANT 1998, BRYANT 1999, BRYANT 2003, BRYANT A, BRYANT B, ECHEBURA 1996, EHLERS 2003A and OST 2003; $n=491$ (one of these studies, BRYANT 2003, was a 4-year follow-up to BRYANT 1998 and BRYANT 1999). These studies involved individuals who had experienced accidents or physical and sexual assaults. In six studies, individuals were identified within 1 month of the trauma occurring and treatment was continued into the period 1–6 months after the trauma. In the other three studies, PTSD sufferers were identified within 3 months and treatment was completed within 6 months. All individuals were included in the studies on the basis of symptomatic criteria, but these varied. Four studies required survivors to have a diagnosis of acute stress disorder; two others required survivors to meet symptomatic diagnostic criteria for PTSD; another two studies required individuals to meet PTSD symptomatic diagnostic criteria and, in addition, to exceed cut-off scores on screening tools; and a final study included individuals on the basis of exceeding cut-off scores on screening tools only. Treatment was delivered to individuals rather than in groups and ranged from 4 sessions to 16 sessions of 1–2 hours' duration, a total time ranging from 4 hours to almost 17 hours of therapy. Treatment also included varied combinations of education, relaxation, imaginal exposure, image habituation training, thought stopping, distraction, cognitive restructuring and *in vivo* exposure. Post-intervention outcomes were reported in four studies at 6 months and in another five studies at 9–13 months. One study reported a further follow-up at 4 years.

7.6.1.1 Trauma-focused CBT versus control

There is limited evidence suggesting a difference favouring trauma-focused CBT over waiting list (random effects) on reducing the likelihood of having a PTSD diagnosis post-treatment (k=3; $n=252$; RR=0.4, 95% CI 0.16 to 1.02). ▮

There is limited evidence suggesting a difference favouring trauma-focused CBT over waiting list (random effects) on reducing the likelihood of having a PTSD diagnosis at 9–13 months' follow-up (k=2; $n=209$; RR=0.41, 95% CI 0.11 to 1.45). ▮

There is limited evidence suggesting a difference favouring trauma-focused CBT over waiting list (random effects) on reducing the severity of PTSD symptoms (self-report measures) (k=3; $n=224$; SMD=−0.98, 95% CI −1.81 to −0.14). ▮

The evidence is inconclusive and so it is not possible to determine if there is a clinically important difference between trauma-focused CBT and waiting list (random effects) on reducing the severity of PTSD symptoms (self-report measures) at 9–13 months' follow-up (k=2; $n=171$; SMD=−0.68, 95% CI −1.23 to −0.12). ▮

There is limited evidence suggesting a difference favouring trauma-focused CBT over waiting list (random effects) on reducing the severity of PTSD symptoms (clinician-rated measures) (k=3; $n=224$; SMD=−0.88, 95% CI −1.72 to −0.04). ▮

There is evidence suggesting there is unlikely to be a clinically important difference between trauma-focused CBT and waiting list (fixed effects) on reducing the severity of PTSD symptoms (clinician-rated measures) at 9–13 months' follow-up (k=2; n=171; SMD=–0.45, 95% CI –0.75 to –0.14). ▪

7.6.2 Prolonged exposure with anxiety management

One study (BRYANT 1999, n=36) compared the effectiveness of prolonged exposure and anxiety management techniques against prolonged exposure. Prolonged exposure entailed a minimum of four 50 min sessions of imaginal exposure to the traumatic memories as part of the five 90 min treatment sessions. Anxiety management included breathing retraining, self-talk and progressive muscular relaxation exercises. Individuals had all experienced road traffic accidents or non-sexual assaults and outcomes were reported at 6 months post-intervention.

There is limited evidence suggesting a difference favouring prolonged exposure over prolonged exposure with anxiety management on reducing the likelihood of having a PTSD diagnosis post-treatment (k=1; n=38; RR=0.58, 95% CI 0.3 to 1.15). ▪

There is limited evidence suggesting a difference favouring prolonged exposure over prolonged exposure with anxiety management on reducing the likelihood of having a PTSD diagnosis as observed at 6 months' follow-up (k=1; n=38; RR=0.64, 95% CI 0.37 to 1.11). ▪

7.6.3 Trauma-focused CBT and hypnotherapy

One study (BRYANT B, n=63) compared the effectiveness of trauma-focused CBT versus trauma-focused CBT with an additional element of hypnotherapy in the form of a 15 min hypnotic induction audiotape recording, for individuals who had experienced road traffic accidents or non-sexual assaults. Outcomes were reported to 6 months post-intervention.

7.6.3.1 Trauma-focused CBT versus trauma-focused CBT and hypnotherapy

The evidence is inconclusive and so it is not possible to determine if there is a clinically important difference between trauma-focused CBT and trauma-focused CBT with hypnotherapy on reducing the likelihood of having a PTSD diagnosis post-treatment (k=1; n=63; RR=1.21, 95% CI 0.6 to 2.46). ▪

The evidence is inconclusive and so it is not possible to determine if there is a clinically important difference between trauma-focused CBT and trauma-focused CBT with hypnotherapy on reducing the likelihood of having a PTSD diagnosis as observed at 6 months' follow-up (k=1; n=63; RR=1.06, 95% CI 0.59 to 1.92). ▪

The evidence is inconclusive and so it is not possible to determine if there is a clinically important difference between trauma-focused CBT and trauma-focused CBT with hypnotherapy on reducing the severity of PTSD symptoms (self-report measures) (k=1; n=47; SMD=0.13, 95% CI –0.45 to 0.7). ▪

The evidence is inconclusive and so it is not possible to determine if there is a clinically important difference between trauma-focused CBT and trauma-focused CBT with hypnotherapy on reducing the severity of PTSD symptoms (self-report measures) as observed at 6 months' follow-up (k=1; n=47; SMD=0.07, 95% CI –0.5 to 0.64). ▪

7.6.4 Relaxation

One study of trauma-focused CBT (ECHEBURA 1996, n=20) used relaxation alone as a comparator condition with a group of female survivors of sexual assault. Relaxation was progressive muscle relaxation training and was delivered in five hour-long sessions. Post-intervention outcomes were reported to 12 months.

7.6.4.1 Trauma-focused CBT versus relaxation

There is limited evidence suggesting a difference favouring trauma-focused CBT over progressive muscular relaxation training on reducing the likelihood of having a PTSD diagnosis post-treatment (k=1; n=20; RR=0.4, 95% CI 0.1 to 1.6). ▪

There is limited evidence suggesting a difference favouring trauma-focused CBT over progressive muscular relaxation training on reducing the likelihood of having a PTSD diagnosis at 12 months' follow-up (k=1; n=20; RR=0.2, 95% CI 0.01 to 3.7). ∎

7.6.5 Supportive psychotherapy

Five studies (BRYANT 1998, BRYANT 1999, BRYANT 2003, BRYANT A and BRYANT B; n=191) involved a comparison of 'supportive psychotherapy' against other treatments. Across the studies, the researchers defined supportive psychotherapy to include active listening, education, problem-solving and unconditional support to individuals.

7.6.5.1 Trauma-focused CBT versus supportive psychotherapy

There is evidence suggesting a difference favouring trauma-focused CBT over supportive psychotherapy on reducing the likelihood of having a PTSD diagnosis at 6 months' follow-up (k=3; n=105; RR=0.51, 95% CI 0.32 to 0.8). ∎

The evidence is inconclusive and so it is not possible to determine if there is a clinically important difference between trauma-focused CBT and supportive psychotherapy on reducing the likelihood of having a PTSD diagnosis at 4 years' follow-up (k=1; n=80; RR=0.9, 95% CI 0.61 to 1.33). ∎

There is evidence suggesting a difference favouring trauma-focused CBT over supportive psychotherapy on reducing the severity of PTSD symptoms (self-report measures) (k=3; n=94; SMD=−1.11, 95% CI −1.55 to −0.67). ∎

There is limited evidence suggesting a difference favouring trauma-focused CBT over supportive psychotherapy on reducing the severity of PTSD symptoms (self-report measures) at 6 months' follow-up (k=3; n=94; SMD=−0.8, 95% CI −1.22 to −0.37). ∎

7.6.6 Self-help

One study of trauma-focused CBT (EHLERS 2003A, n=85) used self-help as a comparator condition for individuals who had experienced road traffic accidents or physical assault. Self-help patients were given a 64-page booklet based on CBT principles, accompanied by one 40 min session with a therapist at the beginning of treatment to explain the book and its content. Post-intervention outcomes were reported to 9 months.

For self-help booklet intervention delivered 1–6 months after the incident, the evidence varies from suggesting that there is not a clinically important difference between the intervention and control, to being inconclusive across the different measures of outcome.

7.6.6.1 Self-help booklet versus control

The evidence is inconclusive and so it is not possible to determine if there is a clinically important difference between self-help booklet and waiting list on reducing the likelihood of having a PTSD diagnosis post-treatment (k=1; n=57; RR=1.09, 95% CI 0.81 to 1.46). ∎

The evidence is inconclusive and so it is not possible to determine if there is a clinically important difference between self-help booklet and waiting list on reducing the likelihood of having a PTSD diagnosis at 9 months' follow-up (k=1; n=57; RR=1.1, 95% CI 0.71 to 1.71). ∎

The evidence is inconclusive and so it is not possible to determine if there is a clinically important difference between self-help booklet and waiting list on reducing the severity of PTSD symptoms (self-report measures) (k=1; n=52; SMD=−0.27, 95% CI −0.81 to 0.28). ∎

There is evidence suggesting there is unlikely to be a clinically important difference between self-help booklet and waiting list on reducing the severity of PTSD symptoms (clinician-rated measures) at 9 months' follow-up (k=1; n=52; SMD=0.07, 95% CI −0.47 to 0.62). ∎

7.7 Clinical summary of early psychological interventions

When trauma-focused CBT is delivered between 1 month and 6 months after the incident, there is evidence suggesting that it is effective for people at risk of developing chronic PTSD, compared with the effect of being on a waiting list, for PTSD diagnosis post-treatment and at 9–13 months' follow-up, as well as a number of other outcomes assessed post-treatment, which included self-report measures of PTSD severity, anxiety and quality of life and clinician-assessed PTSD severity. However, the evidence is inconclusive for a number of outcomes assessed at 9–13 months' follow-up (self-report measures of PTSD severity, anxiety and quality of life) and the evidence suggests that there is no clinically important difference for clinician-assessed PTSD severity at 9–13 months.

Trauma-focused CBT delivered between 1 month and 6 months after the incident is also more effective for people at risk of developing chronic PTSD compared with being on a waiting list or receiving non-trauma-focused interventions such as self-help booklets, relaxation or general supportive counselling.

Although trauma-focused CBT is effective for people at risk of developing chronic PTSD, there is great variation in the dimensions of delivery. The variable response rates in different studies are unexplained and may be due to differences in the PTSD sufferer intake variables (for example, symptomatic PTSD criteria versus diagnoses of acute stress disorder), number of treatment sessions, the expertise of the therapists or the length of individual therapy sessions. The interaction and predictive effects of symptom severity and the duration and number of sessions in trauma-focused CBT are likely to be highly important but have not been systematically varied in controlled trials.

7.8 Early intervention drug treatments for PTSD

There are few trials of early intervention drug treatments and only two studies met the inclusion criteria. The results of the review of these studies are summarised below. For further information on the differences between drug trials and trials of other interventions, see Chapter 6.

7.8.1 Propranolol versus placebo

One study (PITMAN 2002) compared propranolol and placebo. Propranolol is a beta-adrenoceptor blocker and crosses the blood–brain barrier. This trial was based on *a priori* hypotheses about the role of the amygdala in the development of PTSD. Participants were administered propranolol (40 mg four times a day) or placebo, beginning within 6 hours of the traumatic event.

The evidence is inconclusive and so it is not possible to determine if there is a clinically important difference between propranolol and placebo on reducing the likelihood of having a PTSD diagnosis at 1 month (k=1; *n*=41; RR=1.14, 95% CI 0.55 to 2.35). I

There is limited evidence suggesting a difference favouring placebo over propranolol on reducing the likelihood of having a PTSD diagnosis at 3 months' follow-up (k=1; *n*=41; RR=1.28, 95% CI 0.69 to 2.38). I

7.8.2 Hydrocortisone versus placebo

One study (SCHELLING 2001, *n*=20) explored the effect of hydrocortisone (a corticosteroid) and placebo on the reactions to the intense physical and psychological stress during septic shock in the intensive care environment. Studies of hydrocortisone are of particular interest given the evidence of disturbance in the HPA axis in PTSD.

There is limited evidence suggesting a difference favouring hydrocortisone over placebo on reducing the likelihood of having a PTSD diagnosis at approximately 31 months after treatment (k=1; *n*=20; RR=0.17, 95% CI 0.03 to 1.17). I

7.9 Clinical summary of early intervention drug treatments

Given the small number and scale of studies of early intervention drug treatments, it is not possible to draw strong conclusions. At present there is no conclusive evidence that any drug treatment helps as an early intervention for the treatment of PTSD-specific symptoms. However, for sufferers who are acutely distressed, and may in particular be experiencing significant sleep problems, consideration may be given to the use of medication.

7.10 Economic evaluation of early versus later delivery of psychological treatment

7.10.1 Introduction

The phenomenon of spontaneous or natural remission has both health and economic consequences in PTSD as in other conditions. The proposition is that where treatments are given to patients who would otherwise naturally recover, resources could be better spent on patients who need them. The difference between natural remission and treatment-related recovery is critical, and this difference may change with time elapsed since the traumatic event. A large number of mental health economic studies have been conducted generally (see McCrone & Weich, 2001), but none has addressed the incremental costs of alternative interventions, nor the cost-effectiveness of early versus late delivery of cognitive–behavioural therapy, in particular for PTSD. Moreover, few studies have presented a decay curve showing the changing slope of natural remission over time. For example, to examine this phenomenon, Richards (2005) presented 'caseness' data for PTSD, using a General Health Questionnaire (GHQ). At 3 days post-trauma, 60% of the patients who were directly involved in a raid suffered from PTSD symptoms. However, this figure nearly halved to 31% by 2 weeks post-trauma, and again to 17% by 1 month post-trauma (Fig. 7.1, Table 7.1).

7.10.2 Method

For this guideline, all psychological interventions and different service provision options for the treatment of PTSD were briefly reviewed from a health economics perspective. The Guideline Development Group decided to focus on the question of the appropriate time at which to initiate treatment: that is, were there significant additional costs associated with intervening early or later in the course of PTSD? An economic evaluation was therefore undertaken using data from published sources (Bryant *et al*, 1998; Ehlers *et al*, 2003), along with a cost-effectiveness analysis in accordance with the NICE guideline development recommendations (National Institute for Clinical Excellence, 2004). The cost-effectiveness was evaluated to determine the consequences of moving patients from one treatment category to an incrementally earlier treatment category. The NHS perspective was adopted, with only direct staffing costs included in the analysis.

Component costs were measured from the health services perspective based upon 2002–3 prices, and estimated as hours of treatment multiplied by the hourly wage of a clinical psychologist according to the 2002–3 *Unit Costs of Health and Social Care* manual (Netten & Curtis, 2003). According to these estimates, the average annual wage of a clinical psychologist is £33 193 per year and requires £3775 in on-costs, £4230 in direct revenue overheads and £1713 in capital overheads. This translates into £66 per hour of client contact, including these additional expenses.

Using data from Bryant *et al* (1998), total cost was estimated in the instance of early intervention from five 1.5-hour sessions. These earlier timed interventions were evaluated alongside longer-term data from Ehlers *et al* (2003), where total cost was estimated from [(5 x 1.5 h) + (5 x 1 h)] sessions, using the above per-hour costing estimates. Total cost reflected treatment-related recoveries as well as recoveries that might otherwise have occurred naturally in patients who received CBT.

Types of trauma comprised motor vehicle accidents (Ehlers *et al*, 2003) and motor vehicle accidents or industrial accidents (Bryant *et al*, 1998). Treatment-related recoveries were calculated separately for each study by calculating total number of recoveries in the CBT group minus the natural recoveries estimated to arise from the supportive counselling or control groups. Cost-effectiveness ratios comparing treatments of various lengths at 2 weeks versus 12 weeks were estimated and presented as incremental cost per additional treatment-related recovery. Follow-up times ranged from 3 months to 12 months post-trauma.

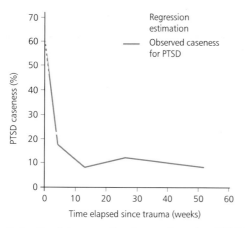

Fig. 7.1 Post-traumatic stress disorder (PTSD) 'caseness' of patients directly involved in a raid (x, weeks post-trauma; y, PTSD % caseness). Data from Richards (1997).

Table 7.1 Data corresponding to decay curve in Figure 7.1

Weeks post-trauma (raid)	GHQ (>3) caseness rates for PTSD
0	60
1	51
2	31
4	17
13	8
26	12
52	8

GHQ, General Health Questionnaire.

Adapted from Richards (1997).

In this analysis, cost was calculated as cost-of-treatment multiplied by the number of sessions, and effectiveness the number of patients who would not otherwise naturally recover (e.g. chronic PTSD sufferers). Uncertainty was estimated in a sensitivity analysis in which the stochastic and deterministic data were varied over plausible ranges.

Incremental cost-effectiveness was determined by dividing the difference between the total costs (TC) of programme 1 and programme 2 by the difference in numbers of treatment-related recoveries (TR) for each programme, to give the incremental cost-effectiveness ratio (ICER):

$$(TC_2 - TC_1)/(TR_2 - TR_1) = ICER$$

This ratio indicates the cost-effectiveness of each timing of programme. In comparing two points in time post-trauma, the ICER indicates the marginal cost necessary to achieve an additional treatment-related recovery. Where the cost is negative, this indicates a reduction in cost per additional treatment-related recovery, relative to the comparator.

Costs and health outcomes were discounted at 3.5%. Discounting is a technique that assumes individuals prefer to delay costs rather than incur them in the present, and forego future benefits in exchange for gaining some benefit in the present. The choice of a discount rate is a disputed issue, however. Although the most common recommendation in health economics literature is that costs and health outcomes should be discounted at the same rate, there is considerable variation in practice, with some studies failing to discount health effects at all, and others citing that different age-groups will discount costs and benefits differently. For instance, younger individuals may be at a disadvantage with respect to the terms on which they can borrow money (i.e. money allocated today is worth far more than it is anticipated to be in the future), and older people or individuals with comorbid conditions that impinge on their quality of life are more aware of their own mortality and therefore may discount benefits more heavily (i.e. an intervention today is worth more than in the future).

Although the effect of discounting was small in this study, the choice to include this method followed NICE recommendations (NICE, 2004) and is common practice in health economic evaluations. Discounting reduced the total cost by £231 in the case of treatment at 12 weeks and by £8 in the case of treatment at 2 weeks post-trauma. Discounting the benefits had no effect on the whole number of treatment-related recoveries on which the cost-effectiveness analyses were based.

7.10.3 Results

The results of this illustrative analysis are presented in Tables 7.2 and 7.3.

Table 7.2	Frequency of recovery and costs at various treatment times						
Weeks post-trauma	Patients treated (n)	Recoveries (n)	Not remitted (n)	Natural remission rate	Treatment-related recoveries (n)	Treatment cost (£ per patient	Total cost (£)
2	12	10	2	0.33	7	495[1]	5932
12	28	25	3	0.42	14	825	22 869

1. Equivalent to five 1.5 h sessions.
Sources – first row: Bryant *et al* (1998); second row: Ehlers *et al* (2003).

Table 7.3	Results of the cost-effectiveness analysis of early versus late intervention	
Weeks post-trauma	Treatment recoveries (n)	Total cost (£)
2	7	5932
12	14	22 869
Incremental cost 2>12		16 937
Incremental recoveries 2>12	7	
ICER 2>12		2420 (cost per additional treatment-related recovery in treating at 12 instead of 2 weeks post-trauma)

ICER, incremental cost-effectiveness ratio, calculated by dividing the difference in total cost by the difference in number of recoveries.

7.10.4 Summary

Assuming a remission is worth more than £2420, then cognitive–behavioural therapy at 12 weeks is the most cost-effective option. Achieving faster recoveries by treating early, however, may provide intangible benefits to those who suffer severe initial PTSD symptoms, particularly by preventing the conditions from becoming chronic. Future early versus late intervention studies should include a waiting list control in order to reduce the uncertainty associated with similar treatments (e.g. psychological debriefing, cognitive–behavioural therapies, self-help booklets and repeated assessments).

7.10.5 Conclusions

The findings of this study strengthen the impression that treating patients with cognitive–behavioural therapy at 12 weeks after the traumatic event is cost-effective, assuming a willngness-to-pay threshold of £2420 per additional treatment-related remission. Of course, caution must be exercised, because the estimates are based on small sample sizes and a select range of traumas. Indeed, the indirect and social costs of treating patients later may present hidden costs that are not included in this analysis (see section 2.7). Further research is needed to evaluate the cost of investing in early PTSD screening and prevention methods compared with the cost of treating PTSD at a later stage. This should be trial-based, where all costing and effectiveness parameters are estimated from data prospectively collected within an RCT. Rigorous health economic evaluations are needed to ensure interventions are cost-effective and equitable in preventing relapses across a wide range of the population.

This analysis does not account for fluctuations in treatment and/or behavioural effects between the two referenced studies. A sensitivity analysis demonstrated that a 10% increase or decrease in caseness, treatment-related recoveries or cost of treatment did not alter the conclusions. Nevertheless, there are certain confounding variables that may limit economic evaluations of the existing samples. These include the type and subtype of trauma; gender, age and other socio-demographic variables; differential study retention and withdrawal rates; differential inclusion criteria; comorbidity factors; time from trauma to presentation and treatment; type of treatment and skill of the person delivering treatment; number and length of sessions; the possibility that some or all of the chronic cases in the 12 week cohort might have recovered equally if given only the number of treatments as in the 2 week cohort; and the fact that patients needed to agree to randomisation. More importantly, this economic evaluation included neither the intangible cost of suffering nor the added financial cost to the patient in terms of work absence and lost opportunities as a consequence.

7.11 Clinical practice recommendations

7.11.1 Immediate interventions for all survivors of traumatic incidents

7.11.1.1 All health and social care workers should be aware of the psychological impact of traumatic incidents in their immediate post-incident care of survivors and offer practical, social and emotional support to those involved. GPP

7.11.1.2 For individuals who have experienced a traumatic event, the systematic provision to that individual alone of brief, single-session interventions (often referred to as debriefing) that focus on the traumatic incident should *not* be routine practice when delivering services. A

7.11.1.3 Drug treatment may be considered in the acute phase of PTSD for the management of sleep disturbance. In this case, hypnotic medication may be appropriate for short-term use but if longer-term drug treatment is required, consideration should also be given to the use of suitable antidepressants at an early stage in order to reduce the later risk of dependence. C

7.11.2 Early interventions for acute PTSD

7.11.2.1 Trauma-focused cognitive–behavioural therapy should be offered to those with severe post-traumatic symptoms or with severe PTSD in the first month after the traumatic event. These treatments should normally be provided on an individual out-patient basis. B

7.11.2.2 Trauma-focused cognitive–behavioural therapy should be offered to people who present with PTSD within 3 months of a traumatic event. A

7.11.2.3 The duration of the trauma-focused cognitive–behavioural therapy should normally be 8–12 sessions, but if the treatment starts in the first month after the event, fewer sessions (about 5) may be sufficient. When the trauma is discussed in the treatment session, longer sessions (for example, 90 min) are usually necessary. Treatment should be regular and continuous (usually at least once a week) and should be delivered by the same person. B

7.11.2.4 Non-trauma-focused interventions such as relaxation or non-directive therapy, which do not address traumatic memories, should not routinely be offered to people who present with PTSD symptoms within 3 months of a traumatic event. B

8 Predictors of PTSD and screening for the disorder

8.1 Introduction

Various factors have been considered as potentially predictive of the development of PTSD and instruments have been developed to screen for it. The benefits of being able to predict accurately those who will develop or have PTSD include the opportunity to focus on individuals at high risk and to contribute to the development of specific interventions.

Screening typically involves testing large numbers of individuals for the presence or absence of a particular condition. Usually a screening test is not diagnostic, but it will detect people at high risk of having the condition under consideration; an example would be mammography to screen for breast cancer. Screening can also be used to identify people at high risk of developing PTSD at a later date, who will perhaps require closer monitoring; this is more comparable to screening for cervical cancer, in which cervical smears identify pre-cancerous changes. In order to be of value, a screening test should be reasonably simple to administer and interpret, and be efficient in discriminating between people with and without the condition under consideration. Brief screening instruments are widely used in other mental health areas, for example the four 'CAGE' questions (Ewing, 1984) and the Alcohol Use Disorders Identification Test (AUDIT) questionnaire (Babor et al, 1992) in the detection of problem drinkers.

The National Screening Committee has set 22 criteria for appraising the viability, effectiveness and appropriateness of a programme for large population screening (http://www.nsc.nhs.uk/pdfs/criteria.pdf). These include: the need for a simple, safe, precise and validated screening test; an agreed policy on the further evaluation of individuals with a positive test result; the availability of an effective intervention for those identified through early detection, with evidence of early treatment leading to better outcomes than late treatment; adequate resources available prior to commencement; and acceptability to the population. It is important that the majority of these criteria are satisfied before a screening programme is adopted, not least because screening can cause adverse effects, including distress secondary to asking specific questions, raising concerns and raising expectations of cure.

Three high-quality systematic reviews have been conducted in this area (Brewin et al, 2000; Ozer et al, 2003; Brewin, 2005). The results of these studies, supplemented by further searches, are discussed below. The search strategies that were used to identify these reviews and subsequent individual studies are described in Chapter 4.

8.2 Risk factors

To determine if any factors or variables predict the development or chronicity of PTSD, large, prospective longitudinal studies are required. Unfortunately no such study has been done and therefore the evidence base is limited and must be interpreted with caution. A number of studies have looked for associations between various factors and the presence or development of PTSD. Although these studies are important, their design does not allow determination of the exact nature of any association with PTSD, for example whether factors are causative of development or chronicity.

Two major systematic reviews of predictors of PTSD have been published (Brewin et al, 2000; Ozer et al, 2003). The main outcome measure considered in the reviews was effect size calculated for the different factors. Effect sizes give an indication of the magnitude of the associations found. A commonly used guideline for interpreting effect sizes is that of Cohen (1988), by which an effect size of 0.25 is considered small, 0.5 is considered medium and 0.8 is considered large (see Chapter 4).

The systematic reviews did not consider all potential predictors of PTSD and only included studies published by the year 2000. Additional factors that have been suggested to have an association with PTSD and key studies published after 2000 are also discussed.

8.2.1 Review by Brewin et al (2000)

The review by Brewin et al (2000) included studies published in English that were designed to detect risk factors for PTSD in populations exposed to trauma in adulthood; there were also ten large epidemiological studies that allowed the trauma to have occurred at any age.

Relevant databases, journals and other sources (for example book chapters) were systematically reviewed using standard methodology. Seventy-seven articles were included, containing a total of 85 data-sets. Potential risk factors were limited to those that had been assessed in at least four of the studies. Fourteen potential risk factors were considered: gender, age at trauma, socio-economic status, education, intelligence, ethnicity, previous psychiatric history, reported abuse in childhood, reported other previous traumatisation, reported other adverse childhood factors (excluding abuse), family history of psychiatric disorder, trauma severity, post-trauma life stress and post-trauma social support. After identification of the factors, all the statistics were converted to obtain a common measure of effect size.

In addition to the risk factors, Brewin et al (2000) considered individual study characteristics and performed analyses to determine if these made a difference to the outcome. The study characteristics considered were: military versus civilian trauma; gender of participants; retrospective versus prospective design; analyses based on presence or absence of diagnosis versus continuous symptom scores; PTSD assessed with interview or questionnaire; traumas that might have occurred in childhood and/or adulthood.

Results

The sample size in the studies ranged from 25 to 4127 with a median of 119. Twenty-eight articles considered service personnel and the trauma was defined as active service. The remaining 49 articles considered civilian trauma victims (13 crime victims, 9 disaster victims, 4 motor vehicle accident victims, 6 burns victims, 7 other specific groups, e.g. terrorist attack victims, and 10 victims of mixed traumas). Fifty-nine articles were retrospective and 18 at least partly longitudinal. The authors produced a combined effect size for all the variables considered (Table 8.1). There was variation between effect sizes for different factors. All were relatively small but strongly statistically significantly associated with PTSD. The factors most associated with PTSD were the three peri-traumatic and post-traumatic ones (greater trauma severity, lack of social support and more subsequent life stress). There was considerable heterogeneity of effect sizes for individual factors, which complicates interpretation. The most homogeneous effect sizes across studies were found for psychiatric history, childhood abuse and family psychiatric history.

With regard to the specific study factors, the greatest number of differences occurred between civilian and military population studies. Female gender was less important in military samples, whereas younger age at trauma, lack of education, ethnicity, childhood adversity, trauma severity and lack of social support were all significantly more important. Younger age at trauma, lower socio-economic status and ethnicity had significantly greater effect sizes among males. Retrospective design was associated with a weaker gender effect but a stronger effect for younger age at trauma and for trauma severity. Continuous measure studies had a weaker female gender effect size but stronger effect sizes for younger age at trauma, lack of education, previous trauma, childhood adversity and trauma severity. Interview PTSD assessment was associated with stronger effect sizes for female gender, younger age at trauma and trauma severity, whereas questionnaire assessment was associated with a stronger effect size for previous trauma. The studies that included trauma at any age found a stronger female gender effect, but weaker effects for lack of education, previous psychiatric history, previous trauma, childhood adversity and trauma severity.

8.2.2 Review by Ozer et al (2003)

The review by Ozer et al (2003) focused on two types of predictor, which the authors labelled as personal characteristics salient for psychological processing and functioning, and aspects of the traumatic event or its sequelae. These were subdivided into seven different factors: a history of at

Table 8.1	Summary of factors considered in the study by Brewin *et al* (2000)				
Risk factor	No. of studies	Population size (*n*)	Range of effect size *r*	Weighted average effect size *r*[1]	95% CI
Gender (female)	25	11 261	−0.04 to 0.31	0.13	0.11 to 0.15
Younger age	29	7 207	−0.38 to 0.28	0.06	0.04 to 0.08
Low socio-economic status	18	5957	0.01 to 0.38	0.14	0.12 to 0.16
Lack of education	29	11 047	−0.11 to 0.37	0.10	0.8 to 0.12
Low intelligence	6	1149	0.08 to 0.38	0.18	0.12 to 0.24
Race (minority status)	22	8165	−0.27 to 0.39	0.05	0.03 to 0.07
Psychiatric history	22	7307	0.00 to 0.29	0.11	0.09 to 0.13
Childhood abuse	9	1746	0.07 to 0.30	0.14	0.09 to 0.19
Other previous trauma	14	5147	−0.05 to 0.36	0.12	0.09 to 0.15
Other adverse childhood	14	6969	0.09 to 0.60	0.19	0.17 to 0.21
Family psychiatric history	11	4792	0.07 to 0.28	0.13	0.10 to 0.16
Trauma severity	49	13 653	−0.14 to 0.76	0.23	0.21 to 0.25
Lack of social support	11	3276	−0.02 to 0.54	0.40	0.37 to 0.43
Life stress	8	2804	0.26 to 0.54	0.32	0.29 to 0.35

1. All these values are statistically significant at *P*<0.001.

From Brewin, C. R., Andrews, B. & Valentine, J. D. (2000) Meta-analysis of risk factors for post-traumatic stress disorder in trauma-exposed adults. *Journal of Consulting and Clinical Psychology*, **68**, 748–766. Copyright © 2000 by the American Psychological Association. Adapted with permission.

least one other trauma prior to the traumatic event, psychological adjustment prior to the traumatic event, family history of psychopathology, perceived life threat during the traumatic event, perceived social support following the traumatic event, peri-traumatic emotionality and peri-traumatic dissociation.

Standard systematic review methods were used to search various databases, journals and other sources such as reference lists. Sixty-eight studies were included and effect size estimates determined for all the factors included. The effect size representing the assessment of PTSD symptoms closest to the time of the traumatic event but after 1 month was included for studies with assessments at multiple time points. The authors also considered the influence of four study factors on outcome: sample type (community, medical patients, or individuals seeking mental health services), length of time between traumatic event and assessment, type of trauma studied as the target incident, and the method used to assess PTSD.

Results

Table 8.2 shows the summary of the effect sizes. All seven risk factors were associated with higher levels of PTSD. Peri-traumatic dissociation was the most strongly associated, closely followed by perceived support and perceived life threat. Pre-trauma factors were also associated with PTSD and the prior trauma and prior adjustment factors included more studies and had tighter 95% confidence intervals than the other factors considered. Whether prior trauma occurred in childhood or in adult life made no difference. However, having a prior trauma was more strongly related to PTSD when the traumatic experience involved non-combat interpersonal violence than when the traumatic experience resulted from combat exposure or an accident.

The prior adjustment grouping included various factors such as previous mental health treatment, previous emotional problems and antisocial personality disorder prior to military service. When the authors considered the four studies that examined pre-trauma depression as a risk factor, this was found to be more strongly associated with PTSD than the other measures of prior adjustment. Having a family history of psychopathology was more significant when the traumatic experience involved non-combat interpersonal violence than when the traumatic experience was combat exposure. Perceived life threat was more associated when assessment was further away from the traumatic event and in non-combat interpersonal violence than in accidents. Perceived social support was also more significant in studies that assessed individuals further away from the time of the traumatic event. Peri-traumatic dissociation was most significantly associated with PTSD in samples seeking mental health treatment, when the assessment time frame was 6 months to 3 years post-trauma and when self-assessment versus interview measures were used.

8.2.3 Comment on the Brewin and Ozer studies

Although the two reviews used a similar design, there are several differences between them. Both reviewed studies published between 1980 and 2000, but Brewin *et al* (2000) included 77 trials, whereas Ozer *et al* (2003) included 68 studies. Nineteen of the studies reviewed by Ozer *et al* (2003) were not reviewed by Brewin *et al* (2000); this might be partly accounted for by the former study not including the demographic factors included by Brewin *et al* such as gender, ethnicity, education and socio-economic status, but it is also likely to reflect more subtle differences in methodology.

Most of the studies included in both reviews used methods by which individuals were asked about potential risk factors after they had developed PTSD or post-traumatic stress symptoms. This design can lead to over-reporting of certain factors and attributions, perhaps particularly of peri- and post-traumatic factors. The review by Brewin *et al* (2000) did not include early emotional symptoms or dissociation. Neither review included other potentially important factors such as the receipt of intervention, comorbidity, physical difficulties, coping strategies and the presence or absence of a compensation claim. Despite these issues the reviews are of high-quality methodologically and seem likely to provide a representative picture of research published between 1980 and 2000.

Reassuringly, there was some consistency in the results of the two reviews. All the factors considered showed relatively small associations with PTSD. Pre-traumatic factors appeared less associated with outcome than peri- and post-traumatic factors, although there was greater homogeneity among the results of the pre-traumatic factors. Of the overlapping factors considered, family psychiatric history was weakly associated with PTSD in both reviews, as was prior psychiatric history (included in prior adjustment in Ozer *et al*, 2003) and prior trauma (considered as three separate factors in Brewin *et al*, 2000). Similar results were obtained for trauma severity (Brewin *et al*, 2000) and perceived life threat (Ozer *et al*, 2003). Reported lack of social support after the traumatic event had the strongest association with PTSD (0.4) in the review by Brewin *et al* (2000) and the second strongest (0.28) in the review by Ozer *et al* (2003). The other measures employed in the two studies did not overlap.

8.2.4 Post-2000 research on risk factors

There have been a few more recent studies of the same risk factors considered by Brewin *et al* (2000) and Ozer *et al* (2003). Holbrook *et al* (2001) diagnosed 261 (32%) of 824 individuals as

Table 8.2 Summary of factors considered in the study by Ozer *et al* (2003)				
Risk factor	No. of studies	Population size (*n*)	Weighted average effect size *r*	95% CI
Prior trauma	23	5308	0.17	0.11 to 0.22
Prior adjustment	23	6797	0.17	0.10 to 0.23
Family history of psychopathology	9	667	0.17	0.04 to 0.29
Perceived life threat	12	3524	0.26	0.18 to 0.34
Perceived support	11	3537	−0.28	−0.40 to −0.15
Peri-traumatic emotions	5	1755	0.26	0.08 to 0.42
Peri-traumatic dissociation	16	3534	0.35	0.16 to 0.52

From Ozer, E. J., Best, S. R., Lipsey, T. L. & Weiss, D. S. (2003) Predictors of post-traumatic stress disorder and symptoms in adults: a meta-analysis. *Psychological Bulletin*, **129**, 52–73. Copyright © 2003 by the American Psychological Association. Adapted with permission.

having PTSD 6 months after major physical trauma. Factors associated with a PTSD diagnosis included perceived threat to life, female gender, younger age and lower income. Mayou *et al* (2002) reported a 3-year follow-up of 546 individuals involved in road traffic accidents: factors associated with increased risk of PTSD at 3 years included female gender, and perceived threat and dissociation during the accident. Van Loey *et al* (2003) found that PTSD symptoms in 301 burn trauma victims were predicted by female gender.

8.2.5 Other factors

In addition to the factors identified in the reviews described above, the Guideline Development Group also considered a number of other factors as being of potential importance. Three of these (the nature of the intervention, comorbidity and cognitive factors) are dealt with elsewhere in the guideline. The fourth and fifth factors – compensation and physical injury – are considered below.

8.2.5.1 Compensation

Compensation issues have been much discussed as a possible maintaining factor for PTSD. However, compensation clearly illustrates why caution is required in suggesting a causative effect of an associated factor. Individuals claiming compensation are presumably more likely to have a psychiatric injury, as this would appropriately be part of the basis of their claim. It has also been argued that individuals claiming compensation are more likely to report higher levels of distress through some manipulation of their symptoms. Additionally, the compensation process often involves regular reminders such as correspondence from lawyers and medico-legal assessments which may re-traumatise individuals.

The concept of 'compensation neurosis' has been challenged by several authors and involves the use of the word 'neurosis' inappropriately and pejoratively. Mendelson (1995) described it as 'simplistic and false' as a result of his follow-up study of 760 litigants and argued that its continued use reflected more on the attitudes and biases of those who used it than on the individuals who were labelled with it. He found that 396 of the 760 litigants he studied had returned to work prior to settlement of the claim. Of the remaining litigants, 99 could not be traced at follow-up, a mean of 23 months post-settlement. Of the 264 who were traced, 198 were still not working; of those who had returned to work the mean time to this was 12.5 months post-settlement. Fontana & Rosenheck (1998) studied 1008 war veterans with PTSD and found no compensation-seeking effect in outcome among out-patients but a significant effect among some in-patients, particularly those on longer-stay units. The reason for this was not clear, but the authors argued that overstatement of symptoms was the most likely explanation. Franklin *et al* (2003) interviewed 204 compensation-seeking US military veterans using the Minnesota Multiphasic Personality Inventory. A large number (84%) had elevated results on at least one scale used to identify overreporting, but Franklin *et al* concluded that the scales appeared to identify both overreporting and extreme pathology. They argued that a majority of compensation-seeking veterans did not overreport their symptoms.

Bryant & Harvey (1995) and Ehlers *et al* (1998) in their studies of motor vehicle accident survivors, and Bisson *et al* (1997) in a study of burns victims, found an association between PTSD and compensation. Mayou *et al* (2002) found that planned or initiated claims at 1 year following road traffic accidents and unsettled claims at 3 years were associated with the presence of PTSD at 3 years. Bryant & Harvey (2003) reported a prospective study of 171 motor vehicle accident survivors, of whom 20 had initiated compensation within 6 months but had settled by 2 years, 73 had initiated claims by 6 months that were ongoing at 2 years, and 13 had not initiated a compensation claim. Post-traumatic stress disorder was less prevalent in those who had never initiated a claim. The majority returned to work within 6 months of the accident irrespective of compensation status. More individuals with settled claims entered psychotherapy than those with unsettled claims. The authors argued that their findings suggested that settlement of compensation claims did not influence reported PTSD.

The studies discussed above support an association between compensation and symptoms of PTSD, but there is a lack of evidence to substantiate the concept of 'compensation neurosis'. Indeed, there appears to be some evidence to support the notion that compensation is not directly causative of chronic PTSD, but the exact nature and direction of the association remains to be determined and may well be heterogeneous. For example, there may be a factor such as anger with others that is related to both PTSD and claiming compensation.

8.2.5.1.1   Healthcare professionals should not delay or withhold treatment for PTSD because of court proceedings or applications for compensation. C

8.2.5.2 Physical injury

Ehlers *et al* (1998) and Mayou *et al* (2002) found that persistent medical problems were associated with PTSD and its severity at 1 year and 3 years after road traffic accidents. Whether or not an individual was admitted to hospital as a result of physical injuries had a smaller association with poorer outcome. Bownes *et al* (1990) found that physical injury was associated with higher rates of PTSD in rape victims. Considerable work has been done in this area with burns trauma victims. There are some conflicting results but overall there appears to be an association between severity of burn and psychological distress, although this association seems unlikely to be a strong one. Of 23 studies identified in one review (Bisson, 2000), one found a relationship between percentage burn and a positive psychological outcome, sixteen found no association and six found an association with increased psychological sequelae. Involvement of hands or face was considered in nine studies, with an association with negative outcome in four and no relationship in five. Van Loey *et al* (2003) found that percentage burn, length of hospital stay and involvement of hands were associated with PTSD symptoms.

The influence of a head injury on outcome is perhaps more contentious. Some studies have suggested that individuals who lost consciousness around the time of a trauma were less likely to develop psychological sequelae (e.g. Adler, 1943). However, more recent studies have challenged this. Chemtob *et al* (1998), in a study of male combat veterans, found that 36 (61%) of those who reported a history of head injury had PTSD compared with 11 (41%) of those who did not. Almost half of those who reported a head injury also reported loss of consciousness. Bryant & Harvey (1998) found that 19 (24%) of 79 consecutive adult patients who sustained a mild traumatic brain injury following a motor vehicle accident satisfied criteria for PTSD at 6 months' follow-up. In a study of 125 male veterans with spinal cord injury, Radnitz *et al* (1998) found that head injury at the time predicted current PTSD symptom severity but not diagnosis or lifetime diagnosis and that loss of consciousness was not consistently associated with PTSD symptom severity or diagnosis. Mayou *et al* (2000) found that PTSD was more commonly found in road traffic accident victims who were rendered unconscious, at both 3 months and 1 year, compared with those who were not. Klein *et al* (2003) reviewed the literature on traumatic brain injury and PTSD, found conflicting evidence but concluded that when traumatic brain injury caused impaired memory of the traumatic event it might protect against the development of PTSD.

8.2.5.2.1   Post-traumatic stress disorder may present with a range of symptoms (including re-experiencing, avoidance, hyperarousal, depression, emotional numbing and anger) and therefore when assessing for PTSD, members of secondary care medical teams should ask in a sensitive manner whether or not patients with such symptoms have suffered a traumatic experience and give specific examples of traumatic events (for example, assaults, rape, road traffic accidents, childhood sexual abuse and traumatic childbirth). GPP

8.3 Screening

In practice, PTSD screening is only likely to be done when someone is felt to be at higher than usual risk of suffering from the disorder. Common reasons for this are known involvement in a major traumatic event, being from a higher-risk group (e.g. refugees, asylum seekers, military/ex-military and emergency services personnel, the bereaved, prison officers and journalists) or the presence of some symptoms of PTSD.

The key measures of effectiveness of a PTSD screening instrument are generally considered to be sensitivity (the probability that someone with a PTSD diagnosis will have tested positive), specificity (the probability that someone without a PTSD diagnosis will have tested negative), the positive predictive power (the probability that someone with a positive test result will receive a diagnosis of PTSD), the negative predictive power (the probability that someone with a negative test result will not receive a PTSD diagnosis) and overall efficiency (percentage of cases correctly classified by the test as having or not having PTSD). A good test will have good results on all these different measures. The relative value placed on each measure in determining which test to use is dependent on several factors, including the prevalence of the disorder among the group being considered and the risks of missing a diagnosis. It can be argued that the positive predictive value is of particular importance. As the prevalence of a condition reduces, so does the positive predictive value, i.e. there are more individuals who have screened positive but do not have the condition (false positives). This has major implications in terms of screening for PTSD, which will usually be expected to occur at a prevalence of less than 50%. One way of addressing this issue would be to screen only populations who are likely to have a high prevalence of PTSD, i.e. targeted screening as opposed to large population screening.

8.3.1 Screening for individuals who may develop PTSD

There has been some interest in determining if the later development of PTSD can be predicted by screening individuals shortly after a traumatic event. One of the major benefits of this would be to allow the identification of high-risk individuals who might benefit from evidence-based brief early interventions such as those discussed in Chapter 7. Most screening instruments have focused on the detection of early psychological distress shortly after the traumatic event rather than the other factors associated with PTSD discussed above.

Perhaps the most studied screening approach to date is that of diagnosing acute stress disorder (ASD) within 1 month of the traumatic event. In the study of 79 consecutive adult patients who sustained a mild traumatic brain injury following a motor vehicle accident (Bryant & Harvey, 1998), ASD was diagnosed in 11 patients within 1 month of the trauma, and at 6 months' follow-up 19 satisfied criteria for PTSD. The latter disorder was diagnosed in 9 (82%) of the patients who had been diagnosed with ASD and in 7 (11%) of those who had not.

Bryant (2003) subsequently reviewed ten prospective studies of ASD to determine if it was predictive of chronic PTSD. The proportion who went on to develop PTSD ranged from 30% to 83% at 6 months, and the proportion of PTSD sufferers at 6 months who had suffered from ASD ranged from 10% to 61%. He concluded that the ASD diagnosis did not have adequate predictive power and postulated that biological and cognitive factors occurring in the acute post-traumatic phase might provide more accurate means of predicting chronic PTSD. Creamer *et al* (2004) found ASD to have low sensitivity in predicting PTSD among 307 consecutive admissions to a critical care unit following severe physical injury. Only 3 (1%) individuals satisfied the criteria for ASD, 29 (9%) suffered from PTSD at 3 months and 32 (10%) at 1 year. Dissociative symptoms were found to be rarely endorsed and therefore particularly unhelpful in predicting PTSD.

Shalev *et al* (1997) interviewed the victims of various traumas who presented to an emergency unit with physical injuries. Of the 239 participants, 191 completed questionnaires and were interviewed at 1 week, 1 month and 4 months after the traumatic event. The study found no significant loss of power between 1 week and 1 month in predicting the presence of PTSD at 4 months. There was no difference in the efficiency of the specific traumatic stress symptom measures used (the Impact of Event Scale and the Mississippi Rating Scale for Combat Related PTSD – Civilian Trauma Version) and the non-specific ones (the State–Trait Anxiety Scale and the Peritraumatic Experiences Scale). The performance of the instruments was considered using various cut-off values. Table 8.3 displays the results obtained by Shalev *et al* using cut-off values that gave a balance between sensitivity and specificity and highlights the limited overall efficiency. The authors concluded that the instruments were better at predicting recovery than predicting individuals who would go on to develop PTSD.

Unfortunately the results of the currently available research on predictive screening are disappointing. No accurate way of screening for the later development of PTSD has been identified. All the instruments considered suffer from limited overall efficiency.

8.3.2 Screening for the presence of PTSD

Several screening instruments, mainly questionnaires containing traumatic stress symptoms, have been developed to detect the presence of PTSD. These may be of potential use for screening programmes following major traumatic events and for use in primary and secondary care within the NHS, when usually individuals with PTSD will first present to someone other than a mental health professional, such as a primary care worker or an emergency unit worker.

Scale	Cut-off	Sensitivity	Specificity	PPV	NPV
Table 8.3 Sensitivity, specificity and power of questionnaires to predict the development of PTSD					
Impact of Event Scale	35	0.72	0.67	0.31	0.36
State–Trait Anxiety Scale	55	0.66	0.65	0.28	0.38
Mississippi Rating Scale for Combat Related PTSD[1]	85	0.78	0.69	0.34	0.35
Clinician-Administered PTSD Scale	51	0.74	0.86	0.52	0.15

After Shalev *et al*, 1997.
NPV, negative predictive value; PPV, positive predictive value.
1. Civilian Trauma version.

8.3.2.1 Screening questionnaires

The only systematic review of screening questionnaires for the presence of PTSD is by Brewin (2005), who performed a systematic search of various databases and hand-searched journals, books and reference lists to identify studies that had attempted to validate self-completed questionnaires. Only general questionnaires (as opposed to ones of specific populations) of fewer than 30 items, validated against a structured interview that yielded a diagnosis of PTSD, were included. Twenty-two different data-sets from the 13 instruments listed below were identified.

1. The Impact of Event Scale (IES; Horowitz *et al*, 1979) contains 15 questions about intrusion and avoidance relative to a specified event, which are answered on a four-point scale.

2. The PTSD Checklist – Civilian version (PCL–C; Weathers *et al*, 1991; Weathers & Ford, 1996) contains the 17 DSM–IV PTSD symptoms, which are rated on a scale ranging from 1 ('not at all') to 5 ('extremely').

3. The Posttraumatic Stress Symptom Scale – Self-Report version (PSS–SR) and Post-traumatic Diagnostic Scale (PDS) (Foa *et al*, 1993). Developed from the 17 DSM–III–R PTSD symptoms to the DSM–IV ones rated on a four-point scale. The PDS includes 12 preliminary items inquiring about the occurrence of specific traumatic experiences and a further 9 questions assessing impairment.

4. The Davidson Trauma Scale (DTS; Davidson *et al*, 1997) consists of 17 items corresponding to each of the DSM–IV symptoms scored for both frequency and severity during the previous week on scales of 0–4.

5. The SPAN test (Meltzer-Brody *et al*, 1999) comprises the 'startle', 'physiological upset on reminders', 'anger' and 'numbness' questions derived from the DTS, scored for both frequency and severity during the previous week on scales of 0–4.

6. The Self-Rating Scale for Post-traumatic Stress Disorder (SRS–PTSD; Carlier *et al*, 1998) contains 17 items corresponding to the DSM–III–R symptoms of PTSD using a three-point scale.

7. The Brief DSMPTSD–III–R (Ursano *et al*, 1995) and DSMPTSD–IV (BPTSD–6; Fullerton *et al*, 2000) are based on the IES and the Symptom Checklist (SCL–90–R; Derogatis, 1983) as core instruments, supplemented by 12 PTSD-specific items scored on a five-point scale. Fullerton *et al* (2000) reported on the use of these 12 items alone in screening for PTSD.

8. The Screen for Post-traumatic Stress Symptoms (SPTSS; Carlson, 2001) is not tied to a single traumatic event and covers the 17 DSM–IV items using an 11-point scale.

9. The Post-traumatic Stress Disorder Questionnaire (PTSD–Q; Cross & McCanne, 2001) has the 17 DSM–IV symptoms and uses a seven-point scale.

10. The Penn Inventory (Hammarberg, 1992) has questions with options of four sentences, modelled on the Beck Depression Inventory (Beck *et al*, 1961), which measure the presence or absence of PTSD symptoms as well as their degree, frequency or intensity.

11. The Trauma Screening Questionnaire (TSQ; Brewin *et al*, 2002) consists of the ten re-experiencing and arousal items from the PSS–SR (Foa *et al*, 1993), modified to provide only two response options. Respondents indicate whether or not they have experienced each symptom at least twice in the past week.

12   The Disaster-Related Psychological Screening Test (DRPST; Chou *et al*, 2003) consists of seven items (three re-experiencing symptoms, three arousal symptoms, and one arousal symptom answered present or absent) derived from the 17 PTSD symptoms and nine symptoms of major depression.

13   The Self-Rating Inventory for Post-traumatic Stress Disorder (SRIP; Hovens *et al*, 2002) consists of 22 items based on DSM–IV symptoms using a four-point intensity scale.

The results of the various screening instruments used were impressive, with an overall mean diagnostic efficiency of 86.5%. Given the relatively uniform results obtained across the instruments it seems appropriate to follow Brewin's advice in determining which instruments to recommend in routine practice. He argued that the ideal instrument would have fewer items, simpler response scales, simple scoring methods and perform as well if not better than longer and more complex measures. Such instruments are likely to be more acceptable and provide less scope for error or uncertainty in terms of answering the questions. Another important consideration on which we have little information is their acceptability to individuals with and without PTSD who are asked to complete them.

The questionnaires that appear to have the greatest potential for routine use in primary care are the Trauma Screening Questionnaire and the SPAN, although both have their limitations. The TSQ has ten questions requiring yes/no answers, which, for example, may be considered too many in a busy primary care setting. The SPAN has only four questions but the nature of the SPAN symptoms (e.g. numbing) is not so straightforward, and the response scales (0–4 ratings for both frequency and severity) and scoring are more complicated than is the case for the TSQ. The other instrument that performed well was the Impact of Event Scale. Many individuals will be familiar with this scale and, like the TSQ, it has the advantage of having been validated on independent samples and within 1 year of a traumatic event. Table 8.4 lists the relative efficiencies of the IES, SPAN and TSQ. Unfortunately, several studies determined the cut-off point *post hoc*, i.e. they determined the 'best fit' with the results they obtained rather than stating *a priori* what the cut-off value was to be; this potentially reduced the reliability of the results and increased the apparent efficiency of the scale.

8.3.2.2 Other studies

Screening for psychological illness, including PTSD, has been evaluated in the British army (Rona *et al*, 2004*a*). In this study 314 service personnel completed a 17-item PTSD checklist as part of a longer screening document that covered other psychological and physical symptoms as well as alcohol use. The participants were subsequently assessed by a medical officer masked to the screening results, who determined if further help was required. The positive predictive value for the PTSD checklist was 67%, somewhat better than the performance of the other screening measures. However, the screening programme did not appear to be acceptable to service personnel. Less than 30% of individuals invited to attend a medical centre for further evaluation after screening attended. It was noted that those who screened positive for PTSD were less likely to attend than controls (Rona *et al*, 2004*b*).

8.3.2.3 Conclusions

So far there is no sound evidence to support a national or large population screening programme for PTSD. None of the screening questionnaires considered would fulfil all of the relevant National Screening Committee criteria. There is evidence that several measures can aid the detection of PTSD, but they require refinement and crucially integration into a screening programme with appropriate follow-up before routine, large-scale administration can be seriously considered. Indeed, the National Steering Committee guidelines state that no such screening programme will be implemented in the NHS without evidence from a properly conducted, randomised controlled trial.

This raises important questions as to how proactive to be in trying to identify individuals with PTSD following traumatic events. The case for screening in large populations where a low prevalence or rapidly decreasing prevalence of PTSD is expected is weak, not least because of the large number of 'false positives' that would be generated. A stronger case can be made to consider targeted screening when high prevalence rates are expected, for example for those directly involved in the heart of an extremely traumatic event. The strength of the case will also depend on various factors including the simplicity of administration of the screening tool,

Table 8.4 Sensitivity, specificity and predictive power of screening tests for PTSD

Reference	Instrument	Number of items	Sample	Prevalence of PTSD (%)	Sensitivity	Specificity	Positive predictive power	Negative predictive power	Overall efficiency
Neal et al (1994)	IES/cut-off 35[1]	15	Mixed trauma (n=70)	51	0.89	0.88	0.89	0.88	0.89
Wohlfarth et al (2003)	IES/cut-off 35	15	Crime victims (n=79)[2]	13	0.89	0.94	0.67	0.99	0.94
Meltzer-Brody et al (1999)	SPAN/cut-off 5[1]	4	Mixed trauma (n=121)	46	0.84	0.91	0.89	0.87	0.88
Meltzer-Brody et al (1999)	SPAN/cut-off 5	4	Mixed trauma (n=122)	51	0.77	0.82	0.81	0.78	0.80
Brewin et al (2002)	TSQ/cut-off 6[1]	10	Rail crash survivors (n=41)[2]	34	0.86	0.93	0.86	0.93	0.90
Brewin et al (2002)	TSQ/cut-off 6	10	Crime victims (n=157)[2]	27	0.76	0.97	0.91	0.92	0.92
Mean performance of all measures					0.83	0.85	0.70	0.90	0.86

IES, Impact of Event Scale; SPAN, Startle, Physiological arousal, Anger and Numbness items from the Davidson Trauma Scale; TSQ, Trauma Screening Questionnaire.
1. Cut-off value determined *post hoc*.
2. Administered within 1 year of trauma.

cultural validity and acceptability to the population being considered, and the existence of easily accessible full assessment and effective management options for those who screen positive.

It can be argued that until a screening programme has been shown to be effective, resources should first be focused on raising awareness. This would involve the provision of information to those affected and their families, and the education of those most likely to be confronted by individuals with symptoms, such as general practitioners and employers.

8.4 Clinical practice recommendations

8.4.1 Individuals at high risk

8.4.1.1   For individuals at high risk of developing PTSD following a major disaster, consideration should be given (by those responsible for coordination of the disaster plan) to the routine use of a brief screening instrument for PTSD at 1 month after the disaster. C

8.4.1.2   For programme refugees and asylum seekers at high risk of developing PTSD, consideration should be given (by those responsible for management of the refugee programme) to the routine use of a brief screening instrument for PTSD as part of the initial refugee healthcare assessment. This should be a part of any comprehensive physical and mental health screen. C

8.5 Research recommendations

8.5.1 Screening

8.5.1.1   An appropriately designed longitudinal study should be conducted to determine if a simple screening instrument, acceptable to those receiving it, can identify individuals who develop PTSD after traumatic events and can be used as part of a screening programme to ensure individuals with PTSD receive effective interventions.

Rationale

Post-traumatic stress disorder is a common and potentially disabling condition. It has been shown that some individuals are more likely to develop PTSD following traumatic events than others (e.g. Brewin *et al*, 2000) and that individuals with acute PTSD respond to trauma-focused psychological interventions (e.g. Bryant *et al*, 1998; Ehlers *et al*, 2003). Interventions for everyone following a traumatic event have not been shown to be effective (Rose *et al*, 2004). It has therefore been argued that a standard response following a traumatic event should be to detect individuals who develop PTSD and offer them trauma-focused psychological interventions (e.g. Bisson *et al*, 2003). Trials of screening programmes should determine if this approach is feasible and effective and is consistent with the criteria for such screening programmes developed by the National Screening Committee (2003).

9 Children and young people with PTSD

9.1 Introduction

When the diagnosis of PTSD was first formulated in 1980 (American Psychiatric Association, 1980) it was initially believed that it would not be relevant to children and young people. This was soon demonstrated to be false and it is now accepted that children and young people can develop PTSD following traumatic events. For the purposes of this guideline, 'children' refers to ages 2–12 years and 'young people' (adolescents) to ages 13–18 years.

9.2 Developmental differences

9.2.1 Post-traumatic stress reactions in children

The broad categories of PTSD symptoms (re-experiencing, avoidance/numbing and increased arousal) are present in children as well as in adults. The requirements of DSM criteria for the diagnosis of PTSD in children are that children must exhibit at least one re-experiencing symptom, three avoidance/numbing symptoms and two increased arousal symptoms. From the age of 8–10 years, following traumatic events, children display reactions closely similar to those manifested by adults. Below 8 years of age, and in particular below the age of 5 years, there is less agreement as to the range and severity of the reactions. Scheeringa *et al* (1995) have suggested an alternative set of criteria for the diagnosis of PTSD in children, placing more emphasis on regressive behaviours and new fears, but these have yet to be fully validated.

Traumatic reactions in children have been less extensively studied than in adults and there are few naturalistic, longitudinal studies mapping the natural history of these reactions. It has long been recognised (Eth, 2001) that it is much more difficult to elicit evidence of emotional numbing in young children. Other items indicating avoidance reactions in children simply are not relevant, thereby making it difficult for children to meet DSM criteria for that part of the diagnostic algorithm (although this does not apply to the ICD diagnosis).

In general, it is agreed that children display a wide range of stress reactions. To some extent these vary with age, with younger children displaying more overt aggression and destructiveness. They may also show more repetitive play about the traumatic event, and this may even be reflected in repetitive drawing.

9.2.2 Family influences

As with other anxiety disorders, children's reactions are influenced by parental reactions. In addition to modelling on their parents' reactions (social influence) there are probably also inherited dispositions to react adversely to traumatic events (genetic influence). This has not been adequately studied in relation to PTSD in children.

What is clinically described and widely accepted is that children are very sensitive to their parents' reactions – both to the event itself and to talking about it afterwards. Children often say that they choose not to discuss a traumatic event and/or their reactions to it with their parents, as they do not wish to upset the parents further. This is, in part, one of the reasons for the finding that even more than with other anxiety disorders, parents grossly underestimate the degree of stress reactions experienced by their children. Thus, one cannot rely solely on parental report when making diagnoses or estimating prevalence. A study by McFarlane (1987) suggested that in an Australian bush fire, the children's reactions to the event were fully accounted for by the mothers' own mental health, rather than by the exposure to the fire. However, as mothers had rated both their own adjustment and that of their children, this finding was suspect. Subsequent studies (for example Smith *et al*, 2001) have found that direct exposure is usually a stronger determinant of child reaction, with maternal reactions being important modifying influences.

It is important therefore always to consider the nature and extent of a child's exposure to a traumatic event.

9.2.3 Multiple versus single trauma

Many children presenting with symptoms of PTSD may have been subjected to multiple traumas such as childhood sexual abuse or domestic violence. The most common form of multiple trauma for children that has been studied and investigated is childhood sexual abuse, which often occurs in secret and is repeated over a long period. The traumatic reactions associated with such multiple trauma can be usefully construed as similar to those that follow from single traumas, although issues of abuse of power, loss of trust and so on do make them different. Although there is evidence that the social circumstances and events surrounding multiple traumas for children may have consequences for their future management (Ramchandani & Jones, 2003), the evidence does not support the idea that multiple traumas are associated with significantly different outcomes or that the treatment required for PTSD is significantly different when compared with single traumas.

9.3 Incidence, prevalence and natural history

9.3.1 Prevalence

Most epidemiological studies have been of older young people and adults. Giaconia *et al* (1995) reported a lifetime prevalence of 6% in a community sample of older young people. Kessler *et al* (1995) reported a lifetime prevalence of 10% using data collected from older young people and adults in the US National Comorbidity Survey. In contrast, the British National Survey of Mental Health of over 10 000 children and young people (Meltzer *et al*, 2000) reported that 0.4% of children aged 11–15 years were diagnosed with PTSD, with girls showing twice the rate of boys. Below the age of 10 years, PTSD was scarcely registered. This lower rate is, of course, a point prevalence estimate and is bound to be lower than a lifetime prevalence estimate. Moreover, the screening instrument employed was not specifically developed to screen for PTSD.

9.3.2 Incidence

Estimates of the incidence of PTSD are more frequently reported after various natural and other disasters. Rates vary enormously, partly as a result of different methodologies and partly as a result of different types of traumatic event. In various studies of the effects of road traffic accidents (not resulting in an overnight stay in hospital) rates of 25–30% are reported. The study of 200 young survivors of the sinking of the cruise ship *Jupiter* (Yule *et al*, 2000) reported an incidence of PTSD of 51%. Most cases manifested within the first few weeks, with delayed onset being rare. Other disorders such as anxiety and depression were common as well. Studies of the mental health of child refugees from war-torn countries find the incidence to be close to 67% (W. Yule, personal communication, 2004). Therefore, significantly increased demands may be made at all levels of primary and secondary child and adolescent mental health services following traumatic events.

The implication of this for the NHS is that while the numbers of children and young people experiencing PTSD at any one point in time may be approaching 1% and represents a significant level of morbidity in any community, by way of comparison, in adults PTSD has a point prevalence of 1.5–3%, and schizophrenia in adults has a prevalence of 1%.

9.3.3 Natural history

The follow-up study of young people who survived the sinking of the *Jupiter* found that 15% still met criteria for PTSD 5–7 years after the event. More recently, a 33-year follow-up of the children who survived the Aberfan landslide disaster found that 29% of those traced and interviewed still met criteria for PTSD (Morgan *et al*, 2003). In other words, in the absence of effective therapy, the long-term effects of life-threatening, traumatic events in childhood can be severe.

9.4 Diagnostic and assessment measures

9.4.1 Children over 7 years old

More is known about screening, assessment and diagnosis in children over the age of 7 years because above that age many children can read independently and can complete self-rating scales. It is much more time-consuming and expensive to conduct standardised clinical interviews with both parent and child to establish a diagnosis in large groups of children.

9.4.1.1 Self-completed PTSD scales

The most widely used self-report scales in research and clinical settings are the Children's Impact of Event Scale, the Child Post Traumatic Stress Reaction Index and the Child PTSD Symptom Scale. For a detailed recent review of self-completed scales, see Ohan et al (2002).

The Children's Impact of Event Scale was developed from the widely used adult self-report PTSD measure, the Impact of Event Scale (Horowitz et al, 1979). The adult version has been used with children and young people in its original 15-item version. Following two large principal component analyses, a briefer eight-item version was developed for children (Yule, 1997) and subsequently expanded to a 13-item version to include five items attempting to measure arousal (see http://www.childrenandwar.org).

The Child Post Traumatic Stress Reaction Index (CPTS–RI) was originally rated following interview by a clinician with the carer and sometimes the child. More recently it has been modified to be a self-report instrument (Pynoos et al, 1987; Pynoos, 2002).

The Child PTSD Symptom Scale (CPSS; Foa et al, 2001) is a 17-item scale used both in initial diagnosis and in monitoring progress. It contains a brief functional impairment rating.

9.4.1.2 Structured interviews for PTSD in children and young people

Structured interviews for children are not well developed; three of the more commonly used scales are described below.

- The Clinician-Administered PTSD Scale for Children and Adolescents for DSM–IV (CAPS–CA; Nader et al, 2002) is modelled on the adult CAPS and is widely regarded as the gold standard measure to diagnose DSM–IV PTSD in children.
- The Anxiety Disorders Interview Schedule for Children for DSM–IV (ADIS–C; Silverman & Albano, 1996) can be used to diagnose a range of anxiety disorders and has a specific module for PTSD symptoms.
- The Schedule for Affective Disorders and Schizophrenia for School Age Children (K–SADS; Kaufman et al, 1997) can be used to diagnose a range of anxiety disorders and has specific supplementary questions for measuring PTSD symptoms. Both the parent and the child are interviewed.

Trauma-specific PTSD measures

The Children's Impact of Traumatic Events Scale – Revised (CITES–R; Wolfe et al, 1991) is a measure of PTSD symptoms arising from sexual abuse and measures aspects such as social reactions to disclosure, eroticism and abuse-related attributions in addition to non-trauma-specific PTSD symptoms.

9.4.2 Children aged 7 years or younger

No consensus has emerged as to how to measure PTSD symptoms in children aged 7 years or younger. In the recent past a range of scales measuring behavioural problems have been adopted such as the Child Behaviour Checklist (CBCL; Achenbach & Edelbrock, 1983) and, for children who have suffered sexual abuse, the Child Sexual Behaviour Inventory (CSBI; Friedrich et al, 1992).

9.4.2.1 Measures of outcome for children within this review

Given the lack of consensus about the measurement of PTSD for younger children, a range of child-specific measures were included in this review (Table 9.1).

Table 9.1	Measures of PTSD in children			
Scale	Age range	No. of items and score range	Self-report/interview	Notes
Children's Impact of Event Scale	8–18 years	15–13 items depending on version, 4-point range	Self-report	
Child Post Traumatic Stress Reaction Index (CPTS–RI)	8–18 years	20 items, 5-point range	Clinician-rated and self-report versions	
Child PTSD Symptom Scale (CPSS)	8–15 years	24 items, 4-point range	Self-report	
Clinician-Administered PTSD Scale for Children and Adolescents for DSM–IV (CAPS–CA)	8–18 years	32 items, 5-point range	Clinician-rated	
Anxiety Disorders Interview Schedule for Children (ADIS–C) (PTSD module)	Not specified	(PTSD module only) 24 items, scale 'yes'/'no'/'other'	Clinician-rated (child and parent/caretaker interviewed)	
Schedule for Affective Disorders and Schizophrenia for School-Age Children (K–SADS; K–SADS–E; K–SADS–PL) (PTSD supplement)	6–18 years	Variable, approximately 17 items with varying scales, typically a 4-point scale	Clinician-rated (child and parent/caretaker interviewed)	PL, Present and Lifetime version; E, Epidemiological version
Children's Impact of Traumatic Events Scale – Revised	8–16 years	78 items, 3-point scale	Clinician-rated	Trauma-specific (sexual abuse)
Child Behavior Checklist (CBCL) parent version	2–16 years	113 items, 3-point scale	Parent-rated	Measures adaptive competencies and behavioural problems
Child Sexual Behavior Inventory (CSBI)	Not specified	42 items, 4-point scale	Parent-rated	Measures sexual behaviours
Child Report of PTSD Symptoms (CROPS)[1]	7–17 years	24 items	Self-report	
Parent Report of PTSD Symptoms (PROPS)[1]	7–17 years	28 items	Parent-rated	Designed to be used as companion instrument to CROPS

1. Greenwald & Rubin, 1999.

In addition to PTSD scales, a range of child measures of depression, anxiety and quality of life were included within the review.

9.4.2.2 Measures of exposure to traumatic events

The structured interviews indicate the most likely adverse life events that may result in PTSD in children and young people, but they do not constitute formal measures. General practitioners, paediatricians and child mental health workers who see a child presenting with a sudden change in sleep pattern, nightmares and jumpiness should enquire about intrusive images and then ask whether the child has experienced any threatening life event such as a bad accident, natural disaster, or physical or sexual abuse.

9.4.2.3 Measures of process and related aspects

Increasing attention is being paid to cognitive factors such as the way in which children attribute blame for an event or the extent to which they erroneously believe that they might have died in the accident. The effective social support that is available to the child is also likely to be a key determinant of whether the child continues to respond adversely (Joseph et al, 1993). Standard measures of these aspects are still being developed.

9.5 Psychological interventions

Early intervention would be attractive if it could be shown that it prevented later development of PTSD or other disorders, but, as with adult studies, there have been few properly controlled trials of any early intervention. The only one known is that of Stallard *et al* (2005), which is discussed below.

Ramchandani & Jones (2003) reported a systematic review of RCTs treating a range of psychological symptoms in sexually abused children. They identified 12 RCTs: three investigating group CBT; six investigating individual CBT; one of adding group therapy to a family therapy intervention; and two comparing individual (non-CBT) therapy with group therapy. However, the dependent (outcome) measures were very varied, and only five studies looked at recognised, specific measures of PTSD.

9.5.1 Studies included

The inclusion criteria that 70% of participants within a study have a PTSD diagnosis was not applied for the review of children and young people because, as discussed above, diagnosis of child and adolescent PTSD is still evolving and is relatively undeveloped for younger children. Otherwise the inclusion criteria were identical to those for adults (see Chapter 4). However, all studies had to include a measure of the child's PTSD symptoms, although as discussed above (see section 9.4.5) a wider range of measures was deemed more acceptable than for adult PTSD scales.

From the main search for RCTs (see Appendix 6), 11 studies of psychological interventions were identified by the Guideline Development Group as meeting the inclusion criteria: CELANO 1996, COHEN 1996, COHEN 1997 (COHEN 1997 is a follow-up study to COHEN 1996), COHEN 1998, COHEN 2004, DEBLINGER 1999, JABERGHADERI[1], KING 2000, STALLARD, STEIN 2003 and TROWELL 2002. References given in shortened format and summary characteristics of individual included trials are given in Appendix 14.

9.5.1.1 Interventions considered

Broadly, four different psychological interventions were covered within the included studies: one early intervention treatment (debriefing), cognitive–behavioural therapy, eye movement desensitisation and reprocessing (EMDR) and supportive therapy (fuller definitions of these treatment classifications, as they apply to adults, are given in Chapter 5).

Within these broad categories of treatments there was considerable variation in how treatments were delivered, with many studies allowing for some part of treatment being delivered to the caretaker as well as the child, either individually or in sessions for both the child and the caretaker. Two studies involved treatment arms that consisted of treatments delivered to groups of children (STEIN 2003, TROWELL 2002). Given the many different formats in which the four treatments were delivered, it was not possible to combine many of the studies for the purpose of this review. Table 9.2 provides a summary of the range of interventions and delivery formats (treatment delivered to both the caretaker/parent and the child, to the child individually, etc.) for which eligible studies were available.

9.5.1.2 Populations – childhood sexual abuse and other traumas

Nine of the studies related to childhood sexual abuse and were analysed separately from the remaining studies, which covered a range of traumatic events including witnessing violence, natural disaster, war and burns.

9.5.2 Childhood sexual abuse

Trials comparing different forms of CBT with waiting list or supportive therapy

Seven of the trials covering childhood sexual abuse compared different forms of CBT therapies against waiting list, supportive therapy or another mode of delivering CBT (CELANO 1996, COHEN 1996, COHEN 1997, COHEN 1998, COHEN 2004, DEBLINGER 1999, KING 2000).

---

1. Data from this study have now been published as Jaberghaderi *et al* (2004).

Table 9.2 Interventions for which eligible studies were available

Intervention	Debriefing	EMDR	CBT (child and carer)	CBT (child only)	CBT (mother only)	CBT (for carer and child)	CBT (child only but group format)	Individual psychotherapy
Supportive therapy	STALLARD (age 7–18, n=158)[1]		CELANO 1996, COHEN 2004 (CSA, age 8–16, n=276) COHEN 1998 (CSA, age 7–14, n=82) COHEN1996/7 (CSA, age 2–7 approx., n=86)					
Community care				DEBLINGER 1999 (CSA, age 7–13, n=50)	DEBLINGER 1999 (CSA, age 7–13, n=50)	DEBLINGER 1999 (CSA, age 7–13, n=50)		
Waiting list				KING 2000 (CSA, age 5–17, n=24)		KING 2000 (CSA, age 5–17, n=24)	STEIN 2003 (age about 10–12, n= 126)	
CBT (child only)		JABER-GHADERI (CSA, age 12–13, n=14)				KING 2000 (CSA, age 5–17, n=24)		
Group psycho-therapy								TROWELL 2002 (CSA, age 6–14, n=71)

CBT, cognitive–behavioural therapy; CSA, childhood sexual abuse (where not specified, participants had experienced a range of other traumas); EMDR, eye movement desensitisation and reprocessing.
1. Note: n denotes number of participants in the intent-to-treat sample (those randomised to a treatment condition whether or not they completed any treatment sessions).

Children over 7 years old

One large study (COHEN 2004) compared trauma-focused CBT with supportive therapy for children aged 8–14 years and a parent. Each treatment arm consisted of 12 weekly sessions of 45 min for the child individually and 45 min for the parent, although three of the weekly sessions involved 30 min of joint parent–child therapy. Supportive therapy was child- and parent-centred, allowing the child or parent to guide the structure and content of the treatment, supplemented by the provision of written psychoeducational information. Trauma-focused therapy worked on expression of feelings, coping skills and gradual exposure, whereby the children were assisted in developing their own trauma narrative as well as some psychoeducation. An earlier smaller study by COHEN 1998 of CBT versus supportive therapy for children aged 7–14 years compared similar interventions but used a behavioural-based measure to assess PTSD symptoms. Each treatment arm consisted of 12 individual treatment sessions of 90 min (45 min for the child individually and 45 min for the parent individually). Another study (CELANO 1996) compared developmentally appropriate cognitive–behavioural techniques and metaphoric techniques with supportive therapy for girls aged 8–13 years and their carers. Each treatment arm consisted of eight 1-hour weekly sessions. Sessions were split with 30 min of treatment each for the child and the carer individually, although two or three sessions included some joint work. For this review the COHEN 1998, COHEN 2004 and CELANO 1996 studies were combined.

There was limited evidence that CBT for children over 7 years old and their carers was better than supportive therapy in reducing the severity of PTSD symptoms post-treatment. For the other outcome measures post-treatment, the evidence was either inconclusive (child-rated depression, parent-rated internalising and externalising behaviours, sexualised behaviours and likelihood of leaving the study early) or indicated that there was unlikely to be a clinically important difference (child-rated anxiety). Unfortunately we do not know how sustained these improvements are because no follow-up data are currently available.

There is limited evidence favouring CBT for children over 7 years old and their parents/carers over supportive therapy on reducing the severity of PTSD symptoms (k=2; *n*=212; SMD=−0.55, 95% CI −0.83 to −0.28). ▌

The evidence is inconclusive and so it is not possible to determine if there is a clinically important difference between CBT for children over 7 years old and their parents/carers and supportive therapy on reducing self-rated post-treatment depression symptoms as measured by the Child Depression Inventory (k=2; *n*=232; SMD=−0.44, 95% CI −0.7 to −0.18). ▌

The evidence is inconclusive and so it is not possible to determine if there is a clinically important difference between CBT for children over 7 years old and their parents/carers and supportive therapy on reducing the likelihood of leaving the study early for any reason (k=2; *n*=276; RR=1.18, 95% CI 0.77 to 1.82). ▌

Children under 7 years old

The study by COHEN 1996 and its follow-up study (COHEN 1997) compared CBT with supportive therapy for children under 7 years old. Each treatment arm consisted of 12 weekly sessions of 50 min for the parent individually and 30–40 min for the child. Measurement of PTSD symptoms in very young children is still evolving, and for this study there was no direct measure of PTSD but rather a range of behavioural measures such as CBCL and CSBI. There is limited evidence favouring CBT over supportive therapy for reducing parent-rated externalising symptoms and sexualised behaviour both post-treatment and at 1-year follow-up.

There is limited evidence favouring CBT for children under 7 years old and their parents/carers over supportive therapy on reducing parent-rated externalising behaviours post-treatment as measured by the CBCL (k=1; *n*=67; SMD=−0.79, 95% CI −1.29 to −0.28). ▌

There is limited evidence favouring CBT for children under 7 years old and their parents/carers over supportive therapy on reducing parent-rated externalising behaviours at 1-year follow-up as measured by the CBCL (k=1; *n*=43; SMD=−0.53, 95% CI −1.17 to 0.11). ▌

One study (DEBLINGER 1999) compared CBT treatments with community care. Community care consisted of support from child protection workers and victim witness advocates and encouragement to seek therapists within the local community, and was treated as an active intervention for this review. There were three CBT treatment arms comprising CBT for the child only, CBT for the mother only and CBT for child and mother. Individual treatment consisted of 12 treatment sessions of 45 min. The joint treatment condition comprised 12 sessions of 90 min with individual sessions for the child and mother and some joint sessions. Children ranged in age from 7 years to 13 years.

CBT for the child versus community care

On the clinician-rated K–SADS–E, there is limited evidence favouring CBT for the child only over community care on reducing the severity of PTSD symptoms both immediately post-treatment and 6 months post-treatment. However, by the 2-year follow-up the difference between the groups had diminished. There are similar results for the CDI (self-report) measure of depression, and the advantage of CBT for child only is present at the end of treatment and at the 6-month and 2-year post-treatment evaluations. Given the nature of the community care, evidence on tolerability (leaving the study early) is difficult to interpret.

There is limited evidence favouring CBT for the child only over community care on reducing the severity of PTSD symptoms post-treatment as measured by K–SADS–E (clinician-rated measure) (k=1; *n*=35; SMD=−0.96, 95% CI −1.68 to −0.24). ▌

The evidence is inconclusive and so it is not possible to determine if there is a clinically important difference between CBT for the child only and community care on reducing the severity of PTSD symptoms at 2 years post-treatment as measured by K–SADS–E (clinician-rated measure) (k=1; *n*=35; SMD=−0.45, 95% CI −1.14 to 0.24). ▌

CBT for the mother only versus community care

Cognitive–behavioural therapy with the mother alone does not appear to have any advantage over community treatment as far as the severity of PTSD symptoms as measured by the K–SADS–E is concerned, either immediately post-treatment or at 6 months. However, somewhat surprisingly, at 2 years' follow-up the reduction in the severity of PTSD symptoms was clinically significant. For children's self-report depression symptoms the pattern is similar, with clinically significant effects occurring at 2 years' follow-up but not for earlier assessments.

The evidence is inconclusive and so it is not possible to determine if there is a clinically important difference between CBT for the mother only and community care on reducing the severity of PTSD symptoms post-treatment as measured by K–SADS–E (clinician-rated measure) (k=1; *n*=34; SMD=−0.43, 95% CI −1.13 to 0.26). ▌

There is limited evidence favouring CBT for the mother only over community care on reducing the severity of PTSD symptoms at 2 years post-treatment as measured by K–SADS–E (clinician-rated measure) (k=1; *n*=34; SMD=−0.77, 95% CI −1.48 to −0.06). ▌

Mother and child CBT versus community care

On the clinician-rated K–SADS–E there is limited evidence favouring CBT for the child and mother over community care on reducing the severity of PTSD symptoms both immediately post-treatment and at 6 months' follow-up, and this improvement was quite well sustained at 2 years' follow-up. The results for depression (child-rated) showed clinically significant improvement at the post-treatment and 2-year follow-up assessments but did not reach the threshold for clinical significance at the intervening assessments.

There is limited evidence suggesting a difference favouring mother and child CBT over community care on reducing the severity of PTSD symptoms post-treatment as measured by K–SADS–E (clinician-rated measure) (k=1; *n*=33; SMD=−0.86, 95% CI −1.58 to −0.13). ▌

There is limited evidence suggesting a difference favouring mother and child CBT over community care on reducing the severity of PTSD symptoms at 2 years post-treatment as measured by K–SADS–E (clinician-rated measure) (k=1; *n*=33; SMD=−0.64, 95% CI −1.35 to 0.07). ▌

9.5.2.3 Child only and child and mother CBT versus waiting list

One study (KING 2000) compared CBT intervention for the child individually with CBT for the child and mother jointly. The interventions consisted of 20 weekly sessions of 50 min; however, the child and mother joint intervention arm consisted of a further 20 weekly 50 min sessions of training for the parents in child behaviour management skills. Children ranged in age from 5 years to 17 years.

Individual child CBT versus waiting list

There was limited evidence of a clinically important improvement for PTSD severity, although this was not sustained at 3 months' follow-up. Effect sizes for depression and anxiety did not reach the threshold for clinical importance.

There is limited evidence suggesting a difference favouring child CBT over waiting list on reducing the severity of PTSD symptoms post-treatment as measured by the ADIS–C (clinician-rated measure) (k=1; n=24; SMD=−1.05, 95% CI −1.92 to −0.19). I

The evidence is inconclusive and so it is not possible to determine if there is a clinically important difference between child CBT and waiting list on reducing depression symptoms as measured by the CDI (k=1; n=24; SMD=−0.29, 95% CI −1.1 to 0.51). I

Child and mother CBT versus waiting list

The results were similar to those for individual child CBT versus waiting list, with limited evidence of a clinically important improvement for PTSD severity, although this was not sustained at 3 months' follow-up. Effect sizes for depression and anxiety did not reach the threshold for clinical importance.

There is limited evidence suggesting a difference favouring child and mother CBT over waiting list on reducing the severity of PTSD symptoms post-treatment as measured by the ADIS–C (clinician-rated measure) (k=1; n=24; SMD=−1.19, 95% CI −2.08 to −0.31). I

The evidence is inconclusive and so it is not possible to determine if there is a clinically important difference between child and mother CBT and waiting list on reducing depression symptoms post-treatment as measured by the CDI (k=1; n=24; SMD=−0.28, 95% CI −1.09 to 0.52). I

Individual child CBT versus child and mother CBT

Direct comparison of individual child CBT versus CBT for the child and mother did not yield evidence of clinically important differences between the two treatment conditions for PTSD severity, depression, anxiety or tolerability (leaving the study early).

9.5.2.4 Individual versus group psychotherapy for children

One study (TROWELL 2002) compared group psychotherapy with individual psychotherapy for sexually abused girls aged 6–14 years. Individual psychotherapy entailed up to 30 weekly sessions, compared with up to 18 sessions for those completing group psychotherapy. Unfortunately data were not available for total PTSD symptoms (arousal symptoms data were not reported). There was limited evidence that individual therapy was better than the group delivery in terms of reducing re-experiencing and avoidance symptoms at 12 months and 24 months post-therapy, although effect sizes were borderline for clinical importance. The evidence suggests that neither treatment was substantially better tolerated than the other.

There is limited evidence suggesting a difference favouring individual psychotherapy over group psychotherapy on reducing re-experiencing and avoidance symptoms at 12 months using the K–SADS-based Orvaschel scale (Orvaschel, 1989) (k=1; n=56; SMD=−0.49, 95% CI −1.02 to 0.05). I

9.5.2.5 Comparing EMDR with other treatment (CBT)

One unpublished study (JABERGHADERI) compared EMDR with CBT. Each treatment arm entailed up to 12 sessions (duration not specified) and CBT incorporated a degree of exposure work. The evidence was inconclusive for both child-reported and parent-reported PTSD severity, using the Child Report and the Parent Report of PTSD Symptoms, respectively (Greenwald & Rubin, 1999), and there was no evidence that one treatment was better tolerated.

The evidence is inconclusive and so it is not possible to determine if there is a clinically important difference between EMDR and CBT on reducing child self-report PTSD severity as measured by CROPS (k=1; n=14; SMD=−0.49, 95% CI −1.55 to 0.58). I

The evidence is inconclusive and so it is not possible to determine if there is a clinically important difference between EMDR and CBT on reducing parent-rated PTSD severity as measured by PROPS (k=1; n=14; SMD=−0.18, 95% CI −1.23 to 0.87). I

9.5.3 Other trauma

9.5.3.1 Debriefing

One unpublished study (STALLARD) compared single-session debriefing with a generally supportive talk to children aged 7–18 years who had been involved in road traffic accidents, within approximately 2 weeks of the accident occurring. The interventions were of approximately equal duration (68 min). The evidence suggested that there is unlikely to be a clinically important difference at 8 months' follow-up between single-session debriefing and supportive talk for self-rated measures of PTSD severity, depression and anxiety. The evidence was inconclusive for PTSD diagnosis and tolerability.

There is evidence suggesting there is unlikely to be a clinically important difference between structured debriefing and attention control on reducing child self-rated PTSD severity at 8 months' follow-up (k=1; n=132; SMD=−0.05, 95% CI −0.39 to 0.3). I

The evidence is inconclusive and so it is not possible to determine if there is a clinically important difference between structured debriefing and attention control on reducing PTSD diagnosis at 8 months' follow-up (k=1; n=158; RR=0.97, 95% CI 0.58 to 1.62). I

9.5.3.2 CBT interventions

One study (STEIN 2003) compared group CBT against waiting list (delayed intervention) for children who had been exposed to violence. The intervention consisted of ten group sessions and was delivered in a school mental health clinic. The children were approximately 10–12 years old.

Group CBT versus waiting list
The evidence is inconclusive and so it is not possible to determine if there is a clinically important difference between group CBT and waiting list on reducing the severity of PTSD symptoms post-treatment as measured by CPSS (self-report) (k=1; n=117; SMD=−0.71, 95% CI −1.08 to −0.33). I

The evidence is inconclusive and so it is not possible to determine if there is a clinically important difference between group CBT and waiting list on depressive symptoms as measured by CDI (k=1; n=117; SMD=−0.38, 95% CI −0.74 to −0.01). I

9.6 Clinical summary of psychological interventions

The above evidence suggests that psychological interventions, specifically trauma-focused cognitive–behavioural psychotherapy, can be effective for the treatment of post-traumatic stress symptoms in children and young people who have been sexually abused.

In contrast, there is very little evidence from RCTs for the efficacy of any psychological interventions for children or young people who suffer from PTSD arising from other forms of trauma. This reflects not the inconclusive nature of the evidence but rather the lack of RCTs. This means that conclusions about the effectiveness of psychological interventions for this group are reliant on extrapolation from other areas, principally work on PTSD with sexually abused children and psychological interventions for adults. Considerable caution is therefore required in drawing conclusions, particularly when drawing on downward extension of results from work with adults. Nevertheless, the limited psychological trials available suggest that trauma-focused CBT, whether delivered to children and young people with PTSD or to children who have developed PTSD in the context of childhood sexual abuse, may be of value.

Some of the trials involving children who have suffered sexual abuse included in this review specifically considered to whom and in what combination treatment should be given. For children over 7 years old who have suffered sexual abuse, treatment of the mother alone seems to be ineffective when compared with treatment of the child alone. Indeed, delivering CBT to the mother as well as the child does not of itself seem to confer much advantage over treatment of the child alone on PTSD symptoms. The lack of clinically important effects for trauma-focused CBT treatments delivered to the child and non-abusing parent or caretaker are particularly striking, given that for DEBLINGER 1999 and KING 2000 the 'joint' treatment condition essentially entails additional therapeutic time for the parent/caretaker.

No other psychological intervention has yet established a comparable evidence base, but other interventions such as EMDR show some promise, for example in the study by Chemtob *et al* (2002), which we were unable to include in the review owing to insufficient data being available for the control group, as well as in a number of non-randomised studies. The single study providing a comparison of EMDR against trauma-focused CBT (JABERGHADERI) suffered from the use of a non-standard PTSD measure. The single psychotherapy trial (TROWELL 2002) also used non-standard measures, which, combined with the lack of a waiting list or attention control, made drawing any significant clinical conclusions very difficult.

The evidence base from which to draw conclusions about the treatment of children under 7 years old suffering from PTSD is sparse. The lack of agreement on and use of a common set of measures is particularly of concern for studies of PTSD in very young children, and adds to the difficulties of interpreting an extremely limited data-set. All treatments need to be adapted to accommodate young children's less mature ways of thinking about their world, and often clinicians will use play materials and drawings to help children focus on what happened to them and how they feel. However, there is a lack of high-quality (randomised controlled trial) evidence that specific types of play therapy or art therapy have therapeutic value in treating PTSD in young children.

The evidence does not support the use of single-session debriefing for children of any age.

9.7 Pharmacological interventions

Although the use of some psychotropic drugs has increased since the 1990s (Riddle *et al*, 2001; Bramble, 2003; Wolraich, 2003), and there is belief in their efficacy, much of the increase is accounted for by prescribing by doctors who are not child mental health experts. Although drugs are prescribed less often for childhood disorders in the UK than in the USA, there is none the less a considerable rate of prescribing psychotropic drugs for children by general practitioners in the UK (Montoliu & Crawford, 2002).

Few psychotropic medicines are licensed for use with children. Thus, many prescriptions have to be made 'off licence' on a named patient basis. The Royal College of Paediatrics and Child Health (2000) states that:

> 'The use of unlicensed medicines or licensed medicines for unlicensed applications is necessary in paediatric practice where there is no suitable alternative. Such uses are informed and guided by a respectable and responsible body of professional opinion'.

This advice was given prior to the Medicines Control Agency advising against the use of all but one SSRI for the treatment of major depression in young people, following the discovery that reports of adverse reactions indicating an increased risk of self-harm had been suppressed.

There are major difficulties in conducting adequate drug trials with children and young people, but these need to be undertaken responsibly if potentially useful help is to be made available, if only while awaiting the application of more powerful treatments that are less available.

From the main search for randomised controlled trials (see Appendix 6), no study of drug treatments was identified by the Guideline Development Group as meeting the inclusion criteria. Only one RCT (Robert *et al*, 1999) was identified, which compared imipramine with chloral hydrate for 25 child burns victims aged 2–19 years for 1 week of treatment. However, this study did not meet the inclusion criteria as outcomes were recorded in the form of remission rates across a range of symptoms rather than a specific measure of PTSD. Open-label trials suggest that propranolol (Famularo *et al*, 1988), clonidine (Perry, 1994; Harmon & Riggs, 1996; Horrigan, 1996) and carbamazepine (Loof *et al*, 1995) resulted in symptomatic improvement, but no comparison group was studied.

9.8 Clinical summary of pharmacological interventions

At present there is too little evidence from RCTs, controlled trials, open-label studies or case–control studies to recommend the use of any psychotropic medication to treat PTSD in children or young people.

9.9 Clinical practice recommendations

9.9.1 Assessment

9.9.1.1   When assessing a child or young person for PTSD, healthcare professionals should ensure that they separately and directly question the child or young person about the presence of PTSD symptoms. They should not rely solely on information from the parent or guardian in any assessment. **GPP**

9.9.1.2   When a child who has been involved in a traumatic event is treated in an emergency department, emergency staff should inform the parents or guardians of the possibility of the development of PTSD, briefly describe the possible symptoms (for example, sleep disturbance, nightmares, difficulty concentrating and irritability) and suggest that they contact their general practitioner if the symptoms persist beyond 1 month. **GPP**

9.9.2 Early intervention

9.9.2.1   Trauma-focused cognitive–behavioural therapy should be offered to older children with severe post-traumatic symptoms or with severe PTSD in the first month after the traumatic event. **C**

9.9.3 Chronic PTSD

9.9.3.1   Children and young people with PTSD, including those who have been sexually abused, should be offered a course of trauma-focused cognitive–behavioural therapy adapted appropriately to suit their age, circumstances and level of development. **B**

9.9.3.2   Where appropriate, families should be involved in the treatment of PTSD in children and young people. However, treatment programmes for PTSD in children and young people that consist of parental involvement alone are unlikely to be of any benefit for PTSD symptoms. **C**

9.9.3.3   The duration of trauma-focused psychological treatment for children and young people with chronic PTSD should normally be 8–12 sessions when the PTSD results from a single event. When the trauma is discussed in the treatment session, longer sessions than usual are usually necessary (for example, 90 min). Treatment should be regular and continuous (usually at least once a week) and should be delivered by the same person. **C**

9.9.3.4   Drug treatments should not be routinely prescribed for children and young people with PTSD. **C**

9.9.3.5   When considering treatments for PTSD, parents and, where appropriate, children and young people should be informed that, apart from trauma-focused psychological interventions, there is at present no good evidence for the efficacy of widely used forms of treatment of PTSD such as play therapy, art therapy or family therapy. **C**

9.10 Research recommendations

9.10.1 Trauma-focused psychological intervention for children

9.10.1.1   Randomised controlled trials for children of all ages should be conducted to assess the efficacy and cost-effectiveness of trauma-focused psychological treatments (specifically CBT and EMDR). These trials should identify the relative efficacy of different trauma-focused psychological interventions and provide information on the differential effects, if any, arising from the age of the children or the nature of the trauma experienced.

Post-traumatic stress disorder is a common and potentially disabling condition in children as well as adults (Giaconia *et al,* 1995). Although up to 50% of children may develop PTSD following a traumatic event (Yule *et al*, 2000), many individuals recover without specific intervention; however, a significant proportion of individuals, perhaps more than 30% of victims of major disasters, go on to develop a chronic disorder with associated psychological and social handicaps (Morgan *et al*, 2003). Trauma-focused psychological interventions are generally effective for the treatment of PTSD in adults but only a limited evidence base exists for children and young people (Cohen *et al*, 2000). In addition, much of the evidence is drawn from work with children who have experienced childhood sexual abuse as well as developing PTSD (Ramchandani & Jones, 2003) and therefore the evidence base for interventions for PTSD arising from other traumas is weaker. For children aged under 7 years who develop PTSD there are virtually no formal RCTs of appropriate psychological interventions. A number of non-controlled trials suggest that treatments (specifically CBT and EMDR) are efficacious, but these have not been formally tested (Cohen *et al*, 2000).

10 Special considerations

10.1 Introduction

This guideline is concerned with the treatment of PTSD within the National Health Service. However, certain groups such as ex-military personnel, survivors of major disasters and many refugees and asylum seekers typically have some key aspects of their care delivered outside the NHS. In developing guidelines for the NHS it is therefore essential to give special consideration to the role and links with other organisations that play a key part in delivering care (particularly in the immediate aftermath of traumatic events) for those at risk of PTSD within specific populations of ex-military personnel, refugees and survivors of disasters.

10.2 Disaster planning

Health and social services have specific responsibilities for making arrangements for the appropriate social and psychological support of survivors, relatives and other affected individuals following disasters. In order for their input to be effective this support should be evidence based and delivered in a pre-planned, coordinated manner that is integrated into the central disaster plan. Multi-agency social and psychological care steering groups should be part of every area's Disaster Management System with a responsibility to meet regularly, develop and maintain the psychosocial care plan, and have authority to decide on provision. The membership of these groups should include representatives from primary care, adult mental health services, child and adolescent mental health services, social services, non-statutory organisations and the local emergency planning officer.

Social and psychological care ranges from providing immediate comfort and practical help through to longer-term psychological support, which may need to be provided for 18–24 months or even longer. Those involved should not feel rushed to 'restore normality'. Any formal response should be non-intrusive and non-judgemental, and designed to complement and mobilise the excellent support many people will receive from their family and friends. The exact nature of a response will vary in terms of size, management and the extent to which it will be proactive or reactive, depending on the specific circumstances of the disaster. An early meeting of the psychosocial steering group should be held following a disaster to determine the level of input. The response should then be closely monitored to ensure that the planned service is being delivered and to make changes as necessary.

Individuals involved in psychosocial care following disasters should usually have been selected for specific roles and have received appropriate training prior to the event in order to allow rapid deployment of a coordinated, planned response. This may require the release of individuals involved from routine activities and for this workload to be covered by others, possibly on a medium- to long-term basis. Support from senior management in both the planning and operational phases is therefore essential. During the response it is vital to involve sufficient numbers of staff to enable regular rotation to ensure that individuals do not work for excessive periods. Those managing the psychological response need to use their professional judgement to determine what is reasonable. The arrangement of adequate supervision for all personnel will be a key role of the social and psychological care steering group.

It is likely that specific local individuals not already mentioned will be important in a particular response, for example local community leaders, religious leaders and local primary care teams. Social and psychological care steering group representatives should liaise with these individuals, incorporate their skills into the planned response and cater for their training and supervision needs.

Social services will have the overall lead role in the initial psychosocial response, but it is vital that mental health professionals liaise with social services and provide supervision and support. There will be specific roles and responsibilities for healthcare staff and these should be identified clearly in the disaster plan. Typically, healthcare staff will only become directly involved in the initial phase if individuals develop extreme responses that are felt to be unmanageable or present with specific needs. The initial focus is likely to be on immediate practical help, including housing, food, drink, financial issues, providing comfort, helping people to get home, obtaining and providing accurate and timely information, establishing clear communication channels, providing space and privacy for those involved, specialist care of elderly people and children, and support to relatives. In addition it is important to record personal details and create a database of individuals involved (including health and social care staff, emergency services and volunteers as well as the victims of the disaster).

Early interventions should be provided in an empathic manner, but formal counselling or psychological intervention is usually inappropriate at this time (see Chapter 7). Information about the availability of help should be widely circulated and this can be done through distributing leaflets that describe some of the feelings commonly experienced by those involved in disasters and give basic advice and contact numbers for those seeking help. Leaflets should be on each local authority's computer system in readiness for contact telephone numbers to be added on the day and for distribution from day one.

As time progresses, the focus of the response will change and key tasks will include education and reassurance about normal emotional reactions, listening to and absorbing people's accounts of the incident if they want to talk about it, as well as helping them to piece together their experience of the disaster. Those involved (and their families and friends) should be provided with help and information on how to deal with problems arising from the disaster, e.g. family difficulties, insomnia, work problems, working with grief and emotional issues. This should include a role in facilitating individuals to make choices on various issues, including access to the dead, visiting the disaster site and memorials. Additional support may be required for any legal proceedings, inquiries and inquests. The creation of an emotional support telephone helpline should be considered along with the identification of those at highest risk (see Chapter 8) and assessment of their need for more formal intervention. Evidence-based interventions (see Chapter 7) should be offered to those with specific needs through adequately trained and supervised counsellors and clinicians. Mutual support groups and self-help work can be facilitated and the longer-term provision should be planned.

Educational psychology services in conjunction with child and adolescent mental health services (CAMHS), social services and education are likely to coordinate the provision of social and psychological care to children. The model used will be similar to the adult model, with an initial focus on providing emotional and practical support. School nurses can play an important role in this area under the supervision of the educational psychologists and CAMHS. It is often necessary to provide input to whole families.

The disaster plan should also consider and plan for the needs of special groups, such as those with sensory impairments, those who are mentally ill, and frail elderly people.

10.3 Ex-military personnel

The NHS has responsibility for the ongoing healthcare of ex-military personnel as soon as they leave the armed forces. It is also responsible for the healthcare of families of serving military personnel when they live in the UK. When experienced by ex-military personnel, PTSD is frequently comorbid with other disorders (Kulka et al, 1990) and there are often other important psychosocial issues that need to be addressed (including the impact of being discharged from the armed services and all that that entails). The adjustment from military to civilian life can be difficult; problematic social circumstances can occur and these may result in housing problems and financial hardship. These factors and the often prolonged and intense nature of traumatic exposure can result in a complex PTSD presentation that is potentially difficult to treat.

It is vital that primary and secondary health services in the UK are familiar with the specific needs of ex-military personnel and their families, and are equipped to deal with them. Ideally every local mental health service should be able to offer evidence-based treatments to ex-military personnel with PTSD. It is likely that this will require increased education and liaison between the military and the NHS. It is hoped that the new Department of Defence Mental Health in London will provide a focus for this.

When an individual is discharged from the military it is the military health service's responsibility to ensure that appropriate aftercare has been arranged. For individuals with PTSD this should involve close liaison with the local NHS service and a comprehensive handover. Many ex-service personnel report feeling better understood by healthcare professionals who are ex-military themselves. This probably mainly relates to difficulty in trusting someone who does not seem to understand the military way of life, and can usually be overcome by improved knowledge and a willingness to deal with issues relating to the individual's military background.

Primary and secondary care practitioners should be aware that ex-military personnel are at higher risk of having or developing PTSD (and other mental health problems) than most civilian populations and should consider assessing for this when they present with other problems (see Chapter 2). It is also important that local mental health services are aware of national bodies that can help ex-military personnel. In addition to the Department of Defence Mental Health, Combat Stress is a charity that was created to help ex-military personnel with mental health difficulties (http://www.combatstress.com). There are also other charities and former military personnel with personal experience of PTSD and difficulties accessing appropriate help who can be contacted for advice (see http://www.ptsd.org.uk for further information).

10.4 Phased interventions in settings of continuing threat

There are situations in which people do not experience a neat termination of a traumatic experience. Here, a phased intervention is appropriate. This has been well described by Herman (1997), especially for women who have been subjected to domestic violence and may experience further risk as long as they stay with their abusive partner.

Where there is ongoing violence at home, the first step of the practitioner is to deal with the dual issues of safety from further harm and trust in the therapist. Typically, achieving safety requires that the victim of violence has to make tough choices – including separation from the perpetrator – and so the task is to help such people to clarify their own wishes, free from external pressures. To negotiate this stage is hard and it does require a trusting, therapeutic and non-judgemental relationship. Although it may be hard to trust a stranger, there are cues that may help. Making it obvious that the therapist has experience of work with other survivors of violence – usually through the use of non-verbal behaviour or choice of questions – is almost always important. A common barrier to trust is a sense of alienation from others. Appropriate use of empathy can be a powerful means of demonstrating understanding. If appropriate, an explicit commitment to the rights of women – perhaps by undertaking work in a refuge setting – can also be helpful.

If the person decides to stay in a situation where violence will continue, then the aims of any further psychological intervention are limited. It is generally not possible to process fully the emotional consequences of a past event if it continues to recur. It may be possible to help to stabilise the psychological symptoms and, of course, to hold open the door for return and re-engagement. To achieve a more fundamental resolution, however, will require the person to take steps to reduce the risk of further violence. This is a crucial phase of any intervention and is often not given enough attention.

Only after this stage has been successfully negotiated can active psychological treatment (seeking fundamental change) really take place. This is when the specific interventions become appropriate. These may take a number of forms. These are the subject of scientific enquiry (efficacy trials) and may appear to carry greater respectability than a consideration of therapeutic process. However, realistically, they can only be approached if the first stage has been successfully negotiated. They have been summarised in other parts of this guideline.

The final phase of treatment is concerned with (re)integration or adaptation to what has happened. The process of therapeutic change does not end, therefore, until the individual is back in the world and can function as an effective agent again.

It has been suggested that the phased approach goes back to the days of Pierre Janet (van der Hart et al, 1989). Herman herself attributes some of her thinking to Janet, although she has certainly enhanced and enlarged on this early thinking. Janet's work on dissociation not only helps explain crucial elements of the dissociative trauma response, it also paved the way for a phased model of intervention, with three phases:

- stabilisation, symptom-oriented treatment
- exploration of traumatic memories
- personality reintegration and rehabilitation (Janet, 1889, cited by Herman, 1997).

A staged model has formed the basis of most treatments for complex trauma reactions, such as Linehan's dialectical behaviour therapy (DBT) model (Linehan, 1993). Similarly, in settings where there is a risk of child abuse, the first step is to achieve safety and then consideration can be given to the processes of treatment and recovery.

10.5 Working with refugees and asylum seekers

Refugees and asylum seekers often present another example of a complex problem. Being a refugee is not a diagnosis, and refugees may present with any of the psychiatric disorders or none at all. Some may develop other specific responses, such as 'enduring personality change after catastrophic experience', and may require long-term treatments, but to discuss these would go beyond the scope of this guideline. There is an important need to ensure a comprehensive assessment and to plan treatment with the refugee or asylum seeker in the light of that assessment.

By virtue of their experiences (e.g. war, imprisonment and torture), these people are more likely to experience PTSD than the general population. Often this is comorbid with depression (Turner et al, 2003; Turner, 2004). The expression of emotional disturbance may be modified by cultural and linguistic factors, as well as by the beliefs of the sufferer concerning health services and their willingness to work across cultures.

This is another situation in which a phased model may be appropriate (although there is no trial evidence to support this contention and it therefore reflects a pragmatic approach). Typically, the first need is to achieve safety from further persecution. This may not be possible until the person has legal status – and this may take a long time to obtain. Clinicians working with refugees should not only have knowledge of the complexity of the emotional reaction that many experience (going well beyond PTSD in many cases), but should also have an awareness of immigration law, welfare rights and cultural and political diversities. Until there is safety from further persecution, there may be a limit to the depth of therapeutic work that can be delivered. It can be hard to confront trauma memories anyway, but if the PTSD sufferer faces a realistic prospect of being returned to face more trauma, then it can be impossible. As asylum seekers who flee civil war in their own country often do not meet the criteria for refugee status (although they are not, as often portrayed in the media, 'bogus'), this is a realistic possibility for some.

In the first phase, primary needs are often focused on accommodation, benefits and continued family separation. These are phase one problems. At this stage, it is typically inappropriate and ineffective to attempt a trauma-focused therapy. (This is something to be considered once the individual has achieved a sufficient sense of stability and security, and this is a subjective state that will vary from person to person.) Interventions in phase one are likely to be practical, supportive, involve medication (see Chapter 6) to help with emotional stabilisation, and may involve psychoeducation (possibly in a group format). A priority is to support the development of a trusting relationship that can help in the provision of other phases of the intervention.

The phase two interventions are similar to those described elsewhere in this review. There has long been interest in the use of narrative approaches ('testimony', e.g. Cienfuegos & Monelli, 1983), although in the context of the evidence statements made earlier about psychological treatments, these can be construed as including important elements of trauma-focused CBT with exposure and cognitive restructuring. There are few good efficacy trials applying treatments to refugee populations. Neuner et al (2004) have reported encouraging data in a trial of 'narrative exposure therapy' (similar to testimony); this is discussed in Chapter 5. Often, in the context of a phase two treatment, a crisis will emerge and it will be necessary to return to phase one stabilisation and crisis management work. In this phase, issues concerning loss and bereavement are also often encountered.

With refugees, it is not a question of reintegration in phase three so much as integration into a new community, but this, too, is an important element of the therapeutic approach and should not be neglected. Some refugees later have the option to return to their own country and they may have reintegration needs to deal with there as well.

There are some subgroups with special needs. Head injuries are common and some refugee PTSD sufferers also present with subtle cognitive impairment as a consequence. There may be other physical handicaps as a result of injury. Where there is a history of sexual assault, a PTSD with predominant shame may be found. It has been demonstrated that both men and women with histories of sexual assault present with marked avoidance responses – in contrast to survivors of physical torture, which is associated with high intrusion scores (van Velsen et al, 1996). This means that people often present a history of rape late and it is appropriate to maintain an open mind in therapy about this possibility.

Work with survivors of torture (and other forms of malicious abuse) reminds us of the need for an ethical base to all our practice in this field. It is appropriate to declare a commitment to human rights. The approach should be focused on the refugee rather than on the service and this may mean trying to offer an integrated physical, psychosocial and legal approach within one setting. Finally, there is an overriding need to respect those aspects of the individual that demonstrate these people's resilience and strengths (Schlapobersky, 1990).

10.6 Role of the non-statutory sector

The non-statutory sector and associated community organisations have long played an important part in the treatment and management of trauma. The contributions of the non-statutory sector have been apparent in a number of distinct ways. First, there has been a long-standing tradition of the provision of bereavement counselling and related services which, despite not having a specialist remit for trauma victims, provide services for a number of people who have experienced a range of traumatic events, including (but not restricted to) traumatic bereavements. Second, a number of services in the non-statutory sector have developed specifically in response to the needs of particular traumatised groups. These have included victims of domestic violence and rape, victims of crime, childhood sexual abuse and torture, refugees and individuals who have been involved in large-scale natural or other disasters. These groups may have developed specifically to meet the needs of identified groups of traumatised individuals or may have emerged from existing groups as their remit changed in order to meet a new need.

The range of services provided within the non-statutory sector is considerable and diverse, with a very varied distribution across England and Wales. Many services will provide some form of psychological intervention; often in the early days of such services this was non-directive counselling, but increasingly these services are providing a range of psychological interventions with a stronger evidence base for the treatment of PTSD. The provision of such services may complement or supplement that provided by the NHS; the degree to which this takes place will vary with the availability of local services and the variation in demand – for example, large-scale disasters often place considerable strain on statutory services and it is in such cases that the non-statutory sector may have a vital role.

In addition to the direct provision of psychological interventions, the non-statutory sector can provide several other key services. Many non-statutory organisations provide immediate practical and emotional support for victims of trauma, both individual and large-scale, which builds on and enhances the support available for local communities. Again, this complements the work of the statutory services and in many regions non-statutory organisations will take the lead for local communities in this area of work. Such work will often provide not just valuable immediate support but also the basis for a better-informed group of trauma sufferers: this has been done both at a local level and at national level, for example through the provision of internet-based information about PTSD. Many non-statutory organisations also take on an advocacy role for PTSD sufferers, working to obtain effective treatment and social and practical support; for some organisations this will be a primary focus of their work. Finally, non-statutory organisations are often the focus for a number of self-help or support groups for PTSD sufferers or their families or carers, which can play a vital part in overcoming the impact of severe trauma.

Non-statutory sector services therefore can make a significant contribution to the care and management of people with PTSD. Given this, it is essential that NHS and related statutory services are aware of the specific contribution that is made in this area by their local non-statutory services. This should then allow for a more integrated approach to the care of PTSD sufferers. As is apparent from this guideline, the effective treatment of many PTSD sufferers depends on their living in a safe and supportive environment, and the non-statutory sector can contribute significantly to this. The NHS services caring for PTSD sufferers should seek to develop effective working links with all relevant non-statutory sector services, which should seek to identify complementary elements of the respective services. The NHS should also support, where appropriate, non-statutory sector services in the provision of effective interventions for PTSD sufferers through educational and training initiatives. An example of this approach can be seen in the *Women's Mental Health Strategy* recently published by the Department of Health (NIMHE, 2003).

10.7 Recommendations

10.7.1 Disaster planning

10.7.1.1   All disaster plans should make provision for a fully coordinated psychosocial response to the disaster. Those responsible for developing the psychosocial aspect of a disaster plan should ensure it contains the following: provision for immediate practical help, means to support the affected communities in caring for those involved in the disaster and the provision of specialist mental health, evidence-based assessment and treatment services. All healthcare workers involved in a disaster plan, should have clear roles and responsibilities, which should be agreed in advance. **GPP**

11 Summary of recommendations

11.1 Key recommendations for implementation

11.1.1 Initial response to trauma

For individuals who have experienced a traumatic event, the systematic provision to that individual alone of brief, single-session interventions (often referred to as debriefing) that focus on the traumatic incident should *not* be routine practice when delivering services.

Where symptoms are mild and have been present for less than 4 weeks after the trauma, watchful waiting, as a way of managing the difficulties presented by people with PTSD, should be considered. A follow-up contact should be arranged within 1 month.

11.1.2 Trauma-focused psychological treatment

Trauma-focused cognitive–behavioural therapy should be offered to those with severe post-traumatic symptoms or with severe post-traumatic stress disorder in the first month after the traumatic event. These treatments should normally be provided on an individual out-patient basis.

All people with PTSD should be offered a course of trauma-focused psychological treatment (trauma-focused CBT or eye movement desensitisation and reprocessing). These treatments should normally be provided on an individual out-patient basis.

11.1.3 Children and young people

Trauma-focused CBT should be offered to older children with severe post-traumatic symptoms or with severe PTSD in the first month after the traumatic event.

Children and young people with PTSD, including those who have been sexually abused, should be offered a course of trauma-focused CBT adapted appropriately to suit their age, circumstances and level of development.

11.1.4 Drug treatments for adults

Drug treatments for PTSD should not be used as a routine first-line treatment for adults (in general use or by specialist mental health professionals) in preference to a trauma-focused psychological therapy.

Drug treatments (paroxetine or mirtazapine for general use, and amitriptyline or phenelzine for initiation only by mental health specialists) should be considered for the treatment of PTSD in adults who express a preference not to engage in trauma-focused psychological treatment.

11.1.5 Screening for PTSD

For individuals at high risk of developing PTSD following a major disaster, consideration should be given (by those responsible for coordination of the disaster plan) to the routine use of a brief screening instrument for PTSD at 1 month after the disaster.

11.2 Guidance

The following guidance is evidence-based. The grading scheme used for the recommendations (A, B, C) or good practice point (GPP) is described in Chapter 4. A summary of the evidence on which the guidance is based is provided in the full guideline (see Chapters 5–10).

11.3 Recognition of PTSD

Effective treatment of PTSD can only take place if the disorder is recognised. In some cases, for example following a major disaster, specific arrangements to screen people at risk may be considered. For the vast majority of people with PTSD, opportunities for recognition and identification come as part of routine healthcare interventions, for example, following an assault or an accident for which physical treatment is required, or when a person discloses domestic violence or a history of childhood sexual abuse. Identification of PTSD in children presents particular problems but is improved if children are asked directly about their experiences.

11.3.1 Recognition in primary care

PTSD can present with a range of symptoms, which in most adults are most commonly in the form of very vivid, distressing memories of the event or flashbacks (otherwise known as intrusive or re-experiencing symptoms). However, at times the most prominent symptoms may be avoidance of trauma-related situations or general social contacts. It is important when recognising and identifying PTSD to ask specific questions in a sensitive manner about both the symptoms and traumatic experiences. A number of problems such as depression are often comorbid with PTSD. Often these problems will improve with the treatment of the PTSD, but where this does not happen or the comorbid disorder impedes the effective treatment of the PTSD, it may be appropriate to consider providing specific treatment for that disorder.

11.3.1.1   PTSD may present with a range of symptoms (including re-experiencing, avoidance, hyperarousal, depression, emotional numbing, drug or alcohol misuse and anger) and therefore, when assessing for PTSD, members of the primary care team should ask in a sensitive manner whether or not patients with such symptoms have suffered a traumatic experience (which may have occurred many months or years before) and give specific examples of traumatic events (for example, assaults, rape, road traffic accidents, childhood sexual abuse and traumatic childbirth). GPP

11.3.1.2   General practitioners and other members of the primary care team should be aware of traumas associated with the development of PTSD. These include single events such as assaults or road traffic accidents, and domestic violence and childhood sexual abuse. GPP

11.3.1.3   For patients with unexplained physical symptoms who are repeated attendees to primary care, members of the primary care team should consider asking whether or not they have experienced a traumatic event, and provide specific examples of traumatic events (for example, assaults, rape, road traffic accidents, childhood sexual abuse and traumatic childbirth). GPP

11.3.1.4   When seeking to identify PTSD, members of the primary care team should consider asking adults specific questions about re-experiencing (including flashbacks and nightmares) or hyperarousal (including an exaggerated startle response or sleep disturbance). For children, particularly younger children, consideration should be given to asking the child and/or the parents about sleep disturbance or significant changes in sleeping patterns. C

11.3.2 Recognition in general hospital settings

Many people attending for medical services in a general hospital setting may have experienced traumatic events. This may be particularly so in emergency departments and in orthopaedic and plastic surgery clinics. For some people with PTSD, this may be the main point of contact with the healthcare system and the opportunity that this presents for the recognition and identification of PTSD should be taken.

11.3.2.1   PTSD may present with a range of symptoms (including re-experiencing, avoidance, hyperarousal, depression, emotional numbing and anger) and therefore when assessing for PTSD, members of secondary care medical teams should ask in a sensitive manner whether or not patients with such symptoms have suffered a traumatic experience and give specific examples of traumatic events (for example, assaults, rape, road traffic accidents, childhood sexual abuse and traumatic childbirth). GPP

11.3.3 Screening of individuals involved in a major disaster, programme refugees and asylum seekers

Many individuals involved in a major disaster will suffer both short- and long-term consequences of their involvement. Although the development of single-session debriefing is not recommended, screening of all individuals should be considered by the authorities responsible for developing the local disaster plan. Similarly, the vast majority of programme refugees (people who are brought to the UK from a conflict zone through a programme organised by an agency such as the United Nations High Commission for Refugees) will have experienced major trauma and may benefit from a screening programme.

11.2.3.1   For individuals at high risk of developing PTSD following a major disaster, consideration should be given (by those responsible for coordination of the disaster plan) to the routine use of a brief screening instrument for PTSD at 1 month after the disaster. **C**

11.2.3.2   For programme refugees and asylum seekers at high risk of developing PTSD, consideration should be given (by those responsible for management of the refugee programme) to the routine use of a brief screening instrument for PTSD as part of the initial refugee healthcare assessment. This should be a part of any comprehensive physical and mental health screen. **C**

11.3.4 Specific recognition issues for children

Children, particularly those aged under 8 years, may not complain directly of PTSD symptoms such as re-experiencing or avoidance. Instead, children may complain of sleeping problems. It is therefore vital that all opportunities for identifying PTSD in children should be taken. Questioning the children as well as parents or guardians will also improve the recognition of PTSD. PTSD is common (up to 30%) in children following attendance at emergency departments for a traumatic injury. Emergency department staff should inform parents or guardians of the risk of their child developing PTSD following emergency attendance for a traumatic injury and advise them on what action to take if symptoms develop.

11.3.4.1   When assessing a child or young person for PTSD, healthcare professionals should ensure that they separately and directly question the child or young person about the presence of PTSD symptoms. They should not rely solely on information from the parent or guardian in any assessment. **GPP**

11.3.4.2   When a child who has been involved in a traumatic event is treated in an emergency department, emergency staff should inform the parents or guardians of the possibility of the development of PTSD, briefly describe the possible symptoms (for example, sleep disturbance, nightmares, difficulty concentrating and irritability) and suggest that they contact their general practitioner if the symptoms persist beyond 1 month. **GPP**

11.4 Assessment and coordination of care

11.4.1 Recommendations

11.4.1.1   For PTSD sufferers presenting in primary care, GPs should take responsibility for the initial assessment and the initial coordination of care. This includes the determination of the need for emergency medical or psychiatric assessment. **C**

11.4.1.2   Assessment of PTSD sufferers should be conducted by competent individuals and be comprehensive, including physical, psychological and social needs and a risk assessment. **GPP**

11.4.1.3   Patient preference should be an important determinant of the choice among effective treatments. PTSD sufferers should be given sufficient information about the nature of these treatments to make an informed choice. **C**

11.4.1.4   Where management is shared between primary and secondary care, there should be clear agreement among individual healthcare professionals about the responsibility for monitoring patients with PTSD. This agreement should be in writing (where appropriate, using the Care Programme Approach) and should be shared with the patient and, where appropriate, their family and carers. **C**

11.5 Support for families and carers

11.5.1 Recommendations

Families and carers have a central role in supporting people with PTSD. However, depending on the nature of the trauma and its consequences, many families may also need support for themselves. Healthcare professionals should be aware of the impact of PTSD on the whole family.

11.5.1.1 In all cases of PTSD, healthcare professionals should consider the impact of the traumatic event on all family members and, when appropriate, assess this impact and consider providing appropriate support. GPP

11.5.1.2 Healthcare professionals should ensure, where appropriate and with the consent of the PTSD sufferer where necessary, that the families of PTSD sufferers are fully informed about common reactions to traumatic events, including the symptoms of PTSD and its course and treatment. GPP

11.5.1.3 In addition to the provision of information, families and carers should be informed of self-help groups and support groups and encouraged to participate in such groups where they exist. GPP

11.5.1.4 When a family is affected by a traumatic event, more than one family member may suffer from PTSD. If this is the case, healthcare professionals should ensure that the treatment of all family members is effectively coordinated. GPP

11.6 Practical support and social factors

Practical and social support can play an important part in facilitating a person's recovery from PTSD, particularly immediately after the trauma. Healthcare professionals should be aware of this and advocate for such support when people present with PTSD.

11.6.1 Recommendations

11.6.1.1 Healthcare professionals should identify the need for appropriate information about the range of emotional responses that may develop and provide practical advice on how to access appropriate services for these problems. They should also identify the need for social support and advocate the meeting of this need. GPP

11.6.1.2 Healthcare professionals should consider offering help or advice to PTSD sufferers or relevant others on how continuing threats related to the traumatic event may be alleviated or removed. GPP

11.7 Language and culture

People with PTSD treated in the NHS come from diverse cultural and ethnic backgrounds and some have no or limited English, but all should be offered the opportunity to benefit from psychological interventions. This can be achieved by the use of interpreters and bicultural therapists. In all cases, healthcare professionals must familiarise themselves with the cultural background of the sufferer.

11.7.1 Recommendations

11.7.1.1 Where a PTSD sufferer has a different cultural or ethnic background from that of the healthcare professionals who are providing care, the healthcare professionals should familiarise themselves with the cultural background of the PTSD sufferer. GPP

11.7.1.2 Where differences of language or culture exist between healthcare professionals and PTSD sufferers, this should not be an obstacle to the provision of effective trauma-focused psychological interventions. GPP

11.7.1.3   Where language or culture differences present challenges to the use of trauma-focused psychological interventions in PTSD, healthcare professionals should consider the use of interpreters and bicultural therapists. **GPP**

11.7.1.4   Healthcare professionals should pay particular attention to the identification of individuals with PTSD where the culture of the working or living environment is resistant to recognition of the psychological consequences of trauma. **GPP**

11.8 Care for all people with PTSD

PTSD responds to a variety of effective treatments. All treatment should be supported by appropriate information to sufferers about the likely course of such treatment. A number of factors, which are described below, may modify the nature, timing and course of treatment.

11.8.1 Care across all conditions

11.8.1.1   When developing and agreeing a treatment plan with a PTSD sufferer, healthcare professionals should ensure that sufferers receive information about common reactions to traumatic events, including the symptoms of PTSD and its course and treatment. **GPP**

11.8.1.2   Healthcare professionals should not delay or withhold treatment for PTSD because of court proceedings or applications for compensation. **C**

11.8.1.3   Healthcare professionals should be aware that many PTSD sufferers are anxious about and can avoid engaging in treatment. Healthcare professionals should also recognise the challenges that this presents and respond appropriately, for example by following up PTSD sufferers who miss scheduled appointments. **C**

11.8.1.4   Healthcare professionals should treat PTSD sufferers with respect, trust and understanding, and keep technical language to a minimum. **GPP**

11.8.1.5   Healthcare professionals should normally only consider providing trauma-focused psychological treatment when the sufferer considers it safe to proceed. **GPP**

11.8.1.6   Treatment should be delivered by competent individuals who have received appropriate training. These individuals should receive appropriate supervision. **C**

11.8.2 Comorbidities

11.8.2.1   When a patient presents with PTSD and depression, healthcare professionals should consider treating the PTSD first, as the depression will often improve with successful treatment of the PTSD. **C**

11.8.2.2   For PTSD sufferers whose assessment identifies a high risk of suicide or harm to others, healthcare professionals should first concentrate on management of this risk. **C**

11.8.2.3   For PTSD sufferers who are so severely depressed that this makes initial psychological treatment of PTSD very difficult (for example, as evidenced by extreme lack of energy and concentration, inactivity, or high suicide risk), healthcare professionals should treat the depression first. **C**

11.8.2.4   For PTSD sufferers with drug or alcohol dependence or in whom alcohol or drug use may significantly interfere with effective treatment, healthcare professionals should treat the drug or alcohol problem first. **C**

11.7.2.5   When offering trauma-focused psychological interventions to PTSD sufferers with comorbid personality disorder, healthcare professionals should consider extending the duration of treatment. **C**

11.7.2.6   People who have lost a close friend or relative due to an unnatural or sudden death should be assessed for PTSD and traumatic grief. In most cases, healthcare professionals should treat the PTSD first without avoiding discussion of the grief. **C**

11.9 Treatment of PTSD

11.9.1 Early interventions

A number of sufferers with PTSD may recover with no or limited interventions. However, without effective treatment, many people may develop chronic problems over many years. The severity of the initial traumatic response is a reasonable indicator of the need for early intervention, and treatment should not be withheld in such circumstances.

Watchful waiting

11.9.1.1 Where symptoms are mild and have been present for less than 4 weeks after the trauma, watchful waiting, as a way of managing the difficulties presented by individual sufferers, should be considered by healthcare professionals. A follow-up contact should be arranged within 1 month. **C**

Immediate psychological interventions for all

As described in this guideline, practical support delivered in an empathetic manner is important in promoting recovery for PTSD, but it is unlikely that a single session of a psychological intervention will be helpful.

11.9.1.2 All health and social care workers should be aware of the psychological impact of traumatic incidents in their immediate post-incident care of survivors and offer practical, social and emotional support to those involved. **GPP**

11.9.1.3 For individuals who have experienced a traumatic event, the systematic provision to that individual alone of brief, single-session interventions (often referred to as debriefing) that focus on the traumatic incident should *not* be routine practice when delivering services. **A**

PTSD where symptoms are present within 3 months of a trauma

Brief psychological interventions (five sessions) may be effective if treatment starts within the first month after the traumatic event. Beyond the first month, the duration of treatment is similar to that for chronic PTSD.

11.9.1.4 Trauma-focused cognitive–behavioural therapy should be offered to those with severe post-traumatic symptoms or with severe PTSD in the first month after the traumatic event. These treatments should normally be provided on an individual out-patient basis. **B**

11.9.1.5 Trauma-focused CBT should be offered to people who present with PTSD within 3 months of a traumatic event. **A**

11.9.1.6 The duration of the trauma-focused CBT should normally be 8–12 sessions, but if the treatment starts in the first month after the event, fewer sessions (about 5) may be sufficient. When the trauma is discussed in the treatment session, longer sessions (for example, 90 min) are usually necessary. Treatment should be regular and continuous (usually at least once a week) and should be delivered by the same person. **B**

11.9.1.7 Drug treatment may be considered in the acute phase of PTSD for the management of sleep disturbance. In this case, hypnotic medication may be appropriate for short-term use but, if longer-term drug treatment is required, consideration should also be given to the use of suitable antidepressants at an early stage in order to reduce the later risk of dependence. **C**

11.9.1.8 Non-trauma-focused interventions such as relaxation or non-directive therapy, which do not address traumatic memories, should not routinely be offered to people who present with PTSD symptoms within 3 months of a traumatic event. **B**

11.9.2 PTSD where symptoms have been present for more than 3 months after a trauma

Most patients presenting with PTSD have had the problem for many months, if not years. The interventions outlined below are effective in treating such individuals and duration of the disorder does not itself seem an impediment to benefiting from effective treatment provided by competent healthcare professionals.

11.9.2.1   All PTSD sufferers should be offered a course of trauma-focused psychological treatment (trauma-focused CBT or eye movement desensitisation and reprocessing). These treatments should normally be provided on an individual out-patient basis. A

11.9.2.2   Trauma-focused psychological treatment should be offered to PTSD sufferers regardless of the time that has elapsed since the trauma. B

11.9.2.3   The duration of trauma-focused psychological treatment should normally be 8–12 sessions when the PTSD results from a single event. When the trauma is discussed in the treatment session, longer sessions than usual are generally necessary (for example, 90 min). Treatment should be regular and continuous (usually at least once a week) and should be delivered by the same person. B

11.9.2.4   Healthcare professionals should consider extending the duration of treatment beyond 12 sessions if several problems need to be addressed in the treatment of PTSD sufferers, particularly after multiple traumatic events, traumatic bereavement or where chronic disability resulting from the trauma, significant comorbid disorders or social problems are present. Trauma-focused treatment needs to be integrated into an overall plan of care. C

11.9.2.5   For some PTSD sufferers it may initially be very difficult and overwhelming to disclose details of their traumatic events. In these cases, healthcare professionals should consider devoting several sessions to establishing a trusting therapeutic relationship and emotional stabilisation before addressing the traumatic event. C

11.9.2.6   Non-trauma-focused interventions such as relaxation or non-directive therapy, which do not address traumatic memories, should not routinely be offered to people who present with chronic PTSD. B

11.9.2.7   For PTSD sufferers who have no or only limited improvement with a specific trauma-focused psychological treatment, healthcare professionals should consider the following options:

- an alternative form of trauma-focused psychological treatment
- the augmentation of trauma-focused psychological treatment with a course of pharmacological treatment. C

11.9.2.8   When PTSD sufferers request other forms of psychological treatment (for example, supportive therapy/non-directive therapy, hypnotherapy, psychodynamic therapy or systemic psychotherapy), they should be informed that there is as yet no convincing evidence for a clinically important effect of these treatments on PTSD. GPP

11.9.3 Drug treatment

The evidence base for drug treatments in PTSD is limited. There is evidence of clinically significant benefits for mirtazapine, amitriptyline and phenelzine. (Dietary guidance is required with phenelzine.) For paroxetine there were statistically but not clinically significant benefits on the main outcome variables. Nevertheless, this drug has also been included in the list of recommended drugs. This is the only drug in the list of recommendations with a current UK product licence for PTSD.

11.9.3.1   Drug treatments for PTSD should not be used as a routine first-line treatment for adults (in general use or by specialist mental health professionals) in preference to a trauma-focused psychological therapy. A

11.9.3.2   Drug treatments (paroxetine or mirtazapine for general use, and amitriptyline or phenelzine for initiation only by mental health specialists) should be considered for the treatment of PTSD in adults where a sufferer expresses a preference not to engage in a trauma-focused psychological treatment. B

11.9.3.3   Drug treatments (paroxetine or mirtazapine for general use, and amitriptyline or phenelzine for initiation only by mental health specialists) should be offered to adult PTSD sufferers who cannot start a psychological therapy because of serious ongoing threat of further trauma (for example, where there is ongoing domestic violence). C

11.9.3.4 Drug treatments (paroxetine or mirtazapine for general use and amitriptyline or phenelzine for initiation only by mental health specialists) should be considered for adult PTSD sufferers who have gained little or no benefit from a course of trauma-focused psychological treatment. C

11.9.3.5 Where sleep is a major problem for an adult PTSD sufferer, hypnotic medication may be appropriate for short-term use but, if longer-term drug treatment is required, consideration should also be given to the use of suitable antidepressants at an early stage in order to reduce the later risk of dependence. C

11.9.3.6 Drug treatments (paroxetine or mirtazapine for general use and amitriptyline or phenelzine for initiation only by mental health specialists) for PTSD should be considered as an adjunct to psychological treatment in adults where there is significant comorbid depression or severe hyperarousal that significantly impacts on a sufferer's ability to benefit from psychological treatment. C

11.9.3.7 When an adult sufferer with PTSD has not responded to a drug treatment, consideration should be given to increasing the dosage within approved limits. If further drug treatment is considered, this should generally be with a different class of antidepressant or involve the use of adjunctive olanzapine. C

11.9.3.8 When an adult sufferer with PTSD has responded to drug treatment, it should be continued for at least 12 months before gradual withdrawal. C

General recommendations regarding drug treatment

11.9.3.9 All PTSD sufferers who are prescribed antidepressants should be informed, at the time that treatment is initiated, of potential side-effects and discontinuation/withdrawal symptoms (particularly with paroxetine). C

11.9.3.10 Adult PTSD sufferers started on antidepressants who are considered to have an increased suicide risk and all patients aged between 18 and 29 years (because of the potential increased risk of suicidal thoughts associated with the use of antidepressants in this age group) should normally be seen after 1 week and frequently thereafter until the risk is no longer considered significant. GPP

11.9.3.11 Particularly in the initial stages of SSRI treatment, practitioners should actively seek out signs of akathisia, suicidal ideation and increased anxiety and agitation. They should also advise PTSD sufferers of the risk of these symptoms in the early stages of treatment and advise them to seek help promptly if these are at all distressing. GPP

11.9.3.12 If a PTSD sufferer develops marked and/or prolonged akathisia while taking an antidepressant, the use of the drug should be reviewed. GPP

11.9.3.13 Adult PTSD sufferers started on antidepressants who are not considered to be at increased risk of suicide should normally be seen after 2 weeks and thereafter on an appropriate and regular basis, for example, at intervals of 2–4 weeks in the first 3 months, and at greater intervals thereafter, if response is good. GPP

Recommendations regarding discontinuation/withdrawal symptoms

11.9.3.14 Discontinuation/withdrawal symptoms are usually mild and self-limiting but occasionally can be severe. Prescribers should normally gradually reduce the dosage of antidepressants over a 4-week period, although some people may require longer periods. C

11.9.3.15 If discontinuation/withdrawal symptoms are mild, practitioners should reassure the PTSD sufferer and arrange for monitoring. If symptoms are severe, the practitioner should consider reintroducing the original antidepressant (or another with a longer half-life from the same class) and reduce gradually while monitoring symptoms. C

11.9.4 Chronic disease management

11.9.4.1   Chronic disease management models should be considered for the management of people with chronic PTSD who have not benefited from a number of courses of evidence-based treatment. C

11.9.5 Children

It is particularly difficult to identify PTSD in children (see section 11.3.4). The treatments for children with PTSD are less developed but emerging evidence provides an indication for effective interventions.

Early intervention

11.9.5.1   Trauma-focused CBT should be offered to older children with severe post-traumatic symptoms or with severe PTSD in the first month after the traumatic event. B

PTSD where symptoms have been present for more than 3 months after a trauma

11.9.5.2   Children and young people with PTSD, including those who have been sexually abused, should be offered a course of trauma-focused CBT adapted appropriately to suit their age, circumstances and level of development. B

11.9.5.3   The duration of trauma-focused psychological treatment for children and young people with chronic PTSD should normally be 8–12 sessions when the PTSD results from a single event. When the trauma is discussed in the treatment session, longer sessions than usual are usually necessary (for example, 90 min). Treatment should be regular and continuous (usually at least once a week) and should be delivered by the same person. C

11.9.5.4   Drug treatments should not be routinely prescribed for children and young people with PTSD. C

11.9.5.5   Where appropriate, families should be involved in the treatment of PTSD in children and young people. However, treatment programmes for PTSD in children and young people that consist of parental involvement alone are unlikely to be of any benefit for PTSD symptoms. C

11.9.5.6   When considering treatments for PTSD, parents and, where appropriate, children and young people should be informed that, apart from trauma-focused psychological interventions, there is at present no good evidence for the efficacy of widely used forms of treatment of PTSD such as play therapy, art therapy or family therapy. C

11.10 Disaster planning

Both health and social services have a role in organising the appropriate social and psychological support for those affected by disasters.

11.10.1 Recommendations

11.10.1.1 Disaster plans should include provision for a fully coordinated psychosocial response to the disaster. Those responsible for developing the psychosocial aspect of a disaster plan should ensure it contains the following: provision for immediate practical help, means to support the affected communities in caring for those involved in the disaster and the provision of specialist mental health, evidence-based assessment and treatment services. All healthcare workers involved in a disaster plan should have clear roles and responsibilities, which should be agreed in advance. GPP

11.11 Research recommendations

11.11.1 Guided self-help

11.11.1.1 A randomised controlled trial, using newly developed guided self-help materials based on trauma-focused psychological interventions, should be conducted to assess the efficacy and cost-effectiveness of guided self-help compared with trauma-focused psychological interventionse for mild and moderate PTSD.

11.11.2 Children and young people

11.11.2.1 Randomised controlled trials for children of all ages should be conducted to assess the efficacy and cost-effectiveness of trauma-focused psychological treatments (specifically CBT and EMDR). These trials should identify the relative efficacy of different trauma-focused psychological interventions and provide information on the differential effects, if any, arising from the age of the children or the nature of the trauma experienced.

11.11.3 Trauma-focused psychological interventions in adults

11.11.3.1 Adequately powered effectiveness trials of trauma-focused psychological interventions for the treatment of PTSD (trauma-focused cognitive–behavioural therapy and eye movement desensitisation and reprocessing) should be conducted. They should provide evidence on the comparative effectiveness and cost-effectiveness of these interventions and consider the format of treatment (type and duration) and the specific populations who might benefit.

11.11.4 Screening programme

11.11.4.1 An appropriately designed longitudinal study should be conducted to determine if a simple screening instrument, which is acceptable to those receiving it, can identify individuals who develop PTSD after traumatic events and can be used as part of a screening programme to ensure individuals with PTSD receive effective interventions.

11.11.5 Trauma-focused psychological treatment versus pharmacological treatment

11.11.5.1 Adequately powered, appropriately designed trials should be conducted to determine if trauma-focused psychological treatments are superior in terms of efficacy and cost-effectiveness to pharmacological treatments in the treatment of PTSD and whether they are efficacious and cost-effective in combination.

Appendices

Appendix 1: Scope for the development of a clinical guideline on the management of post-traumatic stress disorder

1 Guideline title

Post-traumatic stress disorder: the management of PTSD in adults and children in primary and secondary care

2 Short title

PTSD

3 Background

The National Institute for Clinical Excellence ('NICE' or 'the Institute') has commissioned the National Collaborating Centre for Mental Health to develop a clinical guideline on the management of anxiety disorders for use in the National Health Service (NHS) in England and Wales. This follows referral of the topic of anxiety disorders, by the Department of Health and Welsh Assembly Government. This document provides further detail on the specific issues relating to PTSD and is a development of the original scope agreed for the anxiety disorders. The guideline will provide recommendations for good practice that are based on the best available evidence of clinical and cost effectiveness.

The Institute's clinical guidelines will support the implementation of National Service Frameworks (NSFs) in those aspects of care where a Framework has been published. The statements in each NSF reflect the evidence that was used at the time the Framework was prepared. The clinical guidelines and technology appraisals published by the Institute after an NSF has been issued will have the effect of updating the Framework.

4 Clinical need for the guideline

Community-based studies in the USA reveal a lifetime prevalence for PTSD of approximately 8% of the adult population. The disorder can occur at any age, including during childhood, with symptoms usually beginning within the first 3 months after the trauma. However, there may be a delay of months or years before symptoms start to appear.

PTSD presents in a range of populations, including those who have been exposed to or witnessed severe accidents, assault, deliberate acts of torture, disaster or military action; members of the emergency services; and other special populations.

People with post-traumatic stress and related disorders are currently treated in a range of NHS settings, including primary care, general mental health services and specialist secondary care mental health services. The provision and uptake of such services varies across England and Wales and reflects the demands of particular populations (for example refugees or war veterans) and the presence or absence of specialist services. The decade since 1995 has seen a significant expansion of special services, but the provision is still subject to considerable local variation.

A number of guidelines, consensus statements and local protocols exist. This guideline will review evidence of clinical and cost-effective practice, together with current guidelines, and will offer guidance on best practice.

5 The guideline

The guideline development process is described in detail in three booklets that are available from the NICE website (see paragraph 11). *The Guideline Development Process – Information for Stakeholders* describes how organisations can become involved in the development of a guideline.

This document is the scope. It defines exactly what this guideline will (and will not) examine, and what the guideline developers will consider. The scope is based on the referral from the Department of Health and Welsh Assembly Government; these organisations asked the Institute:

> to prepare a clinical guideline and audit tool for the NHS in England and Wales for 'talking' therapies, drug treatments and prescribing for anxiety and related common mental disorders, including generalised anxiety disorder (GAD), panic disorder (with or without agoraphobia), post-traumatic stress disorder, and obsessive–compulsive disorder (OCD). The audit tool should include a dataset, database and audit methodology.

The areas that will be addressed by the guideline are described in the following sections.

6 Population

The recommendations made in the guideline will cover management of the following groups:
- Adults and children of all ages who meet or are at risk of PTSD.

The guideline developers will be sensitive to the different approaches to PTSD of different races and cultures, and be aware of the issues of both internal and external social exclusion.

Traumatic experiences can affect the whole family and often the community. The guideline will recognise the role of both in the treatment and support of people with PTSD.

The primary focus of the guideline will be PTSD; however, comorbid factors such as drug misuse and alcoholism, pain disorders, major depression and developmental issues including personality disorder will also be considered.

7 Healthcare setting

The guideline will cover the care provided by primary, secondary and other healthcare professionals who have direct contact with, and make decisions concerning the care of, people with PTSD.

The guideline will also be relevant to the work, but will not cover the practice, of those in:
- occupational health services
- social services
- the independent sector.

8 Clinical management: areas that will be covered

The guideline will cover the following areas of clinical practice.

Diagnostic criteria currently in use for PTSD and the diagnostic factors that trigger the use of this guideline. The definition of the condition in relation to other anxiety disorders will be precise.

The guideline will address the issues of diagnosis, detection and the use of screening techniques in high-risk situations and include advice on the appropriate use of early intervention (psychological and pharmacological).

Pharmacological interventions for PTSD (those available in the UK according to the *British National Formulary*). When referring to pharmacological treatments, the guideline will whenever possible recommend within the licensed indications. However, where the evidence clearly supports it, recommendations for use outside the licensed indications may be made in exceptional circumstances. The guideline will expect that prescribers will use the Summary of Product Characteristics to inform their prescribing decisions for individual patients.

The guideline will include advice on the appropriate use of psychological interventions including type, modality, frequency and duration.

The guideline will include the appropriate use of combined pharmacological and psychological interventions.

The guideline will consider the side-effects, toxicity, acceptability and other disbenefits of treatments.

The guideline will recognise the need for people with PTSD to have information and opportunities to discuss with clinicians the advantages, disadvantages and potential side-effects of treatment, so that they can make informed choices about care options.

9 Clinical management: areas that will not be covered

The guideline will not cover treatments that are not normally available on the NHS.

10 Audit support within guideline

The guideline will include key review criteria for audit, which will enable objective measurements to be made of the extent and nature of local implementation of this guidance, particularly its impact upon practice and outcomes for people with PTSD.

11 Status

This is the final version of the scope. It has been derived from the scope on generalised anxiety which formerly included PTSD and which was subject to a 4-week period of consultation with stakeholders and review by the Guidelines Advisory Committee. As a result of that consultation, a decision was taken to prepare a separate guideline for PTSD and this separate scope was drafted and submitted to the Institute's Guideline Programme Director and Executive Lead for approval.

The development of the guideline recommendations began in spring 2003.

Further information on the guideline development process is provided in:
- *The Guideline Development Process – Information for the Public and the NHS*
- *The Guideline Development Process – Information for Stakeholders*
- *The Guideline Development Process – Information for National Collaborating Centres and Guideline Development Groups.*

These booklets are available as PDF files from the NICE website (www.nice.org.uk). Information on the progress of the guideline will also be available from the website.

Appendix 2: Stakeholders who responded to early requests for evidence

ASSIST (Assistance, Support and Self-Help in Surviving Trauma) Trauma Care

British Association for Counselling and Psychotherapy

British Geriatrics Society

College of Occupational Therapists

Eli Lilly

GlaxoSmithKline UK

Inner Cities Mental Health Group

NHS Quality Improvement Scotland

Pfizer

Royal College of Nursing

Solvay Healthcare Limited

Victim Support

Wyeth Laboratories

Appendix 3: Stakeholders and experts who responded to the first consultation draft of the guideline

Stakeholders

ASSIST (Assistance, Support and Self-Help in Surviving Trauma) Trauma Care

Association for Improvements in Maternity Services

Association of the British Pharmaceuticals Industry

Birth Trauma Association

Bolton Salford & Trafford Mental Health

British Association for Behavioural and Cognitive Psychotherapies

British Association for Counselling and Psychotherapy

British Association for Psychopharmacology

British Association of Art Therapists

British Psychological Society

Camden & Islington Mental Health and Social Care Trust

Centre for Trauma Studies/Traumatic Stress Services

Chartered Society of Physiotherapy

Cheshire & Wirral Partnership NHS Trust

CIS'ters

College of Occupational Therapists

Cornwall Partnership Trust

Counselling and Psychotherapy Trust

Department of Health

First Person Plural

GlaxoSmithKline UK

Hampshire Partnership NHS Trust

Human Givens Institute

Institute of Psychotrauma

Janssen-Cilag Ltd

London Ambulance Services NHS Trust

Moving Minds Ltd

National Childbirth Trust

National Mental Health Partnership

North Staffordshire Combined Healthcare NHS Trust

Oxfordshire Mental Health Care NHS Trust

Patient Involvement Unit for NICE

Royal College of Midwives

Royal College of Nursing

Royal College of Paediatrics and Child Health

Survivors Trust

Tavistock and Portman NHS Trust

UK Council for Psychotherapy

UK Society for the Study of Dissociation

Victim Support

West London Mental Health NHS Trust

WISH – Women in Secure Hospitals

Wyeth Laboratories

Experts

Mr Paul Atkinson

Dr Sandra Buck

Dr Judith Cohen

Dr Stephen Davies

Defence Medical Services

Dr Edna Foa

Dr Berthold Gersons

Dr Ben Green

Dr Rahul Kacker

Dr Blanaid Kelly

Dr Mark Mayal

Mr Peter McDermott

Dr Paul Rogers

Dr Barbara Rothbaum

Ms Sue Richardson

Dr Josef Ruzek

Dr Francine Shapiro

Dr Simon Wessely

Appendix 4: Researchers contacted to request information about unpublished or soon-to-be published studies

Arnoud Arntz

Richard Bryant

Willi Butollo

Claude Chemtob

Judith Cohen

Mark Creamer

Jonathan Davidson

Enrique Echeburua

Paul Emmelkamp

Edna Foa

Chris Freeman

Matt Friedman

Berthold Gersons

Louise Humphreys

Terry Keane

Dean Kilpatrick

Merel Kindt

Edward Kubany

Brett Litz

Andreas Maercker

Charles Marmar

Sandy McFarlane

Thomas Mellman

Lars-Göran Öst

Michael Otto

Roger Pitman

Mark Pollack

Patti Resick

David Riggs

Sue Rose

Barbara Rothbaum

Joe Ruzek

Paula Schnurr

Arieh Shalev

Dan Stein

Nick Tarrier

Agnes van der Minnen

Simon Wessely

Patricia White

Rachel Yehuda

Appendix 5: Clinical questions

Psychology

1. For people with PTSD, do psychological treatments improve patient outcomes compared with no treatment?
2. For people with PTSD, does any psychological treatment confer any advantage over any other psychological treatment?
3. For people exposed to trauma, do early psychological interventions improve patient outcomes compared with no intervention?
4. For people exposed to trauma, does any early psychological intervention confer any advantage compared with other psychological intervention?

Pharmacology

1. For people with PTSD, do pharmacological interventions improve patient outcomes compared with placebo?
2. For people with PTSD, do any pharmacological interventions confer any advantage over any other pharmacological interventions?
3. For people exposed to trauma, do early pharmacological interventions improve patient outcomes compared with placebo?
4. For people exposed to trauma, do any early pharmacological interventions confer any advantage over any other pharmacological interventions?

Psychology and pharmacology

1. For people with PTSD, do combinations of pharmacological and psychological interventions improve outcomes over no treatment/placebo?
2. For people with PTSD, do combinations of pharmacological and psychological interventions improve outcomes over psychological or pharmacological treatment alone?

Response to treatment

1. For adults with PTSD, do factors such as traumatic grief, depression, personality disorders, pain and drug and alcohol misuse predict response to treatment?
2. For children with PTSD, do factors such as parental involvement in the traumatic event predict response to treatment?

Screening and diagnosis

1. Are there routine screening methods that may be valuable in predicting who will develop PTSD?
2. Are there routine methods that may be valuable in confirming a clinical diagnosis of PTSD?

Risk factors

1   Do any factors or variables predict the development of PTSD?
2   Do any factors or variables predict the chronicity of PTSD?

Health economics

1   Initiation of treatment: are there significant additional costs associated with intervening early or later in the course of PTSD?

Appendix 6: Search strategies for the identification of clinical studies

General search filters

Medline, EMBASE, PsycINFO, CINAHL–OVID interface

A general search was conducted to extract randomised controlled trials and systematic reviews of randomised controlled trials, from which relevant papers were identified for each of the main chapters within this guideline (psychological interventions, pharmacological interventions, children and early interventions).

1 Stress Disorders, Traumatic/ or Combat Disorders/ or Stress Disorders, Post-Traumatic, Acute/ or Stress Disorders, Post-Traumatic/ or Stress, Psychological/

2 Stress, Psychological/ or Critical Incident Stress/ or Stress Disorders, Post-Traumatic/

3 Posttraumatic Stress Disorder/ or Emotional Trauma/ or Traumatic Neurosis/

4 Posttraumatic Stress Disorder/ or Psychotrauma/

5 (post?traumatic$ or post-traumatic$ or stress disorder$ or acute stress or PTSD or ASD or DESNOS).tw.

6 (combat neuros$ or combat syndrome or concentration camp syndrome or extreme stress or flash?back$ or flash-back$ or hypervigilan$ or hypervigilen$ or psych$ stress or psych$ trauma$ or psycho?trauma$ or psycho-trauma$).tw.

7 (railway spine or (rape adj2 trauma$) or re?experienc$ or re-experienc$ or torture syndrome or traumatic neuros$ or traumatic stress).tw.

8 (trauma$ and (avoidance or grief or horror or death$ or night?mare$ or night-mare$ or emotion$)).tw.

9 or/1–8

10 exp clinical trials/ or cross-over studies/ or random allocation/ or double-blind method/ or single-blind method/

11 random$.pt.

12 exp clinical trial/ or crossover procedure/ or double blind procedure/ or single blind procedure/ or randomization/

13 exp clinical trials/ or crossover design/ or random assignment/

14 exp clinical trials/ or double blind method/ or random allocation/

15 random$.mp.

16 (cross-over or cross?over or (clinical adj2 trial$) or single-blind$ or single?blind$ or double-blind or double?blind$ or triple-blind or triple?blind).tw.

17 or/10–16

18 animals/ not (animals/ and human$.mp.)

19 animal$/ not (animal$/ and human$/)

20 meta-analysis/

21 meta-analysis.pt.

22 systematic review/

23 or/18–22

24 17 not 23

25 9 and 24

26 or/1–5

27 or/6–8

28 26 and 24

29 27 and 24

30 remove duplicates from 29

31 remove duplicates from 28

32   30 or 31

33   remove duplicates from 32

In addition, the Cochrane Database of Systematic Reviews, the Cochrane Controlled Trials Register and the Database of Reviews of Effectiveness of the Cochrane Library were searched.

Narrative review search filters

Medline, EMBASE, PsycINFO–Dialog DataStar interface

Separate searches were conducted to cover narrative reviews for screening and risk factors.

The following search was used to update the systematic review undertaken by Brewin *et al* (2000) for longitudinal prospective studies.

#5 #3 and #4

#4 cohort* or longitudinal or prospective or case control*

#3 #1 and #2 and (PY=2000-2004)

#2 risk or predictor or prediction or predisposition

#1 post traumatic or posttraumatic or ptsd

Additional searches were conducted for specific risk factors such as injury, compensation and litigation and prospective screening tools. These search filters are available on request.

Appendix 7: Systematic review quality checklist

Checklist completed by:	Report reference ID:	
SECTION 1: VALIDITY		
Evaluation criteria	Notes for reviewer	
1.1 Does the review address an appropriate and clearly focused question?	Unless a clear and well-defined question is specified, it will be difficult to assess how well the study has met its objectives or how relevant it is to the question you are trying to answer on the basis of its conclusions.	
1.2 Does the review include a description of the methodology used?	A systematic review should include a detailed description of the methods used to identify and evaluate individual studies. If this description is not present, it is not possible to make a thorough evaluation of the quality of the review, and it should be rejected as a source of Level I evidence (although it may be useable as Level IV evidence, if no better evidence can be found.	
1.3 Was the literature search sufficiently rigorous to identify all relevant studies?	Consider whether the review used an electronic search of at least one bibliographic database (searching for studies dating at least 10 years before publication of the review). Any indication that hand-searching of key journals or follow-up of reference lists of included studies was done in addition to electronic database searches can normally be taken as evidence of a well-conducted review.	
1.4 Was study quality assessed and taken into account?	A well-conducted systematic review should have used clear criteria to assess whether individual studies had been well conducted before deciding whether to include or exclude them. At a minimum, the authors should have checked that there was adequate concealment of allocation, that the rate of withdrawal from the study was minimised, and that the results were analysed on an intention-to-treat basis. If there is no indication of such an assessment, the review should be rejected as a source of Level I evidence. If details of the assessment are poor, or the methods considered to be inadequate, the quality of the review should be downgraded.	
SECTION 2: OVERALL ASSESSMENT	Comments	Code
2.1 Low risk of bias Moderate risk of bias High risk of bias	All or most criteria met Most criteria partly met Few or no criteria met	A B C

Appendix 8: Randomised controlled trial methodological quality checklist

Checklist completed by:	Report reference ID:	
SECTION 1: INTERNAL VALIDITY		
Evaluation criteria	Notes for reviewer	
1.1 Was the assignment of participants to treatment groups randomised?	**If there is no indication of randomisation, the study should be rejected.** If the description of randomisation is poor, or the process used is not truly random (e.g. allocation by date, alternating between one group and another) or can otherwise be seen as flawed, the study should be given a lower quality rating.	
1.2 Was an adequate concealment method used?	Centralised allocation, computerised allocation systems or the use of coded identical containers would all be regarded as adequate methods of concealment, and may be taken as indicators of a well-conducted study. If the method of concealment used is regarded as poor or relatively easy to subvert, the study must be given a lower quality rating, and can be rejected if the concealment method is seen as inadequate.	
SECTION 2: OVERALL ASSESSMENT	Comments	Code
2.1 Low risk of bias Moderate risk of bias High risk of bias	Both criteria met One or more criteria partly met One or more criteria not met	A B C

Appendix 9: Clinical study data extraction form

Appendix 10: Methods for calculating means and standard deviations for pooled treatment groups

For a number of the analyses of psychological interventions, treatment groups within a study were combined for a particular comparison.

Where n_i is the sample size of treatment group i, m_i is the mean of treatment group i and sd_i is the standard deviation of treatment group i, the mean of the combined treatment group is estimated as

$$\Sigma_i \, n_i \, m_i \, / \, \Sigma \, n_i$$

and the standard deviation of the combined treatment group is estimated as

$$\sqrt{[\Sigma_i \, (n_i - 1) \, (sd_i)^2 \, / \, ((\Sigma_i \, n_i) - T)]}$$

where T is the number of treatment groups (all summations from 1 to T).

Appendix 11: Search strategies for the identification of health economics studies

General search filters

Medline, EMBASE, PsycINFO, CINAHL–OVID interface

A general search was conducted to extract randomised controlled trials and systematic reviews of randomised controlled trials, from which relevant papers were identified for each of the main chapters within this guideline (psychological interventions, pharmacological interventions, children and early interventions).

1. Stress Disorders, Traumatic/ or Combat Disorders/ or Stress Disorders, Post-Traumatic, Acute/ or Stress Disorders, Post-Traumatic/ or Stress, Psychological/
2. Stress, Psychological/ or Critical Incident Stress/ or Stress Disorders, Post-Traumatic/
3. Posttraumatic Stress Disorder/ or Emotional Trauma/ or Traumatic Neurosis/
4. Posttraumatic Stress Disorder/ or Psychotrauma/
5. (post?traumatic$ or post-traumatic$ or stress disorder$ or acute stress or PTSD or ASD or DESNOS).tw.
6. (combat neuros$ or combat syndrome or concentration camp syndrome or extreme stress or flash?back$ or flash-back$ or hypervigilan$ or hypervigilen$ or psych$ stress or psych$ trauma$ or psycho?trauma$ or psycho-trauma$).tw.
7. (railway spine or (rape adj2 trauma$) or re?experienc$ or re-experienc$ or torture syndrome or traumatic neuros$ or traumatic stress).tw.
8. (trauma$ and (avoidance or grief or horror or death$ or night?mare$ or night-mare$ or emotion$)).tw.
9. or/1–8
10. exp clinical trials/ or cross-over studies/ or random allocation/ or double-blind method/ or single-blind method/
11. random$.pt.
12. exp clinical trial/ or crossover procedure/ or double blind procedure/ or single blind procedure/ or randomization/
13. exp clinical trials/ or crossover design/ or random assignment/
14. exp clinical trials/ or double blind method/ or random allocation/
15. random$.mp.
16. (cross-over or cross?over or (clinical adj2 trial$) or single-blind$ or single?blind$ or double-blind or double?blind$ or triple-blind or triple?blind).tw.
17. or/10–16
18. animals/ not (animals/ and human$.mp.)
19. animal$/ not (animal$/ and human$/)
20. meta-analysis/
21. meta-analysis.pt.
22. systematic review/
23. or/18–22
24. 17 not 23
25. 9 and 24
26. or/1–5
27. or/6–8
28. 26 and 24
29. 27 and 24
30. remove duplicates from 29
31. remove duplicates from 28

32   30 or 31
33   remove duplicates from 32

In addition, the Cochrane Database of Systematic Reviews, the Cochrane Controlled Trials Register and the Database of Reviews of Effectiveness of the Cochrane Library were searched.

Narrative review search filters

Medline, EMBASE, PsycINFO–Dialog DataStar interface

Separate searches were conducted to cover narrative reviews for screening and risk factors.

The following search was used to update the systematic review undertaken by Brewin *et al* (2000) for longitudinal prospective studies.

> #5 #3 and #4
> #4 cohort* or longitudinal or prospective or case control*
> #3 #1 and #2 and (PY=2000–2004)
> #2 risk or predictor or prediction or predisposition
> #1 post traumatic or posttraumatic or ptsd

Additional searches were conducted for specific risk factors such as injury, compensation and litigation and prospective screening tools. These search filters are available on request.

Health economics search filters

PTSD – General +

1   (burden adj2 illness).mp.
2   (burden adj2 disease).mp.
3   (cost$ adj2 evaluat$).mp.
4   (cost$ adj2 benefit$).mp.
5   (cost$ adj2 utilit$).mp.
6   (cost$ adj2 minimi$).mp.
7   (cost$ adj2 illness).mp.
8   (cost$ adj2 disease).mp.
9   (cost$ adj2 analys$).mp.
10   (cost$ adj2 assess$).mp.
11   (cost$ adj2 study).mp.
12   (cost$ adj2 studies).mp.
13   (cost$ adj2 allocation).mp.
14   (cost$ adj2 outcome$).mp.
15   (cost$ adj2 consequence$).mp.
16   (cost$ adj2 effect$).mp.
17   (cost$ adj2 treatment$).mp.
18   (economic adj2 evaluat$).mp.
19   (economic adj2 analysis$).mp.
20   (economic adj2 study).mp.
21   (economic adj2 studies).mp.
22   (economic adj2 assess$).mp.
23   (economic adj2 consequence$).mp.
24   (economic adj2 outcome$).mp.
25   (resource$ adj2 allocation$).mp.
26   (resource$ adj2 utili$).mp.
27   expenditure$.mp.
28   exp economics/
29   exp "costs and cost analysis"/
30   exp "health economics"/
31   or/1-30

Appendix 12: Quality checklists for economic studies

Full economic evaluations

Author: **Date:**

Title: Yes   No   NA

Study design

		Yes	No	NA
1	The research question is stated	☐	☐	
2	The viewpoint(s) of the analysis are clearly stated	☐	☐	
3	The alternatives being compared are relevant	☐	☐	
4	The rationale for choosing the alternative programmes or interventions compared is stated	☐	☐	
5	The alternatives being compared are clearly described	☐	☐	
6	The form of economic evaluation used is justified in relation to the question addressed	☐	☐	

Data collection

		Yes	No	NA
1	The source of effectiveness data used is stated	☐	☐	
2	Details of the design and results of effectiveness study are given	☐	☐	☐
3	The primary outcome measure(s) for the economic evaluation are clearly stated	☐	☐	
4	Methods to value health states and other benefits are stated	☐	☐	
5	Details of the subjects from whom valuations were obtained are given	☐	☐	
6	Indirect costs (if included) are reported separately	☐	☐	☐
7	Quantities of resources are reported separately from their unit costs	☐	☐	
8	Methods for the estimation of quantities and unit costs are described	☐	☐	
9	Currency and price data are recorded	☐	☐	
10	Details of currency of price adjustments for inflation or currency conversion are given	☐	☐	☐
11	Details of any model used are given	☐	☐	☐
12	The choice of model used and the key parameters on which it is based are justified	☐	☐	☐

Analysis and interpretation of results

		Yes	No	NA
1	Time horizon of costs and benefits is stated	☐	☐	
2	The discount rate(s) is stated	☐	☐	☐
3	The choice of rate(s) is justified	☐	☐	☐
4	An explanation is given if costs or benefits are not discounted	☐	☐	☐
5	Details of statistical tests and confidence intervals are given for stochastic data	☐	☐	☐
6	The approach to sensitivity analysis is given	☐	☐	
7	The choice of variables for sensitivity analysis is given	☐	☐	
8	The ranges over which the variables are varied are stated	☐	☐	
9	Relevant alternatives are compared	☐	☐	
10	Incremental analysis is reported	☐	☐	☐
11	Major outcomes are presented in a disaggregated as well as aggregated form	☐	☐	
12	The answer to the study question is given	☐	☐	
13	Conclusions follow from the data reported	☐	☐	
14	Conclusions are accompanied by the appropriate caveats	☐	☐	

Partial economic evaluations

Author: **Date:**

Title:

		Yes	No	NA
Study design				
1	The research question is stated	☐	☐	
2	The viewpoint(s) of the analysis are clearly stated and justified	☐	☐	
Data collection				
1	Details of the subjects from whom valuations were obtained are given	☐	☐	
2	Indirect costs (if included) are reported separately	☐	☐	☐
3	Quantities of resources are reported separately from their unit costs	☐	☐	
4	Methods for the estimation of quantities and unit costs are described	☐	☐	
5	Currency and price data are recorded	☐	☐	
6	Details of currency of price adjustments for inflation or currency conversion are given	☐	☐	☐
7	Details of any model used are given	☐	☐	☐
8	The choice of model used and the key parameters on which it is based are justified	☐	☐	☐
Analysis and interpretation of results				
1	Time horizon of costs is stated	☐	☐	
2	The discount rate(s) is stated	☐	☐	☐
3	Details of statistical tests and confidence intervals are given for stochastic data	☐	☐	☐
4	The choice of variables for sensitivity analysis is given	☐	☐	
5	Appropriate sensitivity analysis is performed	☐	☐	
6	The answer to the study question is given	☐	☐	
7	Conclusions follow from the data reported	☐	☐	
8	Conclusions are accompanied by the appropriate caveats	☐	☐	

Appendix 13: Diagnostic criteria

Diagnostic criteria for post-traumatic stress disorder in ICD–10 and DSM–IV

ICD–10 diagnostic guidelines	ICD–10 research diagnostic criteria	DSM–IV criteria
Stressor criterion 1 Event or situation of exceptionally threatening or catastrophic nature 2 Likely to cause pervasive distress in almost anyone	**Stressor criterion** A1 Event or situation of exceptionally threatening or catastrophic nature 2 Likely to cause pervasive distress in almost anyone	A1 The person experienced, witnessed, or was confronted with an event or events that involved actual or threatened death or serious injury, or a threat to the physical integrity of self or others 2 The person's response involved intense fear, helplessness, or horror (or disorganized or agitated behaviour in children)
Symptom criterion *Necessary symptom* 1 Repetitive intrusive recollection or re-enactment of the event in memories, daytime imagery, or dreams *Other typical symptoms* 2 Sense of 'numbness' and emotional blunting, detachment from others, unresponsiveness to surroundings, anhedonia 3 Avoidance of activities and situations reminiscent of trauma *Common symptoms* 4 Autonomic hyperarousal with hypervigilance, enhanced startle reaction, insomnia 5 Anxiety and depression *Rare symptoms* 6 Dramatic acute bursts of fear, panic, or aggression triggered by reminders	*Necessary symptoms* B Persistent remembering or 'reliving' of the stressor in intrusive 'flashbacks', vivid memories, or recurring dreams, and in experiencing distress when exposed to circumstances resembling or associated with the stressor C Actual or preferred avoidance of circumstances resembling or associated with the stressor which was not present before exposure to the stressor D1 Inability to recall, either partially or completely, some important aspects or the period of exposure to the stressor OR 2 Persistent symptoms of increased psychological sensitivity and arousal (not present before exposure to the stressor), shown by any two of the following (a) Difficulty in falling or staying asleep (b) Irritability or outbursts of anger (c) Difficulty in concentrating (d) Hypervigilance (e) Exaggerated startle response	*Necessary symptoms* B The traumatic event is persistently re-experienced in one (or more) of the following ways 1 Recurrent and intrusive distressing recollections of the event, including images, thoughts, or perceptions (or repetitive play in which the themes or aspects of the trauma are expressed in children) 2 Recurrent distressing dreams of the event (or frightening dreams without recognizable content in children) 3 Acting or feeling as if the traumatic event were recurring (or trauma-specific re-enactment in children) 4 Intense psychological distress at exposure to internal or external cues that symbolize or resemble an aspect of the traumatic event 5 Physiological reactivity at exposure to internal or external cues that symbolize or resemble an aspect of the traumatic event C Persistent avoidance of stimuli associated with the trauma and numbing of general responsiveness (not present before trauma), as indicated by three (or more) of the following 1 Efforts to avoid thoughts, feelings, or conversations associated with the trauma 2 Efforts to avoid activities, places, or people that arouse recollections of the trauma 3 Inability to recall an important aspect of the trauma 4 Markedly diminished interest or participation in significant activities 5 Feeling of detachment or estrangement from others 6 Restricted range of affect 7 Sense of foreshortened future D Persistent symptoms of increased arousal (not present before the trauma), as indicated by two (or more) of the following 1 Difficulty falling or staying asleep 2 Irritability or outbursts of anger 3 Difficulty concentrating 4 Hypervigilance 5 Exaggerated startle response

ICD–10 diagnostic guidelines (contd...)	ICD–10 research diagnostic criteria (contd...)	DSM–IV criteria (contd...)
Time frame Symptoms should usually arise within 6 months of traumatic event	Symptoms should usually arise within 6 months of the traumatic event	Symptoms present for at least 1 month
Disability criterion NA	NA	The disturbance causes clinically significant distress or impairment in social, occupational, or other important areas of functioning
Differential diagnosis 1 Acute stress reaction (F43.0) (immediate reaction in the first 3 days after event) 2 Enduring personality change after a catastrophic experience (F62.0) (present for at least 2 years, only after extreme and prolonged stress) 3 Adjustment disorder (less severe stressor or different symptom pattern) 4 Other anxiety or depressive disorders (absence of traumatic stressor or symptoms precede stressor)	Same as ICD–10 diagnostic guidelines	1 Acute stress disorder (duration of up to 4 weeks) 2 Adjustment disorder (less severe stressor or different symptom pattern) 3 Mood disorder or other anxiety disorder (symptoms of avoidance, numbing or hyperarousal present before exposure to the stressor) 4 Other disorders with intrusive thoughts or perceptual disturbances (e.g. obsessive–compulsive disorder, schizophrenia, other psychotic disorders, substance-induced disorders)

Adapted from Ehlers, A. (2000) Post-traumatic stress disorder (Table 1). In *New Oxford Textbook of Psychiatry*, Vol. 1 (eds M. G. Gelder, J. J. Lopez-Ibor & N. Andreasen), pp. 758–771. Oxford: Oxford University Press. Reproduced by permission of Oxford University Press.

References

Achenbach, T. M. & Edelbrock, C. S. (1983) *Manual for the Child Behavior Checklist and Revised Child Behavior Profile.* Burlington, VT: University Associates in Psychiatry.

Adler, A. (1943) Neuropsychiatric complications in victims of Boston's Cocoanut Grove disaster. *JAMA*, **123**, 1098–1101.

AGREE Collaboration (2001) *Appraisal of Guidelines for Research and Evaluation (AGREE) Instrument.* London: St George's Hospital Medical School (http://www.agreecollaboration.org).

Alderson, P., Green, S. & Higgins, J. P. T. (eds) (2004) *Cochrane Reviewers' Handbook 4.2.2.* http://www.cochrane.org/resources/handbook/hbook.htm.

American Psychiatric Association (1980) *Diagnostic and Statistical Manual of Mental Disorders* (3rd edn) (DSM–III). Washington, DC: APA.

American Psychiatric Association (1994) *Diagnostic and Statistical Manual of Mental Disorders* (4th edn) (DSM–IV). Washington, DC: APA.

American Psychiatric Association (2000) *Handbook of Psychiatric Measures.* Washington, DC: APA.

Andrews, G., Slade, T. & Peters, L. (1999) Classification in psychiatry: ICD–10 versus DSM–IV. *British Journal of Psychiatry*, **174**, 3–5.

Avery, A. & Orner, A. A. (1998) First report of psychological debriefing abandoned – the end of an era? *Traumatic Stress Points*, **12**, 3–4.

Babor, T. F., de la Fuente, J. R., Saunders, J., et al (1992) *AUDIT. The Alcohol Use Diorders Identification Test. Guidelines for Use in Primary Health Care.* Geneva: World Health Organization.

Barlow, D. H. & Lehman, C. L. (1996) Advances in the psychosocial treatment of anxiety disorders. Implications for national health care. *Archives of General Psychiatry*, **53**, 727–735.

Basoglu, M., Livanou, M., Salcioglu, E., et al (2003) A brief behavioural treatment of chronic post-traumatic stress disorder in earthquake survivors: results from an open clinical trial. *Psychological Medicine*, **33**, 647–654.

Basoglu, M., Salcioglu, E., Livanou, M., et al (2005) Single-session behavioural treatment of earthquake-related posttraumatic stress disorder: a randomised controlled trial. *Journal of Traumatic Stress*, in press.

Beck, A. T. (1976) *Cognitive Therapy and the Emotional Disorders.* New York: International Universities Press.

Beck, A. T. & Steer, R. A. (1993) *Beck Anxiety Inventory Manual.* San Antonio, TX: Psychological Corporation.

Beck, A. T., Ward, C. H., Mendelson, M., et al (1961) An inventory for measuring depression. *Archives of General Psychiatry*, **4**, 561–571.

Berlin, J. A. (1997) Does blinding of readers affect the results of meta-analyses? University of Pennsylvania Meta-Analysis Blinding Study Group. *Lancet*, **350**, 185–186.

Birnbaum, H. G., Shi, L., Dial, E., et al (2003) Economic consequences of not recognizing bipolar disorder patients: a cross-sectional descriptive analysis. *Journal of Clinical Psychiatry*, **64**, 1201–1205.

Bisson, J. I. (2000) *The effectiveness of psychological debriefing for victims of acute burn trauma.* DM Thesis, Southampton University.

Bisson, J. I., Jenkins, P. L., Alexander, J., et al (1997) Randomised controlled trial of psychological debriefing for victims of acute burn trauma. *British Journal of Psychiatry*, **171**, 78–81.

Bisson, J. I., Roberts, N. & Macho, G. (2003) The Cardiff traumatic stress initiative: an evidence-based approach to early psychological intervention following traumatic events. *Psychiatric Bulletin*, **27**, 145–147.

Blake, D. D., Weathers, F. W., Nagy, L. M., *et al* (1995) The development of a Clinician-Administered PTSD Scale. *Journal of Traumatic Stress*, **8**, 75–90.

Blanchard, E. B. & Hickling, E. J. (2004) *After the Crash. Psychological Assessment and Treatment of Survivors of Motor Vehicle Accidents* (2nd edn). Washington, DC: APA.

Blanchard, E. B., Hickling, E. J., Taylor, A. E., *et al* (1996) Who develops PTSD from motor vehicle accidents? *Behaviour Research and Therapy*, **34**, 1–10.

Blanchard, E. B., Hickling, E. J., Devineni, T., *et al* (2003*a*) A controlled evaluation of cognitive behavioural therapy for posttraumatic stress in motor vehicle accident survivors. *Behaviour Research and Therapy*, **41**, 79–96.

Blanchard, E. B., Hickling, E. J., Malta, L. S., *et al* (2003*b*) Prediction of response to psychological treatment among motor vehicle accident survivors with PTSD. *Behavior Therapy*, **34**, 351–363.

Bond, T. (2000) *Standards and Ethics for Counselling in Action* (2nd edn). London: Sage.

Bownes, I. T., O'Gorman, E. C. & Sayers, A. (1990) Assault characteristics and posttraumatic stress disorder in rape victims. *Acta Psychiatrica Scandinavica*, **83**, 27–30.

Bramble, D. (2003) Annotation: the use of psychotropic medications in children: a British view. *Journal of Child Psychology and Psychiatry and Allied Disciplines*, **44**, 169–179.

Bremner, J. D., Licinio, J., Darnell, A., *et al* (1997) Elevated CSF corticotropin-releasing factor concentrations in posttraumatic stress disorder. *American Journal of Psychiatry*, **154**, 624–629.

Breslau, N., Davis, G. C., Andreski, P., *et al* (1991) Traumatic events and posttraumatic stress disorder in an urban population of young adults. *Archives of General Psychiatry*, **48**, 216–222.

Breslau, N., Davis, G. C., Andreski, P., *et al* (1997) Sex differences in posttraumatic stress disorder. *Archives of General Psychiatry*, **54**, 1044–1048.

Breslau, N., Kessler, R. C., Chilcoat, H. D., *et al* (1998) Trauma and posttraumatic stress disorder in the community: the 1996 Detroit Area Survey of Trauma. *Archives of General Psychiatry*, **55**, 626–632.

Brett, E. (1993) Classifications of post-traumatic stress disorder in DSM–IV: anxiety disorder, dissociative disorder, or stress disorder? In *Post-Traumatic Stress Disorder: DSM–IV and Beyond* (eds J. R. T. Davidson & E. B. Foa), pp. 191–204. Washington DC: APA.

Breuer, J. & Freud, S. (1895) Studies of hysteria. Reprinted (1955) in the *Standard Edition of the Complete Psychological Works of Sigmund Freud* (trans. & ed. J. Strachey), vol. 2, pp. 1–335. London: Hogarth Press.

Brewin, C. R. (2005) Systematic review of screening instruments for the detection of posttraumatic stress disorder in adults. *Journal of Traumatic Stress*, in press.

Brewin, C. R., Dalgleish, T. & Joseph, S. (1996) A dual representation theory of posttraumatic stress disorder. *Psychological Review*, **103**, 670–686.

Brewin, C. R., Andrews, B. & Valentine, J. D. (2000) Meta-analysis of risk factors for post-traumatic stress disorder in trauma-exposed adults. *Journal of Consulting and Clinical Psychology*, **68**, 748–766.

Brewin, C. R., Rose, S., Andrews, B., *et al* (2002) Brief screening instrument for post-traumatic stress disorder. *British Journal of Psychiatry*, **181**, 158–162.

British Psychological Society (2002) *Psychological Debriefing: Professional Practice Board Working Party*. Leicester: BPS.

Brom, D., Kleber, R. J. & Defares, P. B. (1989) Brief psychotherapy for posttraumatic stress disorders. *Journal of Consulting and Clinical Psychology*, **57**, 607–612.

Bryant, R. A. (2003) Early predictors of posttraumatic stress disorder. *Biological Psychiatry*, **53**, 789–795.

Bryant, R. A. & Harvey, A. G. (1995) Avoidant coping style and post-traumatic stress following motor vehicle accidents. *Behaviour Research and Therapy*, **33**, 631–635.

Bryant, R. A. & Harvey, A. G. (1998) Relationship between acute stress disorder and posttraumatic stress disorder following mild traumatic brain injury. *American Journal of Psychiatry*, **155**, 625–629.

Bryant, R. A. & Harvey, A. G. (2003) The influence of litigation on maintenance of posttraumatic stress disorder. *Journal of Nervous and Mental Disease*, **191**, 191–193.

Bryant, R. A., Harvey, A. G., Dang, S. T., *et al* **(1998)** Treatment of acute stress disorder: a comparison of cognitive-behavioural therapy and supportive counselling. *Journal of Consulting and Clinical Psychology*, **66**, 862–866.

Bryant, R. A., Moulds, M. L., Guthrie, R. M., *et al* **(2003)** Imaginal exposure alone and imaginal exposure with cognitive restructuring in treatment of posttraumatic stress disorder. *Journal of Consulting and Clinical Psychology*, **71**, 706–712.

Cahill, S. P., Hembree, E. A. & Foa, E. B. (2005) Dissemination of prolonged exposure therapy for posttraumatic stress disorder: successes and challenges. In *9/11: Public Health in the Wake of Terrorist Attacks* (eds Y. Neria, R. Gross, R. Marshall, *et al*). Cambridge: Cambridge University Press, in press.

Cardeòa, E., Maldonado, J., van der Hart, O., *et al* **(2000)** Hypnosis. In *Effective Treatments for PTSD: Practice Guidelines from the International Society for Traumatic Stress Studies* (eds E. B. Foa, T. M. Keane & M. J. Friedman), pp. 247–279, 350–353. New York: Guilford Press.

Carlier, I. V. E., Lamberts, R. D., Van Uchelen, A. J., *et al* **(1998)** Clinical utility of a brief diagnostic test for posttraumatic stress disorder. *Psychosomatic Medicine*, **60**, 42–47.

Carlson, E. B. (2001) Psychometric study of a brief screen for PTSD: assessing the impact of multiple traumatic events. *Assessment*, **8**, 431–441.

Charney, D., Deutch, A. Y., Krystal, J. H., *et al* **(1993)** Psychobiological mechanisms of posttraumatic stress disorder. *Archives of General Psychiatry*, **50**, 294–305.

Chemtob, C. M., Muraoka, M. Y., Wu-Holt, P., *et al* **(1998)** Head injury and combat-related posttraumatic stress disorder. *Journal of Nervous and Mental Disease*, **186**, 701–708.

Chemtob, C. M., Nakashima, J. & Carlson, J. G. (2002) Brief treatment for elementary school children with disaster-related posttraumatic stress disorder: a field study. *Journal of Clinical Psychology*, **58**, 99–112.

Chou, F. H. C., Su, T. T. P., Ou-Yang, W. C., *et al* **(2003)** Establishment of a disaster-related psychological screening test. *Australian and New Zealand Journal of Psychiatry*, **37**, 97–103.

Cienfuegos, A. J. & Monelli, C. (1983) The testimony of political repression as a therapeutic instrument. *American Journal of Orthopsychiatry*, **53**, 43–51.

Clark, D. M. (1999) Anxiety disorders: why they persist and how to treat them. *Behaviour Research and Therapy*, **37**, S5–S27.

Cochrane Collaboration (2003) *Review Manager (RevMan) Version 4.2 for Windows*. Oxford: Cochrane Collaboration.

Cohen, J. (1988) *Statistical Power Analysis for the Behavioral Sciences*. Hillsdale, NJ: Erlbaum.

Cohen, J. A., Mannarino, A., Berliner, L., *et al* **(2000)** Trauma-focused cognitive behavioural therapy for children and adolescents. *Journal of Interpersonal Violence*, **15**, 1202–1223.

Comijs, H. C., Penninx, B. W. J. H., Knipscheer, K. P. M., *et al* **(1999)** Psychological distress in victims of elder mistreatment: the effects of social support and coping. *Journal of Gerontology, Psychological Sciences*, **54B**, 240–245.

Committee on Safety of Medicines (2004) Safety of SSRI antidepressants. http://www.info.doh.gov.uk/doh/embroadcast.nsf/vwDiscussionAll/9AA9EC56B07B3B4F80256F61004BAA88

Creamer, M., Burgess, P. & McFarlane, A. C. (2001) Post-traumatic stress disorder: findings from the Australian National Survey of Mental Health and Well-being. *Psychological Medicine*, **31**, 1237–1247.

Creamer, M., O'Donnell, M. L. & Pattison, P. (2004) The relationship between acute stress disorder and posttraumatic stress disorder in severely injured trauma survivors. *Behaviour Research and Therapy*, **42**, 315–328.

Cross, M. R. & McCanne, T. R. (2001) Validation of a self-report measure of posttraumatic stress disorder in a sample of college-age women. *Journal of Traumatic Stress*, **14**, 135–147.

Davidson, J. R. T., Book, S. W., Colket, J. T., *et al* **(1997)** Assessment of a new self-rating scale for post-traumatic stress disorder. *Psychological Medicine*, **27**, 153–160.

Davidson, P. R. & Parker, K. C. H. (2001) Eye movement desensitization and reprocessing (EMDR): a meta-analysis. *Journal of Consulting and Clinical Psychology*, **69**, 305–316.

Department of Health (1995) *ABC of Health Promotion in the Workplace. A Resource Pack for Employees*. London: Department of Health.

Department of Health (1996) *Clinical Guidelines: Using Clinical Guidelines to Improve Patient Care Within the NHS*. Leeds: NHS Executive.

Derogatis, L. R. (1983) *SCL-90-R: Administration, Scoring, and Procedures Manual-II for the Revised Version* (2nd edn, revised). Baltimore, MD: Clinical Psychometric Research.

DerSimonian, R. & Laird, N. (1986) Meta-analysis in clinical trials. *Controlled Clinical Trials*, **7**, 177–188.

Devilly, G. J. & Spence, S. H. (1999) The relative efficacy and treatment distress of EMDR and a cognitive-behavior trauma treatment protocol in the amelioration of posttraumatic stress disorder. *Journal of Anxiety Disorders*, **13**, 131–157.

Dreessen, L. & Arntz, A. (1998) The impact of personality disorders on treatment outcome of anxiety disorders: best-evidence synthesis. *Behaviour Research and Therapy*, **36**, 483–504.

Drummond, M. F. & Jefferson, T. O. (1996) Guidelines for authors and peer reviewers of economic submissions to the BMJ. *BMJ*, **313**, 275–283.

Drummond, M., O'Brien, B., Stoddart, G., *et al* **(1997)** *Methods for the Economic Evaluation of Health Care Programmes* (2nd edn). Oxford: Oxford University Press.

Easton, J. A. & Turner, S. W. (1991) Detention of British citizens as hostages in the Gulf: health, psychological, and family consequences. *BMJ*, **303**, 1231–1234.

Eccles, M. & Mason, J. (2001) How to develop cost-conscious guidelines. *Health Technology Assessment*, **5**, 1–69.

Eccles, M., Freemantle, N. & Mason, J. (1998) North of England evidence based guidelines development project: methods of developing guidelines for efficient drug use in primary care. *BMJ*, **316**, 1232–1235.

Ehlers, A. (2000) Post-traumatic stress disorder. In *New Oxford Textbook of Psychiatry* (eds M. G. Gelder, J. J. Lopez-Ibor & N. Andreasen), vol. 1, pp. 758–771. Oxford: Oxford University Press.

Ehlers, A. & Clark, D. M. (2000) A cognitive model of posttraumatic stress disorder. *Behaviour Research and Therapy*, **38**, 319–345.

Ehlers, A., Mayou, R. A. & Bryant, B. (1998) Psychological predictors of chronic posttraumatic stress disorder after motor vehicle accidents. *Journal of Abnormal Psychology*, **107**, 508–519.

Ehlers, A., Maercker, A. & Boos, A. (2000) Posttraumatic stress disorder following political imprisonment: the role of mental defeat, alienation, and permanent change. *Journal of Abnormal Psychology*, **109**, 45–55.

Ehlers, A., Clark, D. M., Hackmann, A., *et al* **(2003)** A randomized controlled trial of cognitive therapy, a self-help booklet, and repeated assessments as early interventions for posttraumatic stress disorder. *Archives of General Psychiatry*, **60**, 1024–1032.

Ehlers, A., Hackmann, A. & Michael, T. (2004) Intrusive re-experiencing in post-traumatic stress disorder: phenomenology, theory, and therapy. *Memory*, **12**, 403–415

Ehlers, A., Clark, D., Hackmann, A., *et al* **(2005)** Cognitive therapy for posttraumatic stress disorder: development and evaluation. *Behaviour Research and Therapy*, in press.

Endicott, J., Spitzer, R., Fleiss, J., *et al* **(1976)** The global assessment scale: a procedure for measuring overall severity of psychiatric disturbance. *Archives of General Psychiatry*, **33**, 766–771.

Eth, S. (ed.) (2001) PTSD in children and adolescents. *Review of Psychiatry*, **20**, 59–86.

Everly, G. S., Boyle, S. & Lating, J. (1999) Effectiveness of psychological debriefing with vicarious trauma: a meta-analysis. *Stress Medicine*, **15**, 229–233.

Ewing, J. A. (1984) Detecting alcoholism: the CAGE questionnaire. *Journal of the American Medical Association*, **252**, 1905–1907.

Famularo, R., Kinscherff, R. & Fenton, T. (1988) Propranolol treatment for childhood posttraumatic stress disorder, acute type. A pilot study. *American Journal of Diseases in Children*, **142**, 1244–1247.

Fecteau, G. & Nicki, R. (1999) Cognitive behavioural treatment of post traumatic stress disorder after motor vehicle accident. *Behavioural and Cognitive Psychotherapy*, **27**, 201–214.

First, M. B., Spitzer, R. L., Gibbon, M., *et al* (1995) *Structured Clinical Interview for DSM–IV Axis I Disorders – Patient Edition (SCID–I/P, Version 2.0).* New York: Biometrics Research Department of the New York State Psychiatric Institute.

Foa, E. B. & Kozak, M. J. (1986) Emotional processing of fear: exposure to corrective information. *Psychological Bulletin*, **99**, 20–35.

Foa, E. B. & Rothbaum, B. O. (1998) *Treating the Trauma of Rape: Cognitive–Behavioral Therapy for PTSD.* New York: Guilford Press.

Foa, E. B., Rothbaum, B. O., Riggs, D. S., *et al* (1991) Treatment of posttraumatic stress disorder in rape victims: a comparison between cognitive–behavioral procedures and counseling. *Journal of Consulting and Clinical Psychology*, **59**, 715–723.

Foa, E. B., Riggs, D. S., Dancu, C. V., *et al* (1993) Reliability and validity of a brief instrument for assessing post-traumatic stress disorder. *Journal of Traumatic Stress*, **6**, 459–473.

Foa, E. B., Cashman, L., Jaycox, L., *et al* (1997) The validation of a self-report measure of posttraumatic stress disorder: the Posttraumatic Diagnostic Scale. *Psychological Assessment*, **9**, 445–451.

Foa, E. B., Ehlers, A., Clark, D. M., *et al* (1999) The Posttraumatic Cognitions Inventory (PTCI): development and validation. *Psychological Assessment*, **11**, 303–314.

Foa, E. B., Keane, T. & Friedman, M. (2000) *Effective Treatments for PTSD: Practice Guidelines from the International Society for Traumatic Stress Studies.* New York: Guilford Press.

Foa, E., Johnson, K., Feeny, N., *et al* (2001) The Child PTSD Symptom Scale: a preliminary examination of its psychometric properties. *Journal of Clinical Child Psychology*, **30**, 376–384.

Fontana, A. & Rosenheck, R. (1998) Effects of compensation-seeking on treatment outcomes among veterans with posttraumatic stress disorder. *Journal of Nervous and Mental Disease*, **186**, 223–230.

Franklin, C. L., Repasky, S. A., Thompson, K. E., *et al* (2003) Assessment of response style in combat veterans seeking compensation for posttraumatic stress disorder. *Journal of Traumatic Stress*, **16**, 251–255.

Freud, S. (1920) Beyond the pleasure principle. Reprinted (1953–1974) in the *Standard Edition of the Complete Psychological Works of Sigmund Freud* (trans. & ed. J. Strachey), vol 18. London: Hogarth Press.

Friedman, M. J., Davidson, J. R. T. & Mellman, T. A. (2000) Pharmacotherapy. In *Effective Treatments for PTSD: Practice Guidelines from the International Society for Traumatic Stress Studies* (eds E. B. Foa, T. M. Keane & M. J. Friedman), pp. 84–105. New York: Guilford Press.

Friedrich, W. N., Grambsch, P., Damon, L., *et al* (1992) Child sexual behavior inventory: normative and clinical findings. *Psychological Assessment*, **4**, 303–311.

Frommberger, U., Stieglitz, R. D., Nyberg, E., *et al* (2004) Comparison between paroxetine and behaviour therapy in patients with posttraumatic stress disorder (PTSD): a pilot study. *International Journal of Psychiatry in Clinical Practice*, **8**, 19–23.

Fullerton, C. S., Ursano, R. J., Epstein, R. S., *et al* (2000) Measurement of posttraumatic stress disorder in community samples. *Nordic Journal of Psychiatry*, **54**, 5–12.

Garland, C. (ed.) (1998) *Understanding Trauma: A Psychoanalytical Approach.* London: Duckworth.

Gersons, B. P. & Carlier, I. V. E. (1992) Post-traumatic stress disorder: the history of a recent concept. *British Journal of Psychiatry*, **161**, 742–748.

Gersons, B. P., Carlier, I. V., Lamberts, R. D., *et al* (2000) Randomized clinical trial of brief eclectic psychotherapy for police officers with posttraumatic stress disorder. *Journal of Traumatic Stress*, **13**, 333–347.

Giaconia, R. M., Reinherz, H. Z., Silverman, A. B., *et al* (1995) Traumas and posttraumatic stress disorder in a community population of older adolescents. *Journal of the American Academy of Child and Adolescent Psychiatry*, **34**, 1369–1380.

Gilbertson, M. W., Shenton, M. E., Ciszewski, A., *et al* (2002) Smaller hippocampal volume predicts pathologic vulnerability to psychological trauma. *Nature Neuroscience*, **5**, 1242–1247.

Gillespie, K., Duffy, M., Hackmann, A., *et al* (2002) Community based cognitive therapy in the treatment of posttraumatic stress disorder following the Omagh bomb. *Behaviour Research and Therapy*, **40**, 345–357.

Gray, M. J. & Acierno, R. (2002) Symptom presentations of older adult crime victims: description of a clinical sample. *Journal of Anxiety Disorders*, **16**, 299–309.

Greenwald, R. & Rubin, A. (1999) Brief assessment of children's post-traumatic symptoms: development and preliminary validation of parent and child scales. *Research on Social Work Practice*, **9**, 61–75.

Haddad, P. M. (2001) Antidepressant discontinuation syndromes. *Drug Safety*, **24**, 183–197.

Hammarberg, M. (1992) Penn Inventory for Posttraumatic Stress Disorder: psychometric properties. *Psychological Assessment*, **4**, 67–76.

Hansard (2004) House of Commons: Written Answers from Mary Eagle, 27 May 2004; col. 1790W. London: Stationery Office.

Harmon, R. J. & Riggs, P. D. (1996) Clonidine for posttraumatic stress disorder in preschool children. *Journal of the American Academy of Child and Adolescent Psychiatry*, **35**, 1247–1249.

Harvey, A. G. & Bryant, R. A. (1998) The relationship between acute stress disorder and posttraumatic stress disorder: a prospective evaluation of motor vehicle accident survivors. *Journal of Consulting and Clinical Psychology*, **66**, 507–512.

Heim, C. & Nemeroff, C. B. (2001) The role of childhood trauma in the neurobiology of mood and anxiety disorders: preclinical and clinical studies. *Biological Psychiatry*, **49**, 1023–1039.

Herman, J. (1993) Sequelae of prolonged and repeated trauma: evidence for a Complex Posttraumatic Syndrome (DESNOS). In *Posttraumatic Stress Disorder: DSM–IV and Beyond* (eds J. R. T. Davidson & E. B. Foa), pp. 213–228. Washington, DC: American Psychiatric Press.

Herman, J. I. (1997) *Trauma and Recovery*. New York: Basic Books.

Higgins, J. P. T. & Thompson, S. G. (2002) Quantifying heterogeneity in a meta-analysis. *Statistics in Medicine*, **21**, 1539–1558.

Holbrook, T. L., Hoyt, D. B., Stein, M. B., *et al* (2001) Perceived threat to life predicts posttraumatic stress disorder after major trauma: risk factors and functional outcome. *Journal of Trauma Injury, Infection and Critical Care*, **51**, 287–293.

Holmes, J. (1994) Psychotherapy – a luxury the NHS cannot afford? More expensive not to treat. *BMJ*, **309**, 1070–1071.

Horowitz, M. J., Wilner, N. & Alvarez, W. (1979) Impact of Event Scale: a measure of subjective stress. *Psychosomatic Medicine*, **41**, 209–218.

Horowitz, M. J., Siegel, B., Holen, A., *et al* (1997) Diagnostic criteria for complicated grief disorder. *American Journal of Psychiatry*, **154**, 904–910.

Horrigan, J. P. (1996) Guanfacine for post-traumatic stress disorder nightmares [letter]. *Journal of the American Academy of Child and Adolescent Psychiatry*, **35**, 975–976.

Hovens, J. E., Bramsen, I. & Van der Ploeg, H. M. (2002) Self-rating Inventory for Posttraumatic Stress Disorder: review of the psychometric properties of a new brief Dutch screening instrument. *Perceptual and Motor Skills*, **94**, 996–1008.

Hoxter, H. Z. (1998) Introductory address to World Conference on Higher Education: 5–9 October 1998. (Reprinted 2003.) *International Journal for the Advancement of Counselling*, **25**, 135–136.

Incomes Data Services (2003) *IDS Report*. R893/2. http://www.incomesdata.co.uk/ indexreport2003/sub2.htm#Earnings%20statistics.

Jadad, A. R., Moore, R. A., Carroll, D., et al (1996) Assessing the quality of reports of randomized clinical trials: is blinding necessary? *Controlled Clinical Trials*, **17**, 1–12.

Jaberghaderi, N., Greenwald, R., Rubin, A., et al (2004) A comparison of CBT and EMDR for sexually abused Iranian girls. *Clinical Psychology and Psychotherapy*, **11**, 358–368.

Janet, P. (1889) Les actes inconscients et la mémoire pendant le somnambulisme. *Revue Philosophique*, **25**, 238–279.

Joseph, S., Yule, W., Williams, R., et al (1993) Crisis support in the aftermath of disaster: a longitudinal perspective. *British Journal of Clinical Psychology*, **32**, 177–185.

Katon, W., von Korff, M., Lin, E., et al (2001) Rethinking practitioner roles in chronic illness: the specialist, primary care physician, and the practice nurse. *General Hospital Psychiatry*, **23**, 138–144.

Kaufman, J., Birmaher, B., Brent, D., et al (1997) Schedule for Affective Disorders and Schizophrenia for School-Age Children – Present and Lifetime Version (K–SADS–PL): initial reliability and validity data. *Journal of the American Academy of Child and Adolescent Psychiatry*, **36**, 980–988.

Keane, T. M. & Kaloupek, D. G. (1982) Imaginal flooding in the treatment of posttraumatic stress disorder. *Journal of Consulting and Clinical Psychology*, **50**, 138–140.

Keane, T. M., Zimering, R. T. & Caddell, J. M. (1985) A behavioural formulation of post-traumatic stress disorder in combat veterans. *Behaviour Therapist*, **8**, 9–12.

Keane, T. M., Fairbank, J. A., Caddell, J. M., et al (1989) Implosive (flooding) therapy reduces symptoms of PTSD in combat veterans. *Behavior Therapy*, **20**, 245–260.

Keller, M. (2003) Past, present and future directions for defining optimal treatment outcome in depression: remission and beyond. *JAMA*, **289**, 3152–3160.

Kessler, R. C., Sonnega, A., Bromet. E., et al (1995) Posttraumatic stress disorder in the National Comorbidity Survey. *Archives of General Psychiatry*, **52**, 1048–1060.

Kinzie, J. D. & Goetz, R. R. (1996) A century of controversy surrounding posttraumatic stress-spectrum syndromes: the impact on DSM–III and DSM–IV. *Journal of Traumatic Stress*, **9**, 159–179.

Kirsch, I. (2000) Are drug and placebo effects in depression additive? *Biological Psychiatry*, **47**, 733–735.

Kirsch, I., Moore, J. T., Scoboria, A., et al (2002) The emperor's new drugs: an analysis of antidepressant medication data submitted to the U.S. Food and Drug Administration. *American Psychiatric Association, Prevention and Treatment*, 5. Electronic journal. http:// www.journals.apa.org/prevention

Klein, E., Caspi, Y. & Gil, S. (2003) The relation between memory of the traumatic event and PTSD: evidence from studies of traumatic brain injury. *Canadian Journal of Psychiatry*, **48**, 28–33.

Knapp, M. (2003) Hidden costs of mental illness. *British Journal of Psychiatry*, **183**, 477–478.

Kubany, E. S., Hill, E. E. & Owens, J. A. (2003) Cognitive trauma therapy for battered women with PTSD (CTT–BW): preliminary findings. *Journal of Traumatic Stress*, **16**, 81–91.

Kubany, E. S., Hill, E. E. & Owens, J. A. (2004) Cognitive trauma therapy for battered women with PTSD (CTT–BW). *Journal of Consulting and Clinical Psychology*, **72**, 3–18.

Kudler, H. S., Blank, A. S. & Krupnick, J. L. (2000) Psychodynamic therapy. In *Effective Treatments for PTSD: Practice Guidelines from the International Society for Traumatic Stress Studies* (eds E. B. Foa, T. M. Keane & M. J. Friedman), pp. 176–198, 339–341. New York: Guilford Press.

Kulka, R. A., Schlenger, W. E., Fairbank, J. A., et al (1990) *Trauma and the Vietnam War Generation: Report of Findings from the Vietnam Veterans Readjustment Study*. Levittown, PA: Brunner/Mazel.

Lange, A., Rietdijk, D., Hudcovicova, M., *et al* **(2003)** Interapy: a controlled randomized trial of the standardized treatment of posttraumatic stress through the internet. *Journal of Consulting and Clinical Psychology*, **71**, 901–909.

Lejoyeux, M. & Ades, J. (1997) Antidepressant discontinuation: a review of the literature. *Journal of Clinical Psychiatry*, **58**, 11–15.

Lejoyeux, M., Ades, J., Mourad, I., *et al* **(1996)** Antidepressant withdrawal syndrome: recognition, prevention and management. *CNS Drugs*, **5**, 278–292.

Levy, S. & Lemma, A. (2004) *The Perversion of Loss: Psychoanalytic Perspectives on Trauma*. London: Whurr.

Lewis, G., Anderson, L., Araya, R., *et al* **(2003)** *Self-help Interventions for Mental Health Problems*. London: Department of Health.

Linehan, M. M. (1993) *Cognitive–Behavioural Treatment of Borderline Personality Disorder*. New York: Guilford Press.

Litz, B. T., Gray, M. J., Bryant, R. A., *et al* **(2002)** Early intervention for trauma: current status and future directions. *Clinical Psychology – Science and Practice*, **9**, 112–134.

Loof, D., Grimley, P., Kuller, F., *et al* **(1995)** Carbamazepine for PTSD [letter]. *Journal of the American Academy of Child and Adolescent Psychiatry*, **34**, 703–704.

Marks, I. M. (1969) *Fears and Phobias*. New York: Academic Press.

Marks, I., Lovell, K., Noshirvani, H., *et al* **(1998)** Treatment of posttraumatic stress disorder by exposure and/or cognitive restructuring: a controlled study. *Archives of General Psychiatry*, **55**, 317–325.

Mayou, R. A., Black, J. & Bryant, B. (2000) Unconsciousness, amnesia and psychiatric symptoms following road traffic accident injury. *British Journal of Psychiatry*, **177**, 540–545.

Mayou, R. A., Ehlers, A. & Bryant, B. (2002) Posttraumatic stress disorder after motor vehicle accidents: 3 year follow-up of a prospective longitudinal study. *Behaviour Research and Therapy*, **40**, 665–675.

McCrone, P. & Weich, S. (2001) The costs of mental health care: paucity of measurement. In *Mental Health Outcome Measures* (eds M. Tansella & G. Thornicroft), 2nd edn, pp. 145–165. London: Gaskell.

McCrone, P., Knapp, M. & Cawkill, P. (2003) Posttraumatic stress disorder (PTSD) in the armed forces: health economic considerations. *Journal of Traumatic Stress*, **16**, 519–522.

McFarlane, A. C. (1987) Posttraumatic phenomena in a longitudinal study of children following a natural disaster. *Journal of the American Academy of Child and Adolescent Psychiatry*, **26**, 764–769.

McNally, R. J. (2003) *Remembering Trauma*. Cambridge, MA: Harvard University Press.

McNally, R. J., Bryant, R. A. & Ehlers, A. (2003) Does early psychological intervention promote recovery from posttraumatic stress? *Psychological Science in the Public Interest*, **4**, 45–79.

Meichenbaum, D. (1985) *Stress Inoculation Training*. Oxford: Pergamon.

Mellman, T. A., Clark, R. E. & Peacock, W. J. (2003) Prescribing patterns for patients with posttraumatic stress disorder. *Psychiatric Services*, **54**, 1618–1621.

Meltzer, H., Gatward, R. & Goodman, R. (2000) *Mental Health of Children and Adolescents in Great Britain*. London: Stationery Office.

Meltzer-Brody, S. E., Churchill, E. & Davidson, J. R. T. (1999) Derivation of the SPAN, a brief diagnostic screening test for post-traumatic stress disorder. *Psychiatry Research*, **88**, 63–70.

Mendelson, G. (1995) 'Compensation neurosis' revisited: outcome studies of the effects of litigation. *Journal of Psychosomatic Research*, **39**, 695–706.

Michelson, D., Fava, M., Amsterdam, J., *et al* **(2000)** Interruption of selective serotonin reuptake inhibitor treatment. Double-blind placebo-controlled trial. *British Journal of Psychiatry*, **176**, 363–368.

Mitchell, J. T. (1983) When disaster strikes…the critical incident stress debriefing process. *Journal of Emergency Medical Services*, **8**, 36–39.

Mitchell, J. T. & Everly, G. S. (1997) The scientific evidence for critical incident stress management. *Journal of Emergency Medical Services*, **22**, 86–93.

Montoliu, L. & Crawford, T. (2002) Prescribing practices of general practitioners for children with mental health problems. *Child and Adolescent Mental Health*, **7**, 128–130.

Morgan, L., Scourfield, J., Williams, D., et al (2003) The Aberfan disaster: 33-year follow-up of survivors. *British Journal of Psychiatry*, **182**, 532–536.

Murray, J., Ehlers, A. & Mayou, R. A. (2002) Dissociation and posttraumatic stress disorder: two prospective studies of road traffic accident survivors. *British Journal of Psychiatry*, **180**, 363–368.

Nader, K., Kriegler, J., Blake, D., et al (2002) *The Clinician-Administered PTSD Scale for Children and Adolescents for DSM–IV (CAPS–CA).* White River Junction, VT: National Centre for PTSD (http://www.ncptsd.org).

Narrow, W. E., Rae, D. S., Robins, L. N., et al (2002) Revised prevalence estimates of mental disorders in the United States: using a clinical significance criterion to reconcile 2 surveys' estimates. *Archives of General Psychiatry*, **59**, 115–123.

National Collaborating Centre for Mental Health (2005) *Depression: Management of Depression in Primary and Secondary Care.* Leicester: British Psychological Society & Gaskell.

National Institute for Clinical Excellence (2002) *The Guideline Development Process: Information for National Collaborating Centres and Guideline Development Groups.* London: NICE.

National Institute for Clinical Excellence (2004) *Guideline Development Methods: Information for National Collaborating Centres and Guideline Developers.* London: NICE.

National Institute for Mental Health in England (2003) *Women's Mental Health Strategy – Mainstreaming Gender and Women's Mental Health Implementation Guide.* London: Department of Health.

National Screening Committee (2003) Criteria for appraising the viability, effectiveness and appropriateness of a screening programme. http://www.nsc.nhs.uk/pdfs/criteria.pdf.

Neal, L. A., Busuttil, W., Rollins, J., et al (1994) Convergent validity of measures of post-traumatic stress disorder in a mixed military and civilian population. *Journal of Traumatic Stress*, **7**, 447–455.

Netten, A. & Curtis, L. (2003) *Unit Costs of Health and Social Care.* Canterbury: University of Kent Personal Social Services Research Unit.

Neuner, F., Schauer, M., Klaschik, C., et al (2004) A comparison of narrative expposure therapy, supportive counseling, and psychoeducation for treating posttraumatic stress disorder in an African refugee settlement. *Journal of Consulting and Clinical Psychology*, **72**, 579–587.

Ohan, J., Myers, K. & Collett, B. R. (2002) Ten-year review of rating scales. IV: Scales assessing trauma and its effects. *Journal of the American Academy of Child and Adolescent Psychiatry*, **41**, 1401–1422.

Orvaschel, H. (1989) *Kiddies SADS–E Section. Designed to Assess PTSD.* Philadelphia, PA: Medical College of Philadelphia.

Ouimette, P., Cronkite, R., Henson, B. R., et al (2004) Posttraumatic stress disorder and health status among female and male medical patients. *Journal of Traumatic Stress*, **17**, 1–9.

Ozer, E. J., Best, S. R., Lipsey, T. L., et al (2003) Predictors of post-traumatic stress disorder and symptoms in adults: a meta-analysis. *Psychological Bulletin*, **129**, 52–73.

Paunovic, N. (1997) Exposure CBT for post-traumatic stress disorder: its relative efficacy, limitations, and optimal applications. *Scandinavian Journal of Behavior Therapy*, **26**, 54–69.

Paunovic, N. & Ost, L. G. (2001) Cognitive-behaviour therapy vs exposure therapy in the treatment of PTSD in refugees. *Behaviour Research and Therapy*, **39**, 1183–1197.

Pelcovitz, D., van der Kolk, B. A., Roth, S. H., et al (1997) Development of a criteria set and a structured interview for disorders of extreme stress (SIDES). *Journal of Traumatic Stress*, **10**, 3–16.

Peniston, E. G. & Kulkosky, P. J. (1991) Alpha-theta brainwave neuro-feedback therapy for Vietnam veterans with combat-related post-traumatic stress disorder. *Medical Psychotherapy*, **4**, 47–60.

Perry, B. D. (1994) Neurobiological sequelae of childhood trauma: post-traumatic stress disorders in children. In *Catecholamines in Post-traumatic Stress Disorder: Emerging Concepts* (ed. M. Murberg), pp. 253–276. Washington, DC: APA.

Pitman, R. K., Altman, B., Greenwald, E., *et al* (1991) Psychiatric complications during flooding therapy for post-traumatic stress disorder. *Journal of Clinical Psychiatry*, **52**, 17–20.

Power, K., McGoldrick, T., Brown, K., *et al* (2002) A controlled comparison of eye movement desensitisation and reprocessing versus exposure plus cognitive restructuring versus waiting list in the treatment of post-traumatic stress disorder. *Clinical Psychology and Psychotherapy*, **9**, 299–318.

Pynoos, R. (2002) *The Child Post Traumatic Stress Reaction Index (CPTS–RI).* Available from Robert Pynoos MD, Trauma Psychiatry Service, 300 UCLA Medical Plaza, Los Angeles, CA 90024-6968, USA (rpynoos@npih.medsch.ucla.edu).

Pynoos R., Frederick, C., Nader, K., *et al* (1987) Life threat and posttraumatic stress in school-age children. *Archives of General Psychiatry*, **44**, 1057–1063.

Rachman, S. J. (1978) *Fear and Courage.* San Francisco: Freeman.

Rachman, S. J. & Hodgson, R. S. (1980) *Obsessions and Compulsions.* Englewood Cliffs, NJ: Prentice-Hall.

Radnitz, C. L., Hsu, L., Willard, J., *et al* (1998) Posttraumatic stress disorder in veterans with spinal cord injury: trauma-related risk factors. *Journal of Traumatic Stress*, **11**, 505–520.

Ramchandani, P. & Jones, D. P. (2003) Treating psychological symptoms in sexually abused children: from research findings to service provision. *British Journal of Psychiatry*, **183**, 484–490.

Raphael, B. (1986) *When Disaster Strikes: A Handbook for Caring Professions.* London: Hutchinson.

Resick, P. A. & Schnicke, M. K. (1993) *Cognitive Processing Therapy for Rape Victims: A Treatment Manual.* Newbury Park, CA: Sage.

Resick, P. A., Nishith, P., Weaver, T. L., *et al* (2002) A comparison of cognitive-processing therapy with prolonged exposure and a waiting condition for the treatment of chronic posttraumatic stress disorder in female rape victims. *Journal of Consulting and Clinical Psychology*, **70**, 867–879.

Richards, D. A. (1997) *The prevention of post-traumatic stress after armed robbery: the impact of a training programme within the Leeds Permanent Building Society.* PhD thesis, Leeds Metropolitan University.

Richards, D. A. (2001) A field study of critical incident stress debriefing versus critical incident stress management. *Journal of Mental Health*, **10**, 351–362.

Riddle, M. A., Kastelic, E. A. & Frosch, E. (2001) Pediatric psychopharmacology. *Journal of Child Psychology and Psychiatry*, **44**, 73–90.

Robert, R., Blakeney, P. E., Villarreal, C., *et al* (1999) Imipramine treatment in pediatric burn patients with symptoms of acute stress disorder: a pilot study [comment]. *Journal of the American Academy of Child and Adolescent Psychiatry*, **38**, 873–882.

Rogers, C. R. (1951) *Client-Centered Therapy: Its Current Practice, Implications and Theory.* Boston: Houghton Mifflin.

Rona, R. J., Hooper, R., Jones, M., *et al* (2004a) Screening for physical and psychological illness in the British Armed Forces: III. The value of a questionnaire to assist a Medical Officer to decide who needs help. *Journal of Medical Screening*, **11**, 158–161.

Rona, R. J., Jones, M., French, C., *et al* (2004b) Screening for physical and psychological illness in the British Armed Forces: I. The acceptability of the programme. *Journal of Medical Screening*, **11**, 148–152.

Rose, S., Bisson, J. & Wessely, S. (2004) Psychological debriefing for preventing post traumatic stress disorder (PTSD) (Cochrane review). *Cochrane Library*, issue 3. Chichester: John Wiley.

Rosenbaum, J. F., Fava, M., Hoog, S. L., *et al* **(1998)** Selective serotonin reuptake inhibitor discontinuation syndrome: a randomised clinical trial. *Biological Psychiatry*, **44**, 77–87.

Rothbaum, R. O., Foa, E. B., Rigge, D. S., *et al* **(1992)** A prospective examination of post-traumatic stress disorder in rape victims. *Journal of Trauma Stress*, **5**, 455–475.

Rothbaum, B. O., Meadows, E. A., Resick, P., *et al* **(2000)** Cognitive-behavioral therapy. In *Effective treatments for PTSD: Practice Guidelines from the International Society for Traumatic Stress Studies* (eds E. B. Foa, T. M. Keane & M. J. Friedman), pp. 60–83. New York: Guilford Press.

Royal College of Paediatrics and Child Health (2000) *The Use of Unlicensed Medicines or Licensed Medicines for Unlicensed Applications in Paediatric Practice.* London: RCPCH.

Scheeringa, M. S., Zeanah, C. H., Drell, M. J., *et al* **(1995)** Two approaches to the diagnosis of posttraumatic stress disorder in infancy and early childhood. *Journal of the American Academy of Child and Adolescent Psychiatry*, **34**, 191–200.

Schlapobersky, J. (1990) Torture as the perversion of a healing relationship. In *Health Services for the Treatment of Torture and Trauma Survivors* (eds J. Gruschow & K. Hannibal), pp. 51–71. Washington, DC: American Association for the Advancement of Science.

Schnurr, P. P. & Green, B. L. (eds) (2003) *Trauma and Health: Physical Consequences of Exposure to Extreme Stress.* Washington, DC: American Psychological Association.

Schnurr, P. P., Friedman, M. J., Foy, D. W., *et al* **(2003)** Randomized trial of trauma-focused group therapy for posttraumatic stress disorder: results from a Department of Veterans Affairs cooperative study. *Archives of General Psychiatry*, **60**, 481–489.

Shalev, A. Y. (1992) Posttraumatic stress disorder among injured survivors of a terrorist attack. Predictive value of early intrusion and avoidance symptoms. *Journal of Nervous and Mental Disease*, **180**, 505–509.

Shalev, A. Y., Freedman, S., Peri, T., *et al* **(1997)** Predicting PTSD in trauma survivors: prospective evaluation of self-report and clinician-administered instruments. *British Journal of Psychiatry*, **170**, 558–564.

Shapiro, F. (1989) Eye movement desensitisation: a new treatment for post-traumatic stress disorder. *Journal of Behavior Therapy and Experimental Psychiatry*, **20**, 211–217.

Shapiro, F. (1996) Eye movement desensitisation and reprocessing (EMDR): evaluation of controlled PTSD research. *Journal of Behavior Therapy and Experimental Psychiatry*, **27**, 209–218.

Shapiro, F. (2001) *Eye Movement Desensitisation and Reprocessing: Basic Principles, Protocols, and Procedures* (2nd edn). New York: Guilford Press.

Silverman, W. & Albano, A. (1996) *The Anxiety Disorders Interview Schedule for Children for DSM-IV, Child and Parent Versions*. San Antonio, TX: Psychological Corporation.

Smith, P., Perrin, S., Yule, W., *et al* **(2001)** War exposure and maternal reactions in the psychological adjustment of children from Bosnia-Hercegovina. *Journal of Child Psychology and Psychiatry*, **42**, 395–404.

Solomon, S. D. & Davidson, J. R. T. (1997) Trauma: prevalence, impairment, service use and cost. *Journal of Clinical Psychiatry*, **58**, 5–11.

Spielberger, C. D., Gorsuch, R. L., Lushene, R., *et al* **(1973)** *Manual for the State-Trait Anxiety Inventory.* Palo Alto, CA: Consulting Psychologist Press.

Stallard, P., Velleman, R., Salter, E., *et al* **(2005)** A randomised controlled trial to determine the effectiveness of an early psychological intervention with children involved in road traffic accidents. *Journal of Child Psychology and Psychiatry*, in press.

Stein, M. B., Walker, J. R., Hazen, A. L., *et al* **(1997)** Full and partial posttraumatic stress disorder: findings from a community survey. *American Journal of Psychiatry*, **154**, 1114–1119.

Stein, D. J., Zungu-Dirwayi, N., Van der Linden, G. J. H., *et al* **(2004)** Pharmacotherapy for post traumatic stress disorder (PTSD) (Cochrane Review). *Cochrane Library*, issue 2. Chichester: John Wiley.

Tarrier, N., Pilgrim, H., Sommerfield, C., *et al* **(1999)** A randomized trial of cognitive therapy and imaginal exposure in the treatment of chronic posttraumatic stress disorder. *Journal of Consulting and Clinical Psychology*, **67**, 13–18.

Taylor, S., Fedoroff, I. C., Koch, W. E. J., *et al* **(2001)** Postttraumatic stress disorder arising after road traffic collisions: patterns of response to cognitive-behavior therapy. *Journal of Clinical and Consulting Psychology*, **69**, 541–551.

Taylor, S., Thordarson, D. S., Maxfield, L., *et al* **(2003)** Comparative efficacy, speed, and adverse effects of three PTSD treatments: exposure therapy, EMDR and relaxation training. *Journal of Consulting and Clinical Psychology*, **71**, 330–338.

Turner, S. W. (2004) Emotional reactions to torture and organized state violence. *PTSD Research Quarterly*, 15. http://www.ncptsd.org/publications/rq/rqpdf/V15N2.PDF

Turner, S. W., Bowie, C., Dunn, G., *et al* **(2003)** Mental health of Kosovan Albanian refugees in the UK. *British Journal of Psychiatry*, **182**, 444–448.

Ursano, R. J., Fullerton, C. S. & Kao, T. (1995) Longitudinal assessment of posttraumatic stress disorder and depression after exposure to traumatic death. *Journal of Nervous and Mental Disease*, **183**, 36–42.

Van der Hart, O., Brown, P. & van der Kolk, B. A. (1989) Pierre Janet's treatment of posttraumatic stress. *Journal of Traumatic Stress*, **2**, 379–395.

Van der Kolk, B. A., Weisaeth, L. & van der Hart, O. (1996) History of trauma in psychiatry. In *Traumatic Stress: The Effects of Overwhelming Experience on Mind, Body, and Society* (eds B. A. van der Kolk, A. C. McFarlane & L. Weisaeth), pp. 47–74. New York: Guilford.

Van Emmerik, A. A., Kamphuis, J. H., Hulsbosch, A. M., *et al* **(2002)** Single session debriefing after psychological trauma: a meta-analysis. *Lancet*, **360**, 766–771.

Van Etten, M. L. & Taylor, S. (1998) Comparative efficacy of treatments for post-traumatic stress disorder: a meta-analysis. *Clinical Psychology and Psychotherapy*, **5**, 126–145.

Van Loey, N. E., Maas, C. J., Faber, A. W., *et al* **(2003)** Predictors of chronic posttraumatic stress symptoms following burn injury: results of a longitudinal study. *Journal of Traumatic Stress*, **16**, 361–369.

Van Minnen, A., Arntz, A. & Keijsers, G. P. J. (2002) Prolonged exposure in patients with chronic PTSD: predictors of treatment outcome and dropout. *Behaviour Research and Therapy*, **40**, 439–457.

Van Velsen, C., Gorst-Unsworth, C. & Turner, S. W. (1996) Working with survivors of torture – demography and diagnosis. *Journal of Traumatic Stress*, **9**, 181–193.

Van Zelst, W. H., de Beurs, E., Beekman, A. T., *et al* **(2003)** Prevalence and risk factors of post traumatic stress disorder in older adults. *Psychotherapy and Psychosomatics*, **72**, 333–342.

Vaughan, K., Armstrong, M. S., Gold, R., *et al* **(1994)** A trial of eye movement desensitization compared to image habituation training and applied muscle relaxation in post-traumatic stress disorder. *Journal of Behavior Therapy and Experimental Psychiatry*, **25**, 283–291.

Veronen, L. J. & Kilpatrick, D. (1983) Stress management for rape victims. In *Stress Reduction and Prevention* (eds D. Meichenbaum & M. E. Jaremko), pp. 341–374. London: Plenum.

Weathers, F. W., Huska, J. A. & Keane, T. M. (1991) *The PTSD Checklist – Civilian Version (PCL-C)*. Boston: National Center for PTSD, Behavioral Science Division.

Weathers, F. W. & Ford, J. (1996) Psychometric properties of the PTSD Checklist (PCL–C, PCL–S, PCL–M, PCL–PR). In *Measurement of Stress, Trauma and Adaptation* (ed. B. H. Stamm). Lutherville, MD: Sidran Press.

Weiss, D. S. & Marmar, C. R. (1997) The Impact of Event Scale – Revised. In *Assessing Psychological Trauma and PTSD* (eds J. P. Wilson & T. M. Keane), pp. 399–411. New York: Guilford Press.

Weissman, M. M. & Paykel, E. S. (1974) *The Depressed Woman: A Study of Social Relations*. Chicago, IL: University of Chicago Press.

Welch, K. L. & Beere, D. B. (2002) Eye movement desensitization and reprocessing: a treatment efficacy model. *Clinical Psychology and Psychotherapy*, **9**, 165–176.

Wessely, S., Rose, S. & Bisson, J. (1998) A systematic review of brief psychological interventions ('debriefing') for the treatment of immediate trauma related symptoms and the prevention of post traumatic stress disorder (Cochrane Review). *Cochrane Library*, issue 3. Oxford: Update Software.

Wohlfarth, T. D., van den Brink, W., Winkel, F. W., *et al* **(2003)** Screening for posttraumatic stress disorder: an evaluation of two self-report scales among crime victims. *Psychological Assessment*, **15**, 101–109.

Wolfe, V. V., Gentile, C., Michienzi, T., *et al* **(1991)** The Children's Impact of Traumatic Events Scale: a measure of post-sexual abuse PTSD symptoms. *Behavioral Assessment*, **13**, 159–383.

Wolpe, J. (1958) *Psychotherapy by Reciprocal Inhibition.* Stanford, CA: Stanford University Press.

Wolraich, M. L. (2003) Annotation: the use of psychotropic medications in children: an American view. *Journal of Child Psychology and Psychiatry*, **44**, 159–168.

World Health Organization (1992) *The ICD–10 Classification of Mental and Behavioural Disorders: Clinical Descriptions and Diagnostic Guidelines.* Geneva: WHO.

World Health Organization (1993) *The ICD–10 Classification of Mental and Behavioural Disorders: Diagnostic Criteria for Research.* Geneva: WHO.

Yehuda, R., Giller, E. L., Levengood, R. A., *et al* **(1995)** Hypothalamic-pituitary-adrenal functioning in posttraumatic stress disorder: expanding the concept of the stress response spectrum. In *Neurobiological and Clinical Consequences of Stress: From Normal Adaptation to Post-Traumatic Stress Disorder* (eds M. J. Friedman, D. S. Charney & A. Y. Deutch), pp. 351–365. Philadelphia: Lippincott–Raven.

Yule, W. (1997) Anxiety, depression, and post-traumatic stress disorder in children. In *The NFER Child Portfolio* (ed. I. Sclare). Windsor: NFER–Nelson.

Yule, W., Bolton, D., Udwin, O., *et al* **(2000)** The long-term psychological effects of a disaster experienced in adolescence. I: The incidence and course of PTSD. *Journal of Child Psychology and Psychiatry*, **41**, 503–511.